THE GOLD COAST, BRITAIN
AND THE NETHERLANDS
1850–1874

WEST AFRICAN HISTORY SERIES

General Editor: GERALD S. GRAHAM

Rhodes Professor of Imperial History, University of London

THE GOLD COAST, BRITAIN AND THE NETHERLANDS 1850–1874

DOUGLAS COOMBS

LONDON
OXFORD UNIVERSITY PRESS

IBADAN   ACCRA

1963

Oxford University Press, Amen House, London E.C.4

GLASGOW NEW YORK TORONTO MELBOURNE WELLINGTON
BOMBAY CALCUTTA MADRAS KARACHI LAHORE DACCA
CAPE TOWN SALISBURY NAIROBI IBADAN ACCRA
KUALA LUMPUR HONG KONG

Preparation and publication of this series has been made
possible by the generous financial assistance of Overseas
Newspapers group, Lagos, Freetown, London and West
Indies

PRINTED IN GREAT BRITAIN

PREFACE

THIS small monograph, the outcome of intermittent activity in two continents and three countries over the space of six years, would not have been completed without a great deal of help which it is a pleasure rather than a duty to acknowledge here.

My thanks are due to the following: His Excellency the Netherlands Minister for Foreign Affairs, for permission to consult documents not at that time open to public inspection; the present Earls of Clarendon and Kimberley, for permission to make use of their family papers; Dr. A. J. Veenendaal, for allowing me to see and make use of the proofs of Dr. Wolteringen's forthcoming volume in the *Rijks Geschiedkundige Publicatien*; Dr. J. D. Fage, for his encouragement and advice; Dr. W. D. McIntyre, for guidance to British archive materials; and Mr. G. E. Metcalfe, for generously giving me the benefit of his unrivalled knowledge of the British connexion with the Gold Coast in the nineteenth century.

I owe a very special debt of gratitude to Miss A. M. P. Mollema, for her expert advice on the Dutch part in the negotiations of the treaty of cession and for allowing me free use of her collection of transcripts; and to Miss J. W. Jurriaanse, Archivist of the Dutch Ministry for Foreign Affairs, whose unfailing kindness I shall always remember.

In thanking the staffs of all the libraries and archives in which I have worked I think particularly of Mr. Richard Burkett of the library of the University College of Ghana, and of those archivists and members of the reading-room staff, too numerous to mention by name, who make the Algemeen Rijksarchief the most pleasant of all state archives. I must add also my thanks to the staff of the National Register of Archives, for both information and assistance.

I am grateful to the Historical Society of Ghana for permission to print here material already used in a paper read to a conference of the Society and in an article published in the Society's *Transactions*. I must also acknowledge a grant-in-aid by the University College of Ghana in 1956 towards expenses incurred while working in Holland.

Finally I must thank Mr. H. P. White for readily undertaking the production of a map, and my wife for her prolonged secretarial labours.

Ibadan,
   Nigeria,
      March 1962

D. S. C.

CONTENTS

ABBREVIATIONS

All abbreviations used in the footnotes are explained in the Bibliography, with the following exceptions :

D.N.B.   Dictionary of National Biography
C.O.   Colonial Office
F.O.   Foreign Office
M.B.Z.   Netherlands Foreign Minister
M.K.   Netherlands Colonial Minister

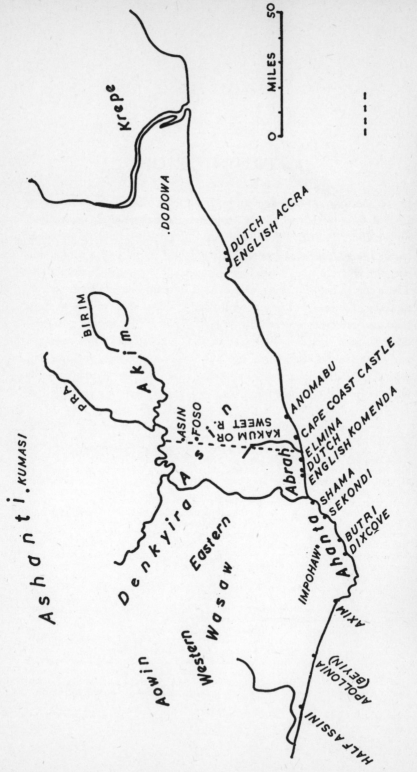

MAP OF THE GOLD COAST showing the places mentioned in the text. The dotted line indicates the boundary laid down by the Anglo-Dutch Convention of 1867.

INTRODUCTION

It is common knowledge among students of nineteenth-century English history that in 1872 Britain acquired the Dutch settlements on the Gold Coast by purchase. Every Dutch schoolboy, on the other hand, knows that this transfer was effected as part of a diplomatic bargain whereby the Netherlands gained a free hand in Sumatra.[1] These contradictory beliefs, each with a long and reputable ancestry,[2] represent the limits of general knowledge about this episode in England and Holland respectively. Which is true? The answer is regrettably simple: neither. This transaction, which marks not only the end of the long Dutch connexion with the Gold Coast (and, indeed, with the African continent), but also a vital stage in the formation of what is now the independent state of Ghana, remains shrouded in

---

[1] *The Oxford History of England* offers not one, but *both* of these conflicting interpretations; cf. E. L. Woodward, *The Age of Reform* (Oxford, 1946: corrected ed.), p. 359, with R. C. K. Ensor, *England, 1870–1914* (Oxford, 1936), p. 27. One could multiply instances of the 'purchase' idea among English writers *ad infinitum*; the most recent examples are in F. Wolfson, *Pageant of Ghana* (London, 1958), p. 21, and E. A. Benians, J. R. M. Butler, and C. E. Carrington (Eds.), *Cambridge History of the British Empire*, iii (Cambridge, 1959), p. 189. This notion is also firmly implanted in Ghana, to judge from the *Gold Coast Calendar, 1957* (Govt. Printer, Accra), and J. M. Akita, 'The Transfer of the Seat of Government from Cape Coast to Accra', *Gold Coast Teachers' Journal*, i (March 1956), p. 46. For the continued acceptance in Holland of the idea of a 'bargain' see A. M. P. Mollema, 'De Afstand der Nederlandse Bezittingen ter Kuste van Guinea aan Engeland in 1872' (offprint from *Varia Historica*, Assen, 1954), pp. 236–7, where it is harshly but truly described as 'an unconscious attempt to sugar the bitter pill of national impotence'. A recent instance of this interpretation is to be seen on p. 40 of the pamphlet, *Ghana, 6 Maart 1957*, issued by the 'Afrika Instituut' of Rotterdam (who should know better!). Other examples from very reputable works are P. J. Blok, *Geschiedenis van het Nederlandsche Volk*, iv (3rd ed., Leiden, [1926]), p. 462; H. T. Colenbrander, *Koloniale Geschiedenis* ('s-Gravenhage, 1925–6), dl. II, p. 30; S. P. L'Honoré Naber (Ed.), *Beschryvinge ende Historische Verhael van het Gout Koninckryck van Guinea* . . . ('s-Gravenhage, 1912), p. xvi; K. A. Ratelband (Ed.), *Vijf Dagregisters van het Kasteel Sao Jorge da Mina* ('s-Gravenhage, 1953), p. lxix.

[2] The British Foreign Secretary himself talked of a 'purchase' (Granville to Gladstone, 8 Oct. 1870, Walmer Castle, A. Ramm (Ed.), *Political Correspondence of Mr. Gladstone and Lord Granville* (London, 1952), i, pp. 140–1), while the 'bargain' idea had the tacit sanction of the responsible Dutch ministers (see below, pp. 87–92).

the mists of ignorance or legend. It is difficult enough to find even the date of the actual cession correctly stated.[1] It is the purpose of this study to dispel at least some of these mists, and above all to show clearly the considerable effect of the cession, together with the events that led up to and followed from it, upon the subsequent development of the Gold Coast and upon British policy there.

In a short but most valuable article Miss A. M. P. Mollema, working from Dutch archive material, has studied the events of 1868–72.[2] Some at least of what follows on the Dutch part in the negotiations of 1869–71 is of necessity a duplication of what Miss Mollema has already said in summary form, and it gives me particular pleasure to acknowledge this debt. But Miss Mollema's article stands virtually alone as the only really serious study of any aspect of the cession. The neglect of this episode by English and Dutch scholars alike is easy enough to explain. To English contemporaries it was 'a very small matter',[3] and this attitude, natural enough in 1872, has persisted, though the events of 1873–4, not to mention subsequent developments, might be thought to have rendered it untenable. Many Dutch contemporaries thought the cession a fairly big matter, but subsequent Dutch historians have shown little interest in this, or indeed (with a few outstanding exceptions such as S. P. L'Honoré Naber and K. A. Ratelband) in any other aspect of the history of the Dutch in West Africa. In this they have no doubt been influenced not only by a certain sensitiveness about 'lost opportunities', but also by those misgivings about the Dutch record on the Coast which led one writer at the time of the cession to advocate the destruction of all relevant documents.[4] It is true, of course, that for Holland the cession never acquired that retrospective importance which its consequences were to give it for Britain; but one might yet have expected a little more interest in the end of a connexion which lasted for two and a half centuries, and which has left behind some still unbroken links

---

[1] Day, month, and even year are frequently mis-stated. Even S. H. Steinberg, in his admirable *Historical Tables* (3rd ed., London, 1949), appears to confuse the ratification of the treaty with the execution of the cession.

[2] Cited in n. 1, page xi, above.

[3] *The Times,* 6 Feb. 1872. I have seen an Elmina Street (in Swindon, Wiltshire), but I take this name to commemorate the successful defence of 1873 rather than the cession of 1872.

[4] Cited in Ratelband, op. cit., pp. xx–xxi.

between Holland and Ghana. Professor Coolhaas has told us that in Holland today there live descendants of the negro recruits who were shipped to Java in the nineteenth century;[1] while in Ghana (where memories are in any case longer than in Europe) the legacy of the Dutch connexion—in such forms as prominent mulatto families, notable historical monuments, and words incorporated into the Akan tongue[2]—is greater than has sometimes been supposed.[3]

I hope that my attempt to deal with this small chapter of West African history will at least bear out my belief that its previous neglect was not completely justified.

[1] W. Ph. Coolhaas, 'Verløren Kansen' (Groningen-Djakarta, 1955: inaugural lecture at Leiden University, 3 Oct. 1955), p. 9.

[2] J. N. Matson, 'History of Akan Words', *Transactions of the Gold Coast and Togoland Historical Society*, ii, 2 (Achimota, 1956).

[3] Trade between Holland and Ghana is also of considerable importance to both countries: in 1955 Holland was the third greatest exporter of goods to the Gold Coast and the fourth greatest buyer of Gold Coast produce (*Ghana, 6 Maart 1957*, pp. 34–5).

1

DUTCH, BRITISH AND ASHANTI

THE Dutch settlements on the Gold Coast were established in the
early seventeenth century. By the middle of the nineteenth century
they could look back upon two centuries of virtually uninterrupted
decline.[1] Undermined almost from the start by English rivalry, by the
end of the eighteenth century it was only thanks to English forbear-
ance that they were able to survive at all. Mere survival was in any
case difficult enough in the Napoleonic period, for most of which
they were cut off from all communication with the home government.
When, with the liberation of Holland and the establishment of the
Kingdom of the Netherlands, contact was resumed, it was accompanied by a final crippling blow: the abolition of the slave
trade.

Henceforth, after a brief and wholly unsuccessful attempt to develop plantations,[2] the home government, despairing of the prospects of legitimate trade, wrote off the settlements as an expensive
nuisance and set about cutting its losses to the minimum. A few
crumbling forts, ill equipped and undermanned (if manned at all);[3]

[1] S. P. L'Honoré Naber's *De Nederlanders in Guineë en Brazilië* ('s-Gravenhage,
1931) is a good short account of the history of the Dutch in West Africa. For
bibliographies of this history see P. J. Veth and C. M. Kan, *Bibliografie van Nederlandsche Boeken, Brochures, Kaarten, enz. over Afrika* (Utrecht, 1876), and Ratelband,
op. cit. The only detailed account of the Dutch in West Africa in the nineteenth
century is H. Herman, *Onze Bezittingen op de Kust van Guinea en de Krijgsverrichtingen aldaar*, dl. ii (typescript, 1926: copy in the Algemeen Rijksarchief), but
this is concerned chiefly with military matters and its usefulness is impaired by a
total absence of references. The bibliography appended to Mollema, op. cit., is of
use not merely for the cession but for the general history of the Dutch Gold Coast
in the nineteenth century.

[2] For which see W. J. Koppius, 'Herman Willem Daendels, Gouv.-Gen. ter Kuste
van Guinea', *De Indische Gids*, Oct. 1930.

[3] Only 6 out of 15 were manned in 1864: (C. J. M. Nagtglas), *What Must the
Netherlands do with her Settlements on the Coast of Guinea?* (translation: London,
1864), p. 1.

an inadequate staff, demoralized when it had the right to engage in private trade and impoverished when it was without it; a small and unreliable native garrison; some ill-defined claims to a 'protectorate' over the coast adjacent to the forts and certain interior districts, which Dutch officials did little to exercise or enforce : this was the state of the Dutch Gold Coast in the nineteenth century.[1] In essentials, it is true, this picture differed little from that presented in the previous century, save for the vital change that, while still a financial burden on the home country, the settlements now offered her no compensatory advantages. By 1857 annual income from local sources was *f*. 4,600, as compared with an expenditure of *f*. 70,000; the deficit was a charge on the Dutch budget.[2] Trade, the whole *raison d'être* of the settlements, was now negligible, thanks perhaps mainly to the fact that the British had almost entirely taken over the once important commerce with Ashanti. In 1858 only 102 ships put in at Elmina, the chief Dutch post, and even of these no more than eleven—less than eight per cent. of the total tonnage—were Dutch.[3] The official figures for this year put the total value of imports at *f*. 988,795, of which Dutch ships carried twenty-six and a half per cent., and of exports at *f*. 342,787, of which Dutch ships carried twenty-nine per cent.[4] Well might the official report for this year describe trade as 'unsatisfactory', and well too might Governor van den Bossche, in the same year, dilate on its insignificance[5]—an opinion borne out by the unanimous testimony of his contemporaries. The returns for the early 1860s, moreover, show a further notable decline in the volume of

[1] For good first-hand evidence of all this see two works by the former official J. S. G. Gramberg: *Schetsen van Afrika's Westkust* (Amsterdam, 1861), and *De Goudkust* (reprint from *De Gids*, 1868). Gramberg was embittered and biased, but his description of the Dutch settlements is substantially confirmed by his *bête noire* Governor Nagtglas (op. cit., *passim*).

[2] *Verslag van het beheer en den staat der West-Indische bezittingen en van die ter Kuste van Guinea over 1857*. . . . See also 'Begrootingen van ontvangsten en uitgaven', Algemeen Rijksarchief/Archief van de Nederlandse Bezittingen ter Kuste van Guinea [=G.] 792.

[3] *Verslag van het Beheer* . . . *der* . . . *bezittingen ter Kuste van Guinea over 1858*. . . .

[4] 'Staten van in- en uitvoer', G. 793.

[5] *Verslag van het beheer* . . . *der* . . . *bezittingen ter Kuste van Guinea over 1858*. . . . The Governor's views are printed in the report on the cession presented to the Second Chamber of the States-General on 30 June 1874, hereafter referred to as the '1874 Report' (*Handelingen der Staten Generaal* [=*Hand. S.G.*], 1873–4, Bijlagen dl. 2, No. 156–1–48), section IA.

trade. Even so all these figures paint an unduly favourable picture, since they in fact include trade with other parts of the Guinea coast (for example, a cargo shown on a bill of lading as taken on at Elmina might well have been picked up elsewhere). They are in any case unimpressive when compared with returns for Dutch trade with the rest of West Africa, Dutch imports from which rose steadily in the 1860s while those from the 'Kust van Guinea' settlements were falling.[1] Meanwhile, further half-hearted attempts to establish plantations and gold-mines had ended in complete failure.[2]

Some Dutchmen, it is true, attached importance to the Gold Coast as a source of soldiers for their East Indian army, and shipments of 'recruits' (partly supplied by the King of Ashanti) were intermittently sent from Elmina to Java. Attempts to recruit on a voluntary basis began in 1831, but not until 1837, when General Verveer arranged with the King of Ashanti for the 'recruitment' of 1,000 slaves at 100 guilders a head, did this scheme begin to bear fruit. When it was ended in 1842, as a result of its slave-trading associations, there were about 1,500 African soldiers serving in the East Indies. After a further fruitless experiment in voluntary recruitment (1850-3), the trade in 'recruits' with Ashanti was revived in 1855, but seems never to have reached its previous level. At the height of this second phase no more than 445 men were shipped from Elmina in the space of four and a half years (1858-mid 1862), and by 1867 there were only about 450 Africans left in the East Indian army.[3] In fact,

[1] Robidé van der Aa, *Afrikaansche Studieën: Koloniaal Bezit en particuliere Handel op Afrika's Westkust* ('s-Gravenhage, 1871), pp. 29, 75-6; 'Memorie van Toelichting', *Hand. S.G.*, 1867, Bijlagen pp. 901-6.

[2] For details see Nagtglas to Colonial Minister [=M.K.] (secret-draft), 25 Nov. 1869, G. 724; '1874 Report', section I A; (Nagtglas), op. cit., 2-3; Gramberg, *Schetsen*, pp. 273-6; *Journal of Royal Society of Arts*, xxiii, pp. 255-7 (remarks by A. Swanzy). Nagtglas attributed these failures to the impossibility of getting reliable, regular labour from free negroes; Gramberg, who ran his own plantation for a time, thought them rather due to mismanagement and the indifference or even hostility of the local authorities.

[3] *Encyclopaedie van Nederlandsch-Indie* (2de druk: 's-Gravenhage-Leiden, 1917), s.v. 'Afrikanen'; Herman, op. cit., ii, pp. 32-6, 60, 62-3; '1874 Report', section I A; C. A. Jeekel, *Onze Bezittingen op de Kust van Guinea* (Amsterdam, 1869: reprinted from *Onze Tijd*), p. 60. Perhaps the only lasting importance of the recruitment was the taste for the 'batiks' of Java which the time-expired 'recruits' brought back with them to Elmina (where they settled on what is still known as 'Java Hill'). This formed the basis of a new and now very important branch of Dutch West African trade, in the so-called 'Dutch wax block prints' (*Ghana 6 Maart 1957*, p. 40).

what with allegations made both at home and abroad[1] of veiled slave-trading, criticisms by East Indian officials of the quality of the recruits, and the difficulties experienced in obtaining and training them, this recruitment never answered the high hopes with which it had begun. In any case, as the Dutch historian Colenbrander once pointed out,[2] their self-appointed mission in the East absorbed the interests and energies of nineteenth-century Dutchmen to the almost complete exclusion of the West, and above all of the derelict settlements of the Guinea coast.

The British settlements, too, had been hard hit by the abolition of the slave trade, as also by Ashanti invasions, but the subsequent growth of their legitimate trade, thanks in part to the enterprise of British merchants and the vigorous administration of President Maclean,[3] was in marked contrast to the experience of their Dutch neighbours. In 1858 the total value of the trade of the British settlements was some five times greater than the inflated official value of that of the Dutch.[4] Moreover, while in the 1860s the share of the Dutch Gold Coast in the overall trade of Holland with West Africa seems to have declined, in the same period the importance of the British Gold Coast in Britain's West African trade rose notably.[5]

If the home government showed little sustained interest in the settlements it was not because these could, like the Dutch Gold Coast, be considered a dead loss, but for rather different reasons. In an era in which the urge to whittle down colonial expenditure and responsibilities was wellnigh universal in Britain, the pestilential, quarrelsome, and subsidy-consuming Coast was regarded with peculiar distaste. Only the pressures of interested merchants, a determination to keep down the slave trade, and a sense of moral obligation to the

---

[1] Especially in England (e.g. 'Dutch Slave-Dealing in Africa,' *Pall-Mall Gazette*, 22 Dec. 1868), though in fact similar dealings in slaves as recruits were not unknown at Cape Coast (B. Cruikshank, *Eighteen Years on the Gold Coast of Africa* (London, 1853), ii, p. 234).

[2] Colenbrander, op. cit., dl. 2, p. 30.

[3] J. D. Fage, 'The Administration of George Maclean on the Gold Coast, 1830–44', *Transactions of the Gold Coast and Togoland Historical Society*, i, 4 (Achimota, 1955), p. 118; H. Swanzy, 'A Trading Family in the Nineteenth Century Gold Coast', ibid., ii, 2 (Achimota, 1956), p. 96.

[4] Compare the details given on pp. 2–3 above with those to be found in Parliamentary Papers 1874, lxx [C. 1037], p. 6.

[5] *Return of Revenue and Expenditure, and Imports and Exports, of the British Possessions in West Africa, for Twenty Years. . . .* (P.P. 1874, xlvi [C. 941]), p. 5.

natives kept Britain there. In the thirties she came as close as was possible, short of complete withdrawal, to leaving the settlements altogether, and although this experiment in 'merchant rule' came to an end in the forties, the Colonial Office still refused to accept full responsibility for the government, and, above all, the defence of peoples to whom it was none the less according 'protection'. In 1853 a Colonial Secretary looked forward to abandoning West Africa once the slave trade was completely suppressed,[1] and it would not be too much to say that the Colonial Office's lack of interest in this area was only excelled by its lack of knowledge. It is scarcely possible to speak of 'British policy' in relation to the Gold Coast in the nineteenth century; it was rather a question of 'groping for an effective policy',[1] which would not be found until it was thrust upon Britain as a result of the events with which this book is concerned.

The merchants had succeeded in keeping Britain on the Coast, but they would have little influence upon this search for a policy. The official British attitude to the Coast in the mid-nineteenth century was typical of the official attitude to the colonies in general, in being governed not by thoughts of economic expansion and penetration, but rather by humanitarian feeling and the desire for economy[2] —two motives which had the unfortunate tendency often (though not always) to seem to point in opposite directions. Commercial interests took a back seat; overt mercantile pressure had little effect, and, indeed, as far as the Coast is concerned it is difficult to find many instances in which it was even applied. The contrast with the Dutch, whose Gold Coast policy, as we shall see, was for many years more or less dictated by Rotterdam merchants, is a striking one.

The record of Anglo-Dutch relations on the Gold Coast had been one of unbroken rivalry interspersed with not a little open hostility and actual violence. Such was the inevitable outcome of the ruthless commercial competition in which the two nations were engaged. In

---

[1] G. E. Metcalfe, 'After Maclean: Some Aspects of British Gold Coast Policy in the mid-Nineteenth Century', *Transactions of the Gold Coast and Togoland Historical Society*, i, 5 (Achimota, 1955), *passim*.

[2] P. G. James, whose thesis 'British policy in relation to the Gold Coast from 1815 to 1858' is summarized in the *Bulletin of the Institute of Historical Research*, xiv (1936), pp. 124–7, sees his period in terms of a conflict between economy and philanthropy, resulting in an attitude of 'parsimonious benevolence'. Cf. *Cambridge History of the British Empire*, iii, p. 17.

the nineteenth century the Dutch had ceased to be serious competitors for the trade of the Gold Coast, but fresh causes of friction had arisen which allowed of little improvement in the relations between the local administrations. In the first place there were the special ties between the Dutch and Ashanti. What these ties were and how they originated are complex problems which for their solution require some discussion of the status and jurisdiction of the European settlements on the Gold Coast. It was arguable that the Dutch had acquired the entire littoral by right of conquest, which was in turn confirmed by treaties with the Portuguese and by 'contracts' with native rulers whereby the latter accepted Dutch jurisdiction.[1] There were, however, two hard facts in conflict with this theory. The first was that, whatever their pretensions of sovereignty, the Dutch had rarely been able to establish effective control beyond the range of their guns. As with all other European nations on the Coast, whatever jurisdiction they enjoyed was ultimately dependent upon the co-operation of the natives. By the nineteenth century this contrast between theory and practice was only too evident. 'Toutes les possessions des Européens là-bas ne sont que tolerées par les indigènes, pour autant qu'ils y ont des avantages', wrote one visitor to the Coast, so that the only true possessions were the forts;[2] and even of these the natives used to say, 'The forts don't protect us—*we* protect the forts'.[3] In 1873 the Elmina chiefs were said to be astonished by the action of the British in bombarding their town after they had failed to respond to an ultimatum. Centuries of Dutch 'rule' had not prepared them for such treatment; 'the Dutch often threatened them,' they said, 'but always gave way at the last.'[4] In West Africa, in fact, as elsewhere, the validity of sovereign rights, whether of conquest or

---

[1] e.g. Gramberg, *Schetsen*, pp. 346–9; J. A. de Marrée, *Reizen op en Beschrijving van de Goudkust van Guinea* ('s-Gravenhage and Amsterdam, 1817–18), i, pp. 39–42, 242, ii, pp. 278–98. For an early statement of this view see the 'Vertoog of Deductie' of Director-General Valckenbergh, in J. K. J. de Jonge, *De Oorsprong van Neerland's Bezittingen op de Kust van Guinea* ('s-Gravenhage, 1871), pp. 51–69.

[2] F. Douchez, *Causeries sur la Côte de Guinée*. . . . ('s-Gravenhage and Amsterdam, 1839), pp. 78–84. Cf. J. van den Bosch, *Nederlandsche Bezittingen in Azië Amerika en Afrika* . . . ('s-Gravenhage, 1818), p. 260.

[3] De Marrée, op. cit., i, pp. 72, 183.

[4] Harley to Kimberley, 23 June 1873, Cape Coast, Parliamentary Papers, *Despatches on the Subject of the Ashantee Invasion and Attack on Elmina. Presented to both Houses of Parliament by Command of Her Majesty, July, 1873* (P.P. 1873, xlix [C. 802]), pp. 1–2.

'contract', depended ultimately upon the ability of their possessor to enforce them, and this was something that the Dutch did not usually enjoy. In any case the 'contracts' themselves were not entirely reassuring; after examining them in 1856 a commission reported that only over the headquarters fort, Elmina Castle itself, did the Netherlands possess sovereign rights.[1] Nine years later a Dutch Colonial Minister, with disarming frankness, declared that it was uncertain by what right the settlements were held![2]

The other great stumbling-block to the notion of Dutch sovereignty over their own settlements—let alone over the whole Coast—was the existence of certain 'notes' by which the Dutch had undertaken to provide regular payments or subsidies to various native rulers. Such payments had long been common practice among the European nations on the Coast, but there was much disagreement, even among men on the spot, as to their precise significance. For some they were all merely gratifications made in furtherance of trade, completely voluntarily and terminable at will.[3] For others, however, these payments represented the ground-rent of the land on which the European forts stood, and thus could be seen as a sort of tribute and an acknowledgment of the suzerainty of the native ruler concerned.[4] The truth of the matter probably lay somewhere between these two extremes. Some at least of the payments made by Europeans (including the Dutch) to natives quite certainly originated as ground-rent, as we know from surviving treaties.[5] On the other hand, for some

---

[1] *Tweede Rapport der Staatscommissie, benoemd . . . tot het Voorstellen van Maatregelen ten Aanzien van de Slaven in de Nederlandsche Kolonien . . .* ('s-Gravenhage, 1856), pp. 76–8.

[2] 'Instructies en Bestuursreglementen nopens het beleid der Regeering ter Kuste van Guinee', *Bijdragen tot de Taal-, Land-, en Volkenkunde van Nederlandsch-Indie,* dl. 86 ('s-Gravenhage, 1930), pp. 40–1. See also M. K. to Foreign Minister [=M.B.Z.], 18 Feb. 1859, encl. in M. B. Z. to Bentinck, 23 Feb. 1859, Algemeen Rijksarchief/Ned. Legatieën, Groot-Brittannië [=N.L.] 198.

[3] e.g. De Marrée, op. cit., i, p. 49; Gramberg, *Schetsen,* pp. 346–8; T. E. Bowdich, *Mission from Cape Coast Castle to Ashantee* (London, 1873, new ed.), p. xii.

[4] This was the prevailing view among the British (e.g. J. Dupuis, *Journal of a Residence in Ashantee* (London, 1824), p. 234 n.; Cruikshank, op. cit., i, pp. 28–9; and see also E. C. Martin, *The British West African Settlements, 1750–1821* (London, 1927), pp. 48–9), who after the Ashanti defeat of 1826 made a distinction between the so-called 'ground-rent' which they had ceased to pay and the dashes or gratifications which they continued to dole out (Fage, op. cit., pp. 113–14).

[5] e.g. the treaty of 1703 between the Dutch and the King of Akwamu, described in I. Wilks, 'The Rise of the Akwamu Empire, 1650–1710', *Transactions of the Historical Society of Ghana,* iii, 2 (Achimota, 1957), p. 128.

of the 'notes' we possess no such clear-cut evidence of origin. The 'notes' themselves seem to have consisted merely of a promise to pay a certain amount at certain intervals to a certain person,[1] so that it was only too easy (failing any other indication of their purport) for payer and payee each to develop his own ideas of the significance of the transaction. It is quite possible that from the very beginning the relationship formed by some of the Dutch 'notes' was founded on a misunderstanding: intended in one sense by the European, it was accepted in a very different one by the African.

It was a 'note' which formed one of the ties that linked the Dutch with Ashanti. The Dutch called their 'notes' *kostbrieven*. A *kostbrief* was a document given to stewards and other employees on the Coast when they were engaged, and bore some such legend as 'Kofi taken on as house-boy at two dollars a month'. On its back was kept a record of wages paid.[2] The use of this name for the 'notes' given to native rulers underlines the fact that, rightly or wrongly, the Dutch tended to think of these as providing 'subsistence' or *kostgeld*,[3] rather than 'tribute'. One of these *kostbrieven* was captured by the Ashantis when they defeated and subjugated the Denkyiras early in the eighteenth century. The Dutch West India Company thereupon proceeded to pay to the King of Ashanti what had previously been due to the King of Denkyira, namely goods to the value of two ounces of gold each month. In return for this the Ashantis may have acknowledged responsibility for an outstanding trade debt owed by Denkyira to the Dutch.[4] This so-called 'Elmina note' continued to be honoured by the Dutch Government when it took over direct control of the settlements in 1791. In the nineteenth

---

[1] Nagtglas to M. K. (draft), 27 March 1871, (Elmina), G. 726. Cf. W. W. Claridge, *History of the Gold Coast and Ashanti* (London, 1915), i, p. 294.

[2] Nagtglas to M. K. (draft), 27 March 1871, (Elmina), G. 726; though cf. Nagtglas's account of 'The Origins of the Ashantee War' in the *Standard* for 18 Feb. 1874, in which he says of the *kostbrief* that 'such an agreement was signed by both parties'.

[3] Nagtglas stated that, according to all the records that he had seen, the payments to Ashanti had always been in the name of 'subsistence': Nagtglas to Ussher, 20 Dec. 1870, Elmina, *Correspondence Relative to the Cession . . . of the Dutch Settlements on the West Coast of Africa, presented to both Houses of Parliament by Command of Her Majesty, February, 1872* (P.P. 1872, lxx [C. 670]), pp. 13–14.

[4] Ibid., pp. 3–4, Nagtglas to Kennedy, 25 Oct. 1870, Elmina; ibid., p. 13, Kofi Karikari to Ussher, 24 Nov. 1870, Kumasi; ibid., pp. 13–14, Nagtglas to Ussher, 20 Dec. 1870, Elmina; Nagtglas to M. K., 21 Dec. 1870, (Elmina), G. 725; 'Certificate of Apologie', 19 Aug. 1871, Kumasi, '1874 Report', App. IIIh; Letter from Nagtglas in *Standard*, 18 Feb. 1874.

century it seems to have been customary for the Ashantis to await the accumulation of several years' arrears before presenting the 'note' for payment at Elmina. The final presentation took place in November 1867, when payment was made of what was due up to the middle of that year.[1] At least six years had elapsed between this and the previous presentation, which was probably that made by Governor Nagtglas in 1860. In 1871 Nagtglas somewhat tentatively recalled that the 'note' which he had seen on that occasion had been worded 'Two ounces of gold dust a month to be paid to Kwaku Dua, King of Ashanti',[2] from which we may deduce that it was the practice to issue a fresh 'note' to each successive king on his accession. But the exact nature of the 'note' will probably never be known, since the current version was destroyed in the sack of Kumasi in 1874[3]—if, indeed, it had not already been lost.[4]

This simple document was seen by the Ashantis as something very different from a mere *kostbrief*. This was to be dramatically underlined in the 1870s,[5] but long before this it had become apparent that they looked upon the European 'notes' in their possession as conferring or confirming some sort of title to the forts and settlements of the powers concerned.[6] Hence the indignation of Osei Bonsu when, after his victories over the coastal Fantes in the early nineteenth

[1] Hamel to Lees, 21 June 1876, Elmina, Algemeen Rijksarchief/Ned. Consulaten: Elmina [=N. C. Elmina] 4.

[2] Nagtglas to M. K., 27 March 1871, (Elmina), G. 726. There is a curious discrepancy between Nagtglas's recollection of 'two ounces a month' and his more or less simultaneous declarations that the Dutch paid the King of Ashanti 'twenty ounces' a year (on one occasion he actually embodied both these statements in one letter: see Nagtglas to Ussher, 20 Dec. 1870, Elmina, P.P. 1872, lxx [C. 670], pp. 13–14). The clue to this may lie in the fact that in 1860 the value of the *kostgeld* was raised from f. 800 to f. 960 in terms of Dutch currency (Nagtglas to M. K., 27 March 1871, (Elmina), G. 726; Herman, op. cit., ii, p. 62), an increase which is in exact proportion to the difference between twenty and twenty-four ounces; thus in the estimates for 1869 (G. 792) it is recorded that 'to the monarch of Ashanti there is granted a *kostgeld* of two ounces of gold/f. 80 a month in trade goods, constituting an amount of f. 960 a year'. But Nagtglas more than once specially associated 'twenty ounces' with f. 960 (as in the letter to Ussher quoted above), and at least one king of Ashanti claimed long before 1860 that the *original* 'note' was for two ounces a month (see below, p. 10).

[3] Osei Mensah to Dutch consul (copy), 7 Feb. 1876, Kumasi, Ministerie van Buitenlandse Zaken/B. 79: Kust van Guinea, Afstand [Afst.] V.

[4] Ibid., Dutch consul to M. B. Z., 8 Oct. 1874, Elmina. Governor Nagtglas at one time searched the Elmina archives for a copy of the 'note', but in vain (Nagtglas to M. B. Z., 14 Oct. 1867, Hague, Algemeen Rijksarchief/Archief van Buitenlandse Zaken [=B.Z.] 3000).

[5] See below, ch. 4.

[6] Cruikshank, op. cit., i, p. 110.

century, the British seemed unwilling to acknowledge Ashanti supremacy in the same way that the Dutch, so he said, had done a century earlier—that is, by transferring to the Ashantis the 'notes' that had hitherto been in the possession of the defeated enemy. As he remarked (speaking indiscriminately of his great ancestor Osei Tutu and himself):

He went to Denkera and fought, and killed the people; then he said, 'Give me the book you get from Elmina', so they did, and now Elmina belongs to him. . . . When the King killed the Denkera caboceer and got two ounces from Elmina, the Dutch Governor said, 'This is a proper King, we shall not play with him', and made the book four ounces. This King has killed all the people, and all the forts are his. . . .[1]

In fact the British seized the opportunity afforded by the shattering defeat inflicted on Ashanti at Dodowa in 1826 to repudiate the 'notes' held by the latter. The Dutch, however, despite the temporary impotence of Ashanti, and although it could now be argued that since Denkyira had been freed from Ashanti domination all claims arising out of that domination were invalid, continued to pay the Ashanti *kostgeld*. At first sight this may seem surprising. After all, although the 'note' had once been valued as contributing to the policy of friendship with Ashanti in the interest of trade, it now seemed to thinking Dutchmen to be a millstone round the neck of the Gold Coast settlements. Even those who insisted most that it was in origin purely an inducement to trade were beginning to see that it was now for the Ashantis and their enemies alike a sign that the Dutch were tributary to the former.[2] As such it was humiliating and also disastrous, in that it brought down on the heads of the Dutch the hatred that the coastal peoples felt for the warlike Ashantis. The feelings of these peoples were well described by Gramberg, sometime Dutch official and planter:

The Dutch pay tribute to the King of Ashanti and the Elminas make

---

[1] Osei Tutu Kwamena (Osei Bonsu) to Govr. Hope Smith, 28 May 1817, Bowdich, op cit., pp. 76–81; see also Dupuis, op. cit., p. 131. I know of no other mention of the 'note' being doubled after the Ashantis had captured it. Since in fact the nominal value of the 'note' in the 1860s was no more than 'two ounces', it is difficult to avoid the impression that the king was somewhat overstating his case.

[2] See the address presented to the king in 1825 by the Colonial Minister Elout ('1874 Report', Section I A); and cf. Nagtglas to M. B. Z., 14 Oct 1867, Hague, B.Z. 3000, and Gramberg, *Schetsen*, p. 321.

custom, that is, mourn, at his death; thus they are the subjects of Ashanti, and consequently our enemies.[1]

It was in fact their relationship with the Elminas which made the Dutch powerless to withdraw the 'note'. It was presumably through the Elminas, traditionally the allies and by their own account the 'blood relations' of the Ashantis,[2] that the Dutch first established those ties with the latter which were formalized (however problematically) by the 'note'. It was inevitable that the Dutch should identify themselves in this manner with the interests of the people upon whose co-operation their peaceful occupation of their settlements ultimately depended, and of course, in the eighteenth century it doubtless seemed expedient to cash in on the Elmina Ashanti connexion in the interest of trade. By the beginning of the nineteenth century, this process of identification had gone so far that the Dutch did not even raise a murmur against the Ashanti attempts to subjugate the Fante coastal regions, which were indeed aided and abetted wherever possible by the Elminas. Their 'neutrality' could be only too readily interpreted as connivance by the enemies of Ashanti, who as a result grew bitterly hostile to them and looked to the British for protection. In this situation the Ashanti connexion, once arguably an asset, was becoming a distinct liability, threatening the isolation and even the annihilation of the Dutch settlements. The Dutch now clung to it only because they dared not risk the repercussions that its abandonment might have on their relationship with the Elminas, on whose goodwill—thus the vicious circle ran—the enmity of the other coastal peoples made them more dependent than ever.

Fortunately for the Dutch the Ashantis were for all practical purposes at peace with the Coast for almost forty years after 1826. Even in this period of quiescence, however, the Fantes did not forget the 'neutrality' of the Dutch during the Ashanti incursions and the continuing Dutch-Ashanti 'alliance' as symbolized by the 'note'. Nor did the British. In fact, this 'alliance' was throughout these years a

---

[1] Gramberg, *De Goudkust*, p. 399.
[2] J. S. Wartemberg, *Sao Jorge d'El Mina, Premier West African Settlement* (Ilfracombe, n.d.), p. 31.

major cause of hostility to the Dutch on the part of the British and their 'protected' tribes alike.[1]

It was in the creation of this British 'protectorate', and the problems that this involved, that lay the second great cause of friction between Dutch and British in the nineteenth century, greater even than the Ashanti 'alliance'. The middle years of the century saw the British engaged in the formalization and extension of the jurisdiction over the tribes *behind* their settlements, which had originally been established largely by the personal influence of Maclean.[2] The higgledy-piggledy fashion in which the Dutch and British stations jostled each other along the coast had long been a fruitful source of dispute, particularly with regard to the responsibility of the European power for the actions of the African inhabitants; but now it was to give rise to much more serious trouble in the interior. One after another the governors of Elmina found themselves the helpless witnesses of the process whereby inland tribes, hitherto considered to be under some sort of Dutch 'influence', were accepting effective British jurisdiction.[3] Neither the British authorities on the Coast nor the Colonial Office in London (however chary it might be of actual territorial expansion) attached any importance to Dutch claims of prior protection.[4] In 1858 Governor van den Bossche reported that British influence had now been extended over the entire area between the Coast and Ashanti.[5] This was certainly an exaggeration, but in the following year Nagtglas, van den Bossche's successor, informed The Hague that the British undoubtedly intended to confine Dutch authority solely to the Coast and thus render their settlements valueless, in that they would be cut off from any share in the eventual opening-up and development of West Africa.[6]

---

[1] For the ill-feeling caused by the Dutch attitude to the Ashanti War of 1863–4 see Herman, op. cit., p. 75; House of Commons, *Report from the Select Committee on Africa (Western Coast)* . . . [P.P. 1865, v, (412)], p. 290; Claridge, op. cit., i, p. 520.

[2] Metcalfe, op. cit., pp. 183–4.

[3] For details see Nagtglas, op. cit., p. 5.

[4] This came out particularly clearly in the dispute over the village of Impohaw, which continued intermittently between 1854 and 1863. Its course between 1859 and 1862 is summarized in a 'Report on the state of the negotiations with England . . .', June 1862, B.Z. 2999.

[5] '1874 Report', section I A.

[6] Nagtglas to M. K. (copy), 9 Feb. 1859, Elmina, B.Z. 2999. Commissioner Ord, writing in 1865, reported that the territory up to 80 miles inland was inhabited by a number of tribes, 'the whole of whom, with the exception of a small number

British officials on the Coast were as conscious as the Dutch of the many difficulties arising from divided jurisdiction, which, as Administrator Conran pointed out in 1866, was the cause of 'troubles and broils constantly arising among all parties'[1]—a situation all the more irritating to these officials in that they firmly believed that it was only *their* presence and *their* authority over the natives that enabled the feeble and unpopular Dutch to maintain their settlements at all.[2] Most galling of all was the reluctance of the Dutch to come into a joint tariff scheme. For twenty years this was the subject of sporadic negotiations which were to culminate in the disastrous 'exchange' of 1868.

---

residing immediately in rear of the Dutch posts, are included in what is termed the [British] "Protectorate" ' (House of Commons, *Report of Colonel Ord, the Commissioner appointed to Inquire into the Condition of the British Settlements on the West Coast of Africa* [P.P. 1865, xxxvii (170)], p. 16).

[1] Conran to Cardwell, 5 Feb. 1866, Cape Coast, House of Commons, *Copies of all Correspondence . . . relative to the Arrest and Deportation of . . . King Aggery . . .* [P.P. 1867, xlix (198)], p. 50.

[2] e.g. Conran to Blackall, 6 Sept. 1866, Cape Coast, Ghana National Archives/ Original Correspondence, ADM.1/688; P.P. 1865, v (412), pp. 115, 129.

2

TARIFFS AND EXCHANGE, 1847–67

NEITHER the Dutch nor the British possessions on the Gold Coast were self-supporting. Expenditure was not very great, but revenue was smaller still. The British settlements consumed an annual grant of £4,000 for civil expenditure alone, which by the 1860s proved totally inadequate,[1] while by 1864 the Dutch settlements, where salaries had been increased but income remained negligible, were running at an annual loss of about ƒ. 120,000.[2] Moreover, the home governments, dubious of the value or desirability of these settlements, grudged even the relatively small sums needed to meet the constant deficit. The obvious remedy for this state of affairs might seem at first glance to have been the imposition of moderate duties on imports, but the fragmentation of the seaboard into dispersed British, Dutch, and (until 1850) Danish 'spheres of influence' made the effective levying of customs duties peculiarly difficult. Unilateral imposition of such duties by any one power seemed quite impracticable, since this could result (it was thought) only in the diversion of trade to some landing-place out of its control a few miles along the coast; and in fact in the 1840s the British levied only one half per cent. *ad valorem*, while Dutch and Danes levied nothing at all. There were two possible solutions to this problem: the first, and by far the more effective, would be for the powers to agree on a uniform tariff; the second, which might at least help to prevent outright evasion of duty, for their respective territories to be consolidated in such a way that each would control a substantial length of coastline, uninterrupted by any enclaves.[3] In the event, twenty years of negotiation

---

[1] 'Return of Revenue and Expenditure . . .', P.P. 1874, xlvi [C. 941].
[2] 'Begrootingen van ontvangsten en uitgaven', G. 792; Nagtglas, op. cit., p. 1.
[3] For a statement of the issues involved see Ord's memorandum enclosed in C.O. to F.O., 31 May 1860, F.O. 97/250.

resulted in an agreement which represented a combination of these alternatives.

As early as 1847 the Dutch and British authorities on the Coast proposed jointly to levy a duty on rum and gin, but the Dutch government considered this pointless unless the Danes followed suit. Subsequent investigation showed that the Danes would have no part of the project, which the Dutch consequently allowed to drop.[1] The British Colonial Secretary, Earl Grey, had already approved the scheme, and in May 1849 he startled the authorities at Cape Coast Castle by sending them an ordinance along the lines of the original proposals.[2] Perhaps he had forgotten, or had never understood, that these proposals had been made on the assumption that they would also be adopted by the Dutch; but a few months later it was with his eyes wide open that he sanctioned an avowedly unilateral scheme of duties on strong drink, tobacco, gunpowder and firearms. This had been drawn up by Governor Winniett, then on leave in London. Winniett was confident that these duties would fall solely upon the consumer, and he also emphasized that the goods concerned were imported principally in foreign ships.[3] This confidence was not, however, shared by the acting Governor at Cape Coast, whose representations persuaded Grey to suspend the operation of both schemes while a request was made to the Dutch Government for co-operation in executing Winniett's proposals.[4] To this application the Dutch replied that they would be ready enough to come into the project if only the continuing opposition of the Danes could be overcome, since for the British and Dutch to act alone would merely drive all Gold Coast trade to the Danish forts.[5]

Almost as soon as this reply had been sent off a totally different complexion was put upon the affair by the news that the British had

[1] Winniett to Grey, 20 May 1847, Cape Coast, C.O. 96/11; M.K. to M. B. Z., 28 Dec. 1849, Hague, B.Z. 2999; ibid., 'Report on state of negotiations with England . . .', June 1862; 'Memorie van Toelichting', *Hand. S.G.*, 1867, Bijlagen pp. 901–6.

[2] Grey to Winniett, 19 Aug. 1847, ADM. 1/9; ibid., Grey to Fitzpatrick, 15 May 1849.

[3] Winniett to Grey, 28 July 1849, Cliffords Inn, C.O. 96/15 (with minute by Grey of 5 Aug. 1849); Grey to Macdonald, 7 Nov. 1849, C.O. 96/17.

[4] Fitzpatrick to Grey, 20 Aug. 1849, Cape Coast, C.O. 96/16; Memo. by Grey ('immediate'), 29 Dec. 1849, C.O. 96/17; Grey to Winniett, 31 Dec. 1849, ADM. 1/9.

[5] Disbrowe to M. B. Z., 21 Dec. 1849, Hague, B.Z. 2999; ibid., M. K. to M. B. Z., 28 Dec. 1849, Hague; 'Memorie van Toelichting', *ut supra*.

agreed to buy the Danish settlements on the Gold Coast.[1] Returning forthwith to the attack, the British envoy at The Hague was rewarded with the assurance that the Dutch Government would stand by its conditional promise and would give Grey's scheme a trial.[2] As soon as detailed negotiations began, however, the Dutch Colonial Minister Pahud began to have second thoughts. Not only did he consider that the British proposals, in singling out a few commodities, discriminated unduly against the staple articles of Dutch trade; he also felt that the presence of near-by French and (so he said) Portuguese[3] trading stations raised dangers that must first be investigated.[4] The views of the Dutch Governor van der Eb more than confirmed these misgivings. In a letter of 1 May 1850 he advised strongly against the whole project, partly because of the nature of the coast, which, he said, would make adequate precautions against smuggling impossible, and partly owing to the cost of instituting the scheme and the harm to trade that would result from it. The enthusiasm of Winniett for the scheme, he alleged, was mainly due to the fact that he expected to have his salary increased by £750 per annum if it went through.[5] Winniett, meanwhile, had informed his government that British merchants on the Coast welcomed the proposals, and had deplored the hostility to them of van der Eb and the Elmina merchants. Van der Eb's attitude, he suggested, was not a little influenced by the fact that he himself was engaged in extensive private trade.[6]

Pahud was now determined to have nothing more to do with Grey's scheme, despite the protests of the Dutch envoy in London who felt that he had been put in a false position and that the whole episode

[1] 'Chiefly because she feared they would be bought by France; though she did not lose sight of the facility they would afford for collection of duty' (James, op. cit.).
[2] M. K. to King (copy), 2 Jan. 1850, Hague, B.Z. 2999.
[3] The nearest Portuguese post was in fact (as it remained until August 1961) at Whydah, more than 170 miles east of Accra—too distant to supply the Gold Coast market, and in any case on a stretch of the Guinea Coast where legitimate trade was at this time virtually unknown.
[4] M. K. to M. B. Z., 16 Jan. 1850, Hague, B.Z. 2999; Disbrowe to Palmerston, 2 Feb. 1850, Hague, F.O. 37/290; same to same, 17 May 1850, Hague, F.O. 37/291.
[5] M. K. to M. B. Z., 22 Aug. 1850, Hague, B.Z. 2999; 'Memorie van Toelichting', ut supra.
[6] Winniett to Grey, 20 May 1850, Cape Coast, C.O. 96/18; Elliott to M. B. Z., 30 Aug. 1850, Hague, B.Z. 2999. Fifteen years later two of van der Eb's successors also impugned his impartiality and the reliability of his figures: Nagtglas and Elias to M. K., 3 Oct. 1865, Hague, B.Z. 2999.

might have a damaging effect on Anglo-Dutch relations.[1] On Pahud's suggestion the British Government was formally told that it could not, for the time being at least, expect Dutch co-operation. The somewhat disingenuous excuse given for this volte-face was that van der Eb's report made it clear that a condition imposed by the Dutch in a note of 8 January—that the measure should not involve any additional expenditure—could not be fulfilled. The real reason for the Dutch change of heart was, however, clearly indicated, namely the unpopularity of the project in Dutch commercial circles, and the consequent unwillingness of the ministry to put it before the States-General.[2]

Grey was still not wholly convinced that Dutch participation was essential for the successful operation of import duties. Anxious that the British Gold Coast should be able to pay for more schools, hospitals and roads,[3] he did not altogether abandon hope of raising a revenue by unilateral moderate duties,[4] as well as by the introduction of a poll-tax. Both schemes were in fact attempted, though not by Grey, and neither achieved its desired end. The hostility of the natives to the ill-fated poll-tax was paralleled by the hostility of the merchants to the three per cent. *ad valorem* duty of 1856, which the Cape Coast authorities consequently found it necessary to reduce to 2 per cent. before the year was out.[5]

The ill success of both the poll-tax and the unilateral duty was

---

[1] He was particularly concerned about the reactions of 'onzen vriend P.'—Palmerston—but was later able to report that the Foreign Secretary seemed fairly satisfied with his explanations: Schimmelpenninck to M. B. Z., 4 and 6 Sept., and 8 Nov. 1850, London, B.Z. 2999.

[2] M. B. Z. to king (draft), 18 Oct. 1850, B.Z. 2999; ibid., M. B. Z. to Elliott (draft), 31 Oct. 1850. For Pahud's motives see also Disbrowe to Palmerston, 14 March 1850, Hague, F.O. 37/290; Elliott to Palmerston, 17 Sept. 1850, F.O. 37/292.

[3] Metcalfe, op. cit., p. 185. He may also have been influenced by the report of the Select Committee of 1842, with its references to the advocacy by the Cape Coast merchants of a tariff discriminating against foreign vessels (House of Commons, *Report from the Select Committee on the West Coast of Africa* . . . [P.P. 1842, xii (551)], i, p. 82, ii, p. 20).

[4] Grey to Winniett, 23 Nov. 1850, ADM. 1/8.

[5] Connor to Russell, 2 and 31 July 1855, Cape Coast, C.O. 96/34; Connor to Labouchere, 5 April, 6 May, 18 June and 1 July 1856, Cape Coast, C.O. 96/38; Labouchere to Officer commanding govt. (copy), 23 May 1856, C.O. 402/5; Connor to Derx (copy), 28 Oct. 1856, Cape Coast, C.O. 96/39. Henceforth the duty in the British settlements remained at 2 per cent. (P.P. 1865, v (412), p. 46), where it had also stood in the time of Maclean (ibid., p. 49). See also E. Baillaud, *La politique indigène de l'Angleterre en Afrique Occidentale* (Paris, 1912), p. 88.

naturally calculated to revive British interest in a joint tariff.[1] Hopes that this might now be achieved seem to have been encouraged by the apparently sympathetic attitude of van der Eb's successor Schomerus,[2] as well as by the report of Major Harry St. George Ord, R.E., who early in 1856 spent three months on the Coast on a special mission of investigation for the Colonial Office.[3] In this report Ord emphasized the importance of the revenue that effective import duties would produce, and to this end recommended *either* the purchase of the Dutch settlements 'in the same manner as we purchased those of the Danes in 1849' *or* the negotiation of a uniform tariff. He was aware, he added darkly, 'to what influence at the Court of The Hague' the rejection of the previous joint tariff proposal had been due, but could not

forego the belief that a clear and impartial exposition of the policy of the measure, and the advantages which it would confer upon the Coast at large by enabling the respective Governments to do so much more for their Settlements than the limited means at their disposal will now admit of, would not be unavailing. . . .[4]

Ord's recommendations were taken to heart at the Colonial Office. The Parliamentary Under-Secretary Ball liked the idea of a purchase which 'would greatly promote the success of our efforts to improve and civilize the people'. He even thought that 'a moderate sum would not be objected to by the H. of C. for this purpose'. But Secretary Labouchere, seeing that there was little hope that the Dutch would sell, favoured instead the alternative proposal for the renewal of tariff negotiations, and a formal approach along these lines was made to the Dutch Government in July 1856.[5]

This application met initially with little favour at the Dutch Colonial Ministry, where the view was taken that the objections put

[1] See, for example, the 'Humble petition of the Merchants and Traders of Cape Coast', 17 Jan. 1856, C.O. 96/40.

[2] Connor to Labouchere, 26 March 1856, Accra, C.O. 96/38.

[3] Ord had previously visited the West African settlements in 1850, on a mission of inspection from the War Office (P.P. 1865, v (412), p. 10). For his varied career in the army and the colonial service see the useful article in the *D.N.B.*

[4] Ord to Labouchere, 15 May 1856, London, C.O. 96/40.

[5] Minutes by Ball (28 May 1856) and Labouchere (31 May 1856) on above; Abercromby to M. B. Z., 4 July 1856, Hague, B.Z. 2999; Labouchere to Clarendon, 7 July 1856, Clarendon MSS. deposited in the Bodleian Library [= MS. Clar. Dep.] C. 48.

forward in 1850 still held good. Of course, it was said, the British were anxious to get Dutch agreement, since their unilateral duties and poll-tax had got them into difficulties and had even led some English merchants to remove their businesses to the Dutch settlements. For Holland the only problem, in the ministry's view, was to find a polite way of declining the British proposal.[1] The British envoy at The Hague had in fact already warned his superiors that the weakness of the Dutch Government was such that it would be inclined 'to reject any proposition, the agreement to wch. may necessitate a Parliamentary discussion and approval'.[2] But the arrival of Major Ord at The Hague to assist in the negotiations led to an important modification of the Dutch attitude. Ord produced evidence to refute the contention that the new British duties had driven away trade; on the contrary, he claimed, the British experiment had shown that such duties, no matter how hostile the merchants might be to them, *could* be imposed without any harmful effects.[3] This evidence greatly impressed the Dutch ministers, who now not only agreed to instruct their Governor to report on the question, but also decided to imitate Britain's example by sending out a Special Commissioner to the Coast. That they were now in earnest was amply demonstrated by their choice as Commissioner of Derx, a former official at Elmina who was known to be an enthusiastic advocate of a joint tariff, and who had already privately engaged himself to Ord to further this cause.[4] Ord, indeed, was told that Derx was being sent out not so much for his opinion as to ensure a favourable report on 'a measure which they [the ministry] wish to put forward in the strongest, and most favourable light . . .'. Unlike Governor Schomerus, Ord was told, Derx would not be influenced by private trading interests.

[1] M. K. to M. B. Z., (15 July 1856), B.Z. 2999.

[2] Abercromby to Clarendon, 4 July 1856, Hague, MS. Clar. Dep. C. 47.

[3] Acting Governor Connor, who imposed the three per cent. duty, always maintained that it had had no adverse effect on trade. Four years later Governor Andrews was seriously concerned at the prospect of the wholesale emigration of merchants from the British to the Dutch settlements (Andrews to Newcastle, 8 Aug. 1860, Cape Coast, C.O. 96/49), but his fears were discounted by the Colonial Office (ibid., Min. by Barrow of 15 Dec. 1860 on Andrews to Newcastle, 8 Nov. 1860, Christiansborg).

[4] Abercromby to Clarendon, 4 July 1856, Hague, MS. Clar. Dep. C. 47; Abercromby to M. B. Z., 26 July 1856, Hague, B.Z. 2999; Ord to Labouchere, 6 Aug. 1856, Hague, C.O. 96/40; Royal Commission for Derx, 18 Aug. 1856, B.Z. 2999. For Derx's previous advocacy of uniform duties see Winniett to Grey, 15 June 1850, Cape Coast, C.O. 96/19.

C

Undoubtedly Meijer, the Colonial Minister, was attracted by the prospect of an increased revenue which would make possible higher salaries for officials and thus enable him to put an end to this pernicious system of private trading. He was therefore determined to approach the States-General with as strong a hand as possible—hence the dispatch of Derx. Even so the British envoy Abercromby had some reservations about the likelihood of success, given the parliamentary weakness of the ministry. 'The whole or nearly so of this question,' he commented,

will . . . probably turn upon the probability of obtaining *without much fighting* the sanction of the Chambers, for you may be assured that rather than have to encounter a struggle there, the Govt. will prefer their own ease. . . .[1]

Derx's report, sent home on 7 November, was very different from that submitted by van der Eb more than five years earlier. So convinced, in fact, was Derx of the desirability and practicability of a uniform tariff that he actually drew up a provisional agreement with Governor Connor for a joint *ad valorem* duty of 3 per cent.[2] Although Ord and Abercromby had hoped for something rather different,[3] negotiations were now resumed at The Hague which resulted in the drawing up of a draft treaty on the lines of Derx's provisional arrangement in March 1857.[4] Once more, however, British hopes were doomed to disappointment, and for much the same reasons as had operated in 1850. As Ord remarked several years later, the parliamentary weakness of successive Dutch Governments made them reluctant to submit to the States-General any agreements with foreign powers unless they could adduce some evidence that

---

[1] Abercromby to Clarendon, 25 July 1856, Hague, MS. Clar. Dep. C. 47; Ord to Labouchere, 6 Aug. 1856, Hague, C.O. 96/40; ibid., same to same, 20 Dec. 1856, Gravesend.

[2] Derx to M. K., 7 Nov. 1856, Elmina, B.Z. 2999; Connor to Labouchere, 7 Nov. 1856, Cape Coast, C.O. 96/39.

[3] They had advocated higher fixed duties on such articles as spirits, gunpowder and firearms, rather than an overall *ad valorem* duty. The British merchants, as Ord knew, preferred the former in the hope that they could be arranged to exclude their staple trade in Manchester goods. By the same token, the Dutch merchants preferred an *ad valorem* duty which would not penalize *their* staple commodities.

[4] Project of Treaty, B.Z. 2999. Before these negotiations were resumed Ord had visited Paris in a fruitless attempt to obtain French participation in the proposed arrangement. This British initiative was taken as a result of the importance attached by Derx to French concurrence. Ord and Abercromby were relieved to find subsequently that the Dutch ministers were not much concerned about this (Ord to Labouchere, 1 and 13 March 1857, Hague, C.O. 96/42).

Holland had got the better of the bargain. This was particularly true, he added, of more than one proposed arrangement concerning the Gold Coast, which, though they had been approved by individual ministers, the government of the day refused to submit to the States-General 'from an avowed fear that they did not look sufficiently favourable to command their approval'.[1]

In 1857 it was the Finance Minister, Vrolik, who was the spokes-man of ministerial misgivings. Above all he pointed to the likelihood of strong opposition from commercial interests which might well decisively influence the deliberations of the Second Chamber.[2] Un-doubtedly he was thinking of the Rotterdam house of van Rycke-vorsel, virtually the only Dutch firm now trading with the Dutch Gold Coast, where, under the system of private trading, the Gov-ernor and his subordinates were in effect van Ryckevorsel's agents. Its head was president of the Rotterdam Chamber of Commerce, and it had already demonstrated its hostility to the tariff scheme in a strongly-worded memorial.[3] The British negotiators retorted that a failure to seize this opportunity of putting an end to a long-standing drain on Dutch revenue would be much more open to criticism at home than the imposition of customs duties, and they had something to say too of the malign influence of van Ryckevorsel, 'the Mon-opolist for whose sole profit the Netherland Government are gener-ous enough to expend the yearly sum of one hundred thousand guilders'.[4] The negotiations were none the less broken off, the Dutch ministers 'freely admitting' that it was van Ryckevorsel's 'consider-able political influence' that had deterred them from proceeding further.[5] The British had the slight consolation of a Dutch assurance that the negotiations would be reopened on the lines laid down in the draft treaty, as soon as 'a favourable opportunity for presenting a measure on this subject to the Chamber shall offer'.[6]

---

[1] Ord to Buckingham, 16 Jan. 1868, Penang, C.O. 273/17.
[2] Finance Minister to M. B. Z. (copy), 23 March 1857, Hague, B.Z. 2999.
[3] Ibid., Memorial from H. van Ryckevorsel, 3 Sept. 1857, Rotterdam.
[4] Abercromby to M. B. Z., 31 March and 16 April 1857, Hague, B.Z. 2999; Ord to Labouchere, 31 March 1857, Hague, C.O. 96/42; ibid., Abercromby to Clarendon (copy), 2 April 1857, Hague.
[5] Ibid., Abercromby to Clarendon (copy), 17 April 1857, Hague; ibid., Ord to Labouchere, 18 April 1857, Hague.
[6] Notes on conference of 17 April 1857, B.Z. 2999; ibid., Abercromby to M. B. Z., 17 April 1857, Hague; ibid., M. B. Z. to Abercromby (draft), 18 April 1857; Memo.

The history of the Derx-Connor proposals disposes of the thesis, current in the Colonial Office in later years, that

if the Netherlands Government had not been under the necessity of consulting the wishes of officers so engaged [*i.e.* in private trading], it is clear that they would have been willing to co-operate with Her Majesty's Government in the imposition of moderate Customs duties.[1]

It was not this but the necessity of consulting the States-General that dictated the attitude of successive Dutch Governments, and thus brought it about that Holland, elsewhere still clinging to some measure of protection, willy-nilly defended the Free Trade cause on the Guinea Coast.

In September 1857 Cornelis Johannes Marius Nagtglas took over the governorship of Elmina.[2] For the next fifteen years this remarkable man devoted himself, whether in a public or a private capacity, to what he saw as the interests of the Dutch Gold Coast. Few Dutch officials were able to inspire so much trust and affection in their British counterparts as Nagtglas, who early in 1859 was able to send home a detailed project for a system of customs duties together with the news that Acting Governor Bird had promised his co-operation in this matter.[3] Nagtglas did not let matters rest here. He had come round to the view, as explained in a further dispatch dated 9 February, that a uniform tariff could be acceptable only if it were accompanied by a regulation of boundaries; that is, by an exchange of territory which would create two well-defined and consolidated 'protectorates' in place of the existing chaotically dispersed and vaguely delimited settlements. As Nagtglas himself remarked, there was nothing new in the idea of an exchange, though this was the first time that it had been formally proposed by the Dutch authorities on

---

from Ord, in C.O. to F.O., 31 May 1860, F.O. 97/250; Nagtglas and Elias to M.K., 3 Oct. 1865, Hague, B.Z. 2999. It was also understood that Vrolik would attempt to get enacted a 'National Financial measure' which would enable the Dutch Government to impose duties without reference to the States-General (Abercromby to Clarendon, 18 April 1857, Hague, MS. Clar. Dep. C. 68), but nothing seems to have come of this.

[1] 'Exchange of settlements with the Dutch in 1867' (by A. W. L. Hemming), April 1874 (Conf. print, African No. 52).

[2] Nagtglas seems first to have come to the Coast in 1837, with Major-General Verveer ('Nominatieve staat der verleende Pensionen', in estimates for 1863, G. 792). In September 1857 he became Acting Governor, and in May 1858 substantive Governor, which he remained until he retired on pension in June 1862 (Herman, op. cit., ii, p. 70).

[3] Nagtglas to M.K. (draft), 10 Jan. 1859, Elmina, G. 398.

the Coast. It had been put before the Dutch Government in a memorial written in about 1816;[1] it had formed the subject of conversations, apparently initiated on the British side, between the authorities at Cape Coast and Elmina as early as 1826;[2] and it had recently been recommended in the report, published in 1856, of the commission set up to deal with the question of slavery in the Dutch colonies.[3] In Nagtglas's opinion the carrying out of such an exchange was now a matter of real urgency if the Dutch Gold Coast was to retain any *raison d'être*. British 'encroachments' had already confined Dutch authority to the coast in the eastern part of the country, and would soon do so in the west if they were not checked, thus making all communication with the interior dependent upon the goodwill of the British and their 'protected' tribes. The only effective method of stopping this process would be an exchange agreement which would confine British authority to the area east of the Sweet River, leaving the western area to Dutch protection. The possession of such a unified protectorate would, moreover, make energetic efforts for improvement and development much more practicable. There would be little objection to such an exchange from the 'English' tribes affected, thought Nagtglas; in particular the chiefs of Wasaw, the inland territory lying between Elmina and Ashanti, could easily be brought to accept Dutch protection by a few gifts or an allowance. He emphasized that a joint tariff could be of little benefit to the Dutch Gold Coast unless such an exchange were first effected, and hoped that the enthusiasm of the British for the former might bring them to agree to the latter if it could be made a pre-condition. The British now seemed confident that they could gain supremacy in the Gold Coast by means of 'illegal encroachments', and hence were no longer interested in an exchange for its own sake; thus, if a joint tariff were agreed to *before* an exchange took place, all hope of the latter would disappear.[4]

---

[1] Said to be the work of W. F. Fennekol, and later published as *Proeve over de Kust van Guinea* . . . ('s-Gravenhage, 1831). See pp. 85–8 for the exchange proposals. A similar suggestion had already been made by the British official H. Meredith in his *Account of the Gold Coast of Africa* . . . (London, 1812), p. 211.

[2] Herman, op. cit., ii, p. 24; Campbell to Bathurst, 14 and 21 Sept. 1826, H.M.S. *Lively* and Cape Coast, C.O. 267/73.

[3] *Tweede Rapport der Staatscommissie* . . . , p. 96.

[4] Nagtglas to M.K. (copies), 9 and 19 Feb. 1859, Elmina, B.Z. 2999.

While Nagtglas was sending home these views the British Government, by a curious coincidence, was sounding the willingness of the Dutch to reopen the negotiations which had been broken off in 1857. The Colonial Minister, Rochussen, showed little interest in the joint tariff project, apparently owing to the same fears of opposition as had been entertained by his predecessors. But this time the British had decided to explore two other possibilities, the purchase of the Dutch Gold Coast, or alternatively the exchange of territory.

This broadening of aims was largely due to the persuasions of Governor Sir Benjamin Pine, who in the course of 1857 had swung from advocating the abandonment of the Gold Coast to stressing the importance of acquiring Dutch Accra. In this he seems to have been influenced by proposals formulated by his subordinate Andrews for the outright purchase of the Dutch settlements east of Cape Coast.[1] The reaction of the Colonial Office to all this was one of caution; one official, indeed, spoke of Andrews' 'wild proposals'.[2] But less than a year later Pine, now on leave, came up with much more detailed and far-reaching recommendations. The present revenue of the settlements, he pointed out, was quite insufficient, the existing 2 per cent. *ad valorem* duty unfair in that (as a result of the proximity of the Dutch) it fell upon the importing merchant rather than the consumer, and the poll-tax ineffective as well as objectionable. What was needed was Dutch co-operation in building up revenues from customs duties. The simplest way, and the best, but probably the most difficult of achievement, would be to induce the Dutch to sell out for, say, £20,000. Failing this, an exchange with the Sweet River as boundary, plus an agreement to impose equal customs duties, would be desirable. Either one of these would be better than nothing; but if neither could be achieved Britain must choose between abandoning the Coast altogether or confining her authority strictly to the forts.[3]

The idea of buying out the Dutch had a fairly long history. Their removal had seemed highly desirable to British abolitionists early

---

[1] Memo. from Andrews to Pine, 4 Dec. 1857, enc. in Pine to Labouchere, 8 Feb. 1858, Cape Coast, C.O. 96/43; Pine to Labouchere, 30 Dec. 1857, Accra, C.O. 96/41.
[2] Min. by Barrow of 19 April 1858 on memo. from Andrews to Pine, 4 Dec. 1857, C.O. 96/43; min. by Merivale on F.O. to C.O., 1 March 1858, C.O. 96/44.
[3] 'Memorandum as to the Revenue of the Gold Coast', by Pine, 11 Nov. 1858, Oriental Club, C.O. 96/46.

in the century,[1] and had commended itself to British commanders engaged in the suppression of the slave trade. In 1822 the ill-fated Governor MacCarthy had joined with the Cape Coast merchants in advocating the purchase of both Dutch and Danish settlements in view of their actual assistance to slave-traders and their potential threat to British commerce, should they, as MacCarthy thought likely, be 'occupied by the Americans'.[2] MacCarthy actually succeeded in persuading the Colonial Secretary of the desirability of purchase,[3] but his subsequent disastrous defeat and death at the hands of the Ashantis put the matter in a very different light. When his successor suggested that *either* the settlements be abandoned *or* the Dutch bought out it was the former alternative which appealed more to the Colonial Office.[4] Thus, when in 1825 the Dutch ambassador in London had been authorized to negotiate the cession of the Dutch Gold Coast to Britain against suitable compensation, the Colonial Office showed little interest.[5] More recently, in 1851, the possibility of purchase had been broached by the Legislative Council at Cape Coast.[6] Now, at last, with Pine's new proposals, it began to receive serious attention in Downing Street, despite the principle of the non-extension of territorial sovereignty.[7] Recent incidents on the Coast had already induced the Under-Secretary Carnarvon to ponder upon 'the difficulties & sometimes risk of collision with foreign Powers from our vague and anomalous jurisdiction',[8] and Secretary Bulwer-Lytton was convinced by Pine that the present state of affairs on the Coast could not and should not last much longer. 'The simplest course' would be to buy out the Dutch; otherwise we should press

[1] House of Commons, *Report from the Select Committee on Papers Relating to the African Forts* [P.P. 1816, iv (470)], Appendix No. 22 (1); Martin, op. cit., p. 102.

[2] MacCarthy to Bathurst, 18 May and 11 November 1822, Sierra Leone and Cape Coast, C.O. 267/56. The possibility of acquiring the Dutch forts had also been mooted by Consul Dupuis after his celebrated sojourn in Kumasi (Dupuis, op. cit., p. lxviii).

[3] Bathurst to MacCarthy, 30 Aug. 1822, C.O. 268/20.

[4] Turner to Bathurst, 24 March 1825, Cape Coast, C.O. 267/65; ibid., same to same, 9 April 1825, Accra (with C.O. memo. of 2 July).

[5] P. H. van der Kemp, 'St. George d'Elmina in 1825', *De Tijdspiegel*, 1910 (1ste dl.), pp. 224–31; Koppius, op. cit., dl. 2 (Nov. 1930), pp. 987, 991.

[6] Minutes of meeting of Leg. Council, 4 March 1851, Cape Coast, Ghana National Archives/Sessional Papers ADM. 5/1; and cf. William Hutton's evidence before the 1842 Select Committee [P.P. 1842, xi (551), i, p. 675].

[7] As enunciated, for example, in Palmerston's instructions to Ord, 31 Oct. 1855, C.O. 96/37.

[8] Min. by Carnarvon of 16 Sept. 1858 on Bird to Bulwer-Lytton, 2 Aug. 1858, Cape Coast, C.O. 96/43.

for an equalization of customs duties. If these alternatives failed then an exchange might be attempted.[1]

This was the basis on which Ward, British chargé d'affaires at The Hague, had been instructed to sound the Dutch. His first report made it clear that the purchase of the Dutch Gold Coast was out of the question. The Dutch constitution of 1815 laid down that no treaty concluded in time of peace which involved the cession or exchange of any part of Netherlands territory could be ratified by the king without the prior approval of the States-General.[2] Ward emphasized that in fact no Dutch Government would dare to propose the cession of territory to this body, where this would be gratefully accepted by the opposition as a stick with which to belabour the ministry. An exchange, however, was a very different matter, above all since the Colonial Office was now ready not merely (as Nagtglas had hoped) to link 'an exchange of territory' with 'an equalization of the Sea customs', but even to regard the former as an alternative to the latter.[3] Rochussen promised to take into serious consideration any overture of this nature, and seemed to entertain the notion of an 'equivalent' in another part of Africa, namely a South African port.[4] There were some second thoughts at the Colonial Office as to how far 'our invariable disclaimer of dominion' over the protected tribes might affect the validity of any exchange which involved the interior, but none the less the British Government showed no hesitation in acting on Rochussen's hint. Its attitude was in accordance with the promptings of Pine, who emphasized that the consolidation of the settlements would not only have fiscal advantages, but would also put an end to the position whereby Dutch 'authority is virtually protected at *our* expense'. Ward was duly sent a memorandum drawn up by Pine, which recommended the Sweet River as a boundary, and was instructed to make an unofficial overture to the Dutch in this sense.[5] To this further proposal the Dutch Government, which

---

[1] C.O. to F.O. (draft), 10 Dec. 1858, C.O. 96/44.
[2] A. Vandenbosch, *Dutch Foreign Policy Since 1815* (The Hague, 1959), p. 9.
[3] C.O. to F.O. (draft), 1 June 1859, C.O. 96/46; Malmesbury to Bentinck (draft), 4 June 1859, F.O. 37/377.
[4] Ward to Malmesbury, 10 Feb. 1859, Hague, F.O. 97/250.
[5] Min. by Merivale of 19 Feb. 1859 on F.O. to C.O., 17 Feb. 1859, C.O. 96/46; ibid., 'Memorandum on the papers relating to the proposed arrangements with the Dutch', by Pine, 6 March 1859 (dated 1858 in error); C.O. to F.O., 19 March 1859,

by now had received Nagtglas's dispatches on this subject, replied
that it was ready to enter into formal negotiations and was hopeful
of the acquiescence of the States-General.[1]

There were still misgivings in Downing Street over the exchange
of territories *behind* the settlements, where Britain exercised some
authority while disclaiming any control, and Holland claimed
sovereignty but possessed little or no authority. These anomalies
worried the Permanent Under-Secretary Merivale, who wrote, after
reading another memorandum from Pine:

We cannot take anything in sovereignty from them [the Dutch], on
account of slavery (unless prepared at once to abolish it unconditionally).
We cannot (technically) give them anything in the way of 'protected'
territory, at least without the consent of the 'protected' parties.

Both Merivale and Pine, however, regarded these as technicalities
which a little ingenuity and co-operation would get round.[2] Thus
matters stood when, on the suggestion of the British Government,
the task of negotiation was delegated to the colonial authorities.

In the negotiations which now opened between himself and Acting
Governor Bird, Nagtglas's hands were tightly tied by the instructions
which Rochussen sent him. The Colonial Minister insisted that the
tariff question should not even be discussed until an exchange had
actually taken place, and that Nagtglas should seek formal British
approval of the Dutch redeeming Ashanti slaves and sending them
as soldiers or 'free labourers' to the East or to Surinam (Dutch
Guiana). Above all he stipulated that 'there should be a clear geo-
graphical line of separation between the territories in the interior
under the jurisdiction of the two nations'.[3]

It was in fact on this question of the interior boundary that the
negotiations on the Coast were to come to grief. Nagtglas set the ball

---

F.O. 97/250; ibid., Memorandum by Pine enclosed in former; ibid., Malmesbury
to Ward (draft), 20 March 1859; note enc. in Ward to M. B. Z., 31 March 1859,
Hague, B.Z. 2999.
  [1] Ibid., M. K. to M. B. Z., 13 April 1859; note enc. in M. B. Z. to Ward (copy),
20 April 1859, Hague, F.O. 97/250.
  [2] Memo. by Pine of 20 May 1859 and min. by Merivale of 21 May 1859 on F.O.
to C.O., 23 April 1859, C.O. 96/46.
  [3] Malmesbury to Ward (draft), 27 May 1859, F.O. 97/250; Ward to M. B. Z.,
30 May 1859, Hague, B.Z. 2999; Ward to Malmesbury, 15 June 1859, Hague, F.O.
97/250; Ward to Russell, 4 July 1859, F.O. 37/373; M.K. to Nagtglas (copy), 20 July
1859, Hague, B.Z. 2999.

rolling by suggesting a boundary running north from the mouth of the Sweet River (which itself extends only a few miles inland) to the Pra, with no restriction on the northward expansion of either protectorate. Despite his previous opinion that the natives would make little trouble about an exchange, he now proposed that the negotiations be kept secret 'so that the passions may not be stirred up from which serious consequences could arise'.[1] Bird countered by arguing that Wasaw (lying to the west of Nagtglas's boundary) should remain under British protection; among other reasons for the retention of this territory (which Pine had been willing to give up)[2] he urged the danger of opposition from the natives to the execution of an exchange, and pointed out that 'the populous district of Wasaw would largely augment the malcontents and therefore tend materially to complicate the difficulties in effecting the proposed exchange'.[3]

It soon became clear that neither side was willing to give way on this vital point of difference. Nagtglas's insistence was due to the importance he attached to free communication with the interior *via* Wasaw. He placed particular emphasis on this, since in his view the main value of the Dutch Gold Coast to the mother country for some years to come would be as a source of recruits and, possibly, emigrant labourers for the colonies. Bird, on the other hand, rejected the Dutch demand for access to the interior as foreign to the purpose of the exchange, nor did he find that Britain would receive any satisfactory equivalent for Wasaw, which, he emphasized, paid a large sum in poll-tax and abounded in gold. In any case, he had now had second thoughts about the desirability of *any* exchange. Rumours of the negotiations had been circulating, and everywhere within the British territories which it was proposed to exchange the peoples were expressing their determination never to submit to Dutch authority. He therefore counselled the abandonment of the project.[4] In this he differed from Nagtglas, who advised his government that if absolutely necessary they should agree to an exchange which did not

---

[1] Nagtglas to Bird (copy), 25 Aug. 1859, Elmina, F.O. 97/250.
[2] Memo. by Pine of 20 May 1859 on F.O. to C.O., 23 April 1859, C.O. 96/46.
[3] Bird to Nagtglas, 6 Sept. 1859, Cape Coast, G. 727.
[4] Bird to Newcastle (copy), 12 Nov. 1859, Cape Coast, F.O. 97/250. Bird was not the first governor to be aware of the dangers of resistance to an exchange; Pine had expressed similar misgivings (Pine to Labouchere, 30 Dec. 1857, Accra, C.O. 96/41), though, as has been seen, he had managed to overcome them.

include Wasaw, so urgent was the need to put an end to British 'encroachments'. He added that in the long run the resources of Apollonia and Aowin might prove as profitable as those of Wasaw. In his opinion, too, the British placed an exaggerated value upon Dutch Accra and it was thus desirable that an agreement should be reached with speed before they discovered their error.[1]

Neither home government followed to the letter the advice sent home by its representatives on the Coast. At The Hague, Rochussen (probably influenced by the views of an experienced official then on leave from Elmina)[2] decided that no project could be accepted which did not include the transfer of Wasaw to Dutch protection.[3] In London the Colonial Office, impressed by Bird's account of the danger of local resistance, decided that it had no right to exchange 'protected' territory, yet felt that a simple exchange of coastal stations might still be possible. The Colonial Secretary Newcastle, after studying the relevant maps, wrote:

We cannot *exchange* Wassaw. We are only protectors and must keep faith with the natives. The only legitimate exchange is that of Forts which are really the possessions of the two countries, and as regards them we propose to give up two (Apollonia and Dixcove) for one (Accra) and thus divide the coast between us without interruption of each by either. More ought not to be attempted or sanctioned.[4]

A proposal in this sense was put before the Dutch Government in April 1860.[5] To this Rochussen replied that he could never present a treaty to the States-General which would leave the Dutch settlements surrounded (*enclavés*) by British territory. How, he asked, could he sign a treaty which he knew 'to be repugnant to the national feeling', adding that in any case his information was that the transfer of Wasaw would not create the difficulties which the British foresaw. In reporting these views, Napier, now British envoy at The Hague, added his own conviction that the British terms 'would be generally unpalatable', and urged the consideration of some middle

[1] Nagtglas to M.K. (draft), 28 Nov. 1859, Elmina, G. 716.
[2] J. A. B. Horton, *West African Countries and Peoples* . . . (London, 1868), p. 255.
[3] M. K. to M. B. Z., 21 Jan. 1860, B.Z. 2999.
[4] C.O. to F.O., 11 Jan. and 17 Feb. 1860, F.O. 97/250; min. by Newcastle of 8 Feb. 1860 on F.O. to C.O., 3 Feb. 1860, C.O. 96/50.
[5] Napier to M. B. Z., 10 April 1860, Hague, B.Z. 2999.

course—perhaps a common protectorate in Wasaw or the *gradual* abandonment of the British protectorate there to the Dutch.[1]

Napier's suggestions found no favour in London, where it was now decided to call once more upon the services of Ord, sending him to The Hague for discussions with Nagtglas, who was coming home on leave after further fruitless negotiations with the Cape Coast authorities.[2] Ord himself, who attached much value to such informal discussions, felt that progress might be made in one of three possible directions: the reopening of the negotiations for a uniform tariff, 'the transfer of the Forts and Settlements "per se", as lately proposed', or

a sale, barter lease or transfer of the Dutch Fort at Accra, which after all is the great thorn in our side, and the possession of which would almost entirely remove the evils complained of.[3]

Rochussen's attitude, however, as revealed in further conversations with Napier, gave little promise of the fulfilment of Ord's hopes, and seemed in London to confirm British suspicions that the main Dutch aim was 'the attainment of extensive Territories in the interior'.[4] The minister showed himself firmly opposed to a common tariff, as well as to any territorial arrangement which did not include a settlement of the interior boundary on the lines of Nagtglas's original proposals. Once more he insisted that to propose anything less to the States-General would be political suicide, and once more this was confirmed by Napier, who added that even a common tariff agreement would probably be rejected by the States-General, 'prompted by commercial jealousy in general, and particularly by the instigation of a house in Rotterdam, which is represented in the First Chamber'.[5] Napier was soon able to compare Rochussen's views with those of Nagtglas, newly-arrived from Elmina. While insisting on the necessity of an interior boundary, and discounting prophecies

---

[1] Napier to Russell, 8 May 1860, Hague, F.O. 97/250; M. K. to M. B. Z., 25 May 1960, B.Z. 2999.

[2] Andrews to Nagtglas, 1 May 1860, Cape Coast, G. 727; ibid., Nagtglas to Andrews (copy), 2 May 1860, Elmina; min. by Barrow of 17 May 1860 on F.O. to C.O., 14 May 1860, C.O. 96/50; C.O. to F.O., 31 May 1860, F.O. 97/250.

[3] Ord to C.O. (16 May 1860, London), C.O. 96/50.

[4] Ibid., Minutes by Barrow of 17 May and 11 June on F.O. to C.O., 14 May and 9 June 1860.

[5] The reference is, of course, to van Ryckevorsel: Napier to Russell, 12 June 1860, Hague, F.O. 97/250.

of trouble with the exchanged peoples, Nagtglas now conceded that only *western* Wasaw need come under Dutch protection. He reiterated his own desire for a common tariff, and added the suggestion (originally made by Pine a year earlier) of a defensive alliance aimed against Ashanti, which would, he asserted, confirm that nation in the pacific course that it had followed under its then ruler.[1]

On 14 July Ord arrived in The Hague, but the ensuing discussions which he and Napier carried on with Nagtglas and the Foreign and Colonial Ministers merely served to make yet more plain the apparently irreconcilable differences between the two governments. Rochussen was now ready to contemplate a common tariff on strong drink and gunpowder, but only after an exchange had been agreed. It was soon realized that Nagtglas's suggestion of a 'partition' of Wasaw was impracticable,[2] and Rochussen proved immovable in his insistence on the 'transfer' of this area. Deadlock was soon reached, with Rochussen demanding that the British negotiators seek fresh instructions. Napier now reported that

as long as Mr. de Rochussen is either in office or in opposition I see no prospect of treating with the Dutch Government on a more advantageous footing,

but Ord realized that the Colonial Minister's attitude was dictated by fear of political repercussions. Moreover, he added,

the same motives and causes are likely to exist in almost every Dutch government, and . . . there is but little prospect of our obtaining from the present, or any future Ministry, the object we seek in its present form.

Wasaw alone was the key to the problem: if Britain abandoned it she could count on Dutch acquiescence in an exchange *and* a joint tariff, if not they would agree to neither. Britain must weigh the material gains that such agreement would bring against the inevitable loss of prestige and influence on the Coast.[3]

---

[1] Ibid., same to same, 23 June 1860, Hague. Cf. Pine's memo. of 20 May 1859 on F.O. to C.O., 23 April 1859, C.O. 96/46.

[2] In this matter Rochussen once more preferred the advice of Nagtglas's subordinate Coulon (see above, p. 29): Ord to C.O., 31 July 1860, Hague, C.O. 96/50.

[3] Napier to Russell, 17 July and 1 Aug. (two dispatches of same date) 1860, Hague, F.O. 97/250; Ord to C.O., 31 July 1860, Hague, C.O. 96/50; 'Memorandum drawn up by Colonel Ord for Lord Napier', n.d. (for use at conference on 1 August), F.O. 97/250: M. B. Z. to Bentinck (draft), 2 Aug. 1860, Hague, B.Z. 2999.

Ord himself was rapidly coming round to the view that Wasaw was expendable. In August he pointed out to the Colonial Office that the condition of the British settlements was 'avowedly unsatisfactory' and that the Dutch proposals seemed to offer a means of improving it. They were, he added, unlikely to be repeated in the future if rejected now. In a private note he expressed the view that the Dutch could offer nothing more even if they wanted to, '& if we don't take this offer what else is open to us?'.[1] Ord's growing willingness to part with Wasaw was not, however, shared at the Colonial Office, where Secretary Newcastle already had doubts as to the wisdom of prolonging the negotiation, and where it was generally agreed that 'we are bound in good faith not to hand over Wasaw to the Dutch without their own consent, or at all events, not against their wishes'.[2] Further consultation with Cape Coast, where Andrews was now Governor, confirmed these views. Sir George Barrow, the senior clerk, thought that the history of the negotiations since 1859 showed 'the futility of making any further attempts', and suspected that a scheme for the so-called 'free emigration' of negro labour was behind the Dutch insistence on the transfer of Wasaw. He supported the suggestion already made by the Foreign Secretary, Lord John Russell, that the negotiation should be allowed to drop, at least for the time being. Both Newcastle and the new Permanent Under-Secretary, Sir Frederic Rogers, concurred, and a formal decision to this effect was taken in January 1861, with Newcastle expressing the belief that self-interest would 'probably induce the Dutch after a time to modify their terms if we show less anxiety for an arrangement which, if fairly carried out, should be & would be mutually advantageous'.[3] Only the Parliamentary Under-Secretary, Chichester Fortescue, was swayed by the pleadings of Ord, who had now come out unequivocally for the abandonment of Wasaw.[4]

---

[1] Ord to C.O. (enc. private note to Unwin), 19 Aug. 1860, Hague, C.O. 96/50.

[2] Ibid., Min. by Newcastle of 21 June on F.O. to C.O., 18 June 1860, Hague; ibid., minutes by Unwin of 7 Aug., Rogers of 10 Aug. and Chichester Fortescue of 11 Aug. on Ord to C.O., 31 July 1860, Hague.

[3] Bentinck to Russell, 7 Aug. 1860, F.O. 97/250; ibid., F.O. to C.O. (drafts), 18 Aug. and 13 Sept. 1860; ibid., C.O. to F.O., 31 Aug. 1860 and 19 Jan. 1861; Andrews to Newcastle, 8 Nov. 1860, Christiansborg, C.O. 96/49 (with minutes by Barrow and Rogers of 15 Dec. 1860 and Newcastle of 4 Jan. 1861).

[4] Ibid., Min. by Chichester Fortescue of 19 Dec. 1860 on Andrews to Newcastle, 8 Nov. 1860, Christianborg.

Ord's arguments, though ineffectual at the time, are of some interest in view of their triumph six years later. For him the advantages
of the Dutch offer 'vastly outweighed' the disadvantages. Even if, as
Andrews had asserted, the Wasaws really hated the Dutch, this
hardly seemed, he remarked, 'a sufficient reason for our insisting on
remaining their protectors', if Britain could 'largely benefit the whole
country by ceasing to be so'. Nor could *Britain* be answerable if, as
Andrews anticipated, the Dixcoves and Apollonias refused to
acknowledge the Dutch. Moreover, 'any evils that may arise there-
from will fall on the Dutch, and not on ourselves'—as, indeed, was
the case with the abandonment of Wasaw! The only real danger to
Britain was that of resistance from former 'Dutch' natives to her poll-
tax, but the latter might well be abandoned completely in the event
of an exchange.

In short, there is nothing in the control or protectorate, which will
of necessity devolve upon us by acquiescence in the Dutch proposals,
which will involve us in any quarrels with the people.

The irresponsible cynicism of these remarks, all the more extraordinary because completely unconscious, throws a curious light upon
the man who had become the Colonial Office's expert adviser on
West Africa. For the moment, however, his recommendations about
Wasaw found no more favour at Downing Street than his accom-
panying hint that he should replace Andrews as Governor.[1]

As Nagtglas wrote some five years later, it was the reluctance of
the British to 'transfer' Wasaw which had led to the failure of the
negotiations of 1859–60. In the Dutch view this reluctance had been
due to the richness of this area in gold and to a desire to cut the
Dutch Gold Coast off from direct communication with the interior
and thus prevent the expansion of its trade; the story that the
Wasaws, who in the past had accepted some form of Dutch protection before falling under British influence, did not wish to submit to
the Dutch, was a mere pretext, and largely an invented one at that.[2]
Governor Andrews, on the other hand, averred that it was the gold

---

[1] Memo. by Ord, 9 Jan. 1861, Brighton, C.O. 96/56.
[2] Nagtglas and Elias to M.K., 3 Oct. 1865, Hague, B.Z. 2999. For general reviews
of these negotiations see '1874 Report', section I A; Herman, op. cit., ii, p. 73;
'Memorie van Toelichting', loc. cit.; P.P. 1865, v (412), p. 52. For an independent
Dutch view of the importance of Wasaw see Gramberg, *Schetsen*, pp. 349–50.

deposits that made the Dutch so insistent, and prophesied 'the sub-jugation of the Dutch sword' for Wasaw should it be abandoned by Britain. *He* was absolutely certain that the Wasaws, like the inhabi-tants of the western settlements, would never submit to the Dutch, so that to give them up 'would . . . retain the unenviable construc-tion of an injudicious and discreditable policy'.[1]

It was to be five more years before negotiation to put the affairs of the Coast on a more settled footing was resumed. Neither side completely lost sight of the desirability of a settlement, and indeed the growing hostility between the coastal authorities over rival claims at Impohaw[2] and elsewhere made this seem yet more necessary, but neither side was willing to take the initiative lest this might impair its bargaining powers. None the less, various tentative approaches to the problem were made in this period that were not without interest. In 1860, before the negotiation for an exchange was formally ended, Governor Andrews suggested to his government that it should offer to purchase the Dutch settlements to the east of Cape Coast for £5,000, payable in five yearly instalments. If this proposal were re-jected, and if it proved impossible to induce the Dutch to agree to an exchange without Wasaw, then the best thing would be for one power to retire completely in favour of the other. It would certainly be worth £50,000 or £60,000 to induce the Dutch to leave.[3] Andrews' proposals, which were accompanied by the suggestion that, if the Dutch sold out, the Gold Coast should be declared a Crown Colony, found little favour at home,[4] and would certainly have been un-acceptable to The Hague at this time. Even Nagtglas, who had little hope that the Dutch Gold Coast in its present form could be of much use or profit to Holland in the foreseeable future, set his face against them. Leaving aside all question of national honour and prestige, he still felt sure that if Holland held firm in her refusal to consider a common tariff without an exchange, Britain was bound eventually to agree to an exchange favourable to Dutch interests, and

[1] Andrews to Newcastle, 8 Aug. 1860, Cape Coast, and 8 November 1860, Chris-tiansborg, C.O. 96/49.
[2] In what the Dutch called the Butri division, a few miles north of Dabokrom.
[3] As n. 1.
[4] Newcastle to Andrews, 23 Nov. 1860, ADM. 1/18; min. by Barrow of 15 Dec. 1860 on Andrews to Newcastle, 8 Nov. 1860, Christiansborg, C.O. 96/49.

then, what with the prospect of development and the revenue to be obtained from duties, the Dutch Gold Coast would cease to be a burden on the mother country.[1]

Disgusted by Nagtglas's attitude, and particularly by his refusal to join in levying an export duty on palm-oil,[2] Andrews now told him that in his opinion the British Government would be willing to cede their settlements to the Dutch on suitable conditions.[3] Meanwhile the Dutch Government was trying to induce Britain to take the initiative in reopening the exchange negotiations by pressing its claims to the Impohaw area while at the same time forbidding Nagtglas to enter into any official discussion of a territorial settlement.[4] Nagtglas's execution of this order was most galling to Andrews,[5] and not without its effect upon him. By April 1862 he could see no prospect of 'any material benefit for the community' unless the 'windward districts . . . eventually yield to accepting the Dutch protection', and he was busy devising schemes whereby this might be achieved without arousing resistance among the peoples affected. For the sake of 'a complete territory and unbroken line of coast . . . in all above 200 miles', he was now ready to contemplate the 'abandonment' that he had hitherto denounced.[6] Soon afterwards, however, Andrews, whose interminable and incoherent dispatches had become the despair of the Colonial Office, left the Coast; London, adducing both the known unwillingness of the Dutch to make any concession and the difficulties anticipated from the natives concerned, showed no readiness whatsoever to resume negotiations.[7] Even Chichester Fortescue, who had previously been under Ord's influence, was so impressed by the trouble that had arisen on the Coast between the British authorities and former 'Danish' natives that he

---

[1] Nagtglas to M.K. (drafts), 8 April and 5 August 1861, Elmina, G. 716.

[2] Andrews to Newcastle, 11 Sept. 1861, Christiansborg, C.O. 96/55; Andrews to Nagtglas (copy), n.d., G. 727.

[3] Ibid., Nagtglas to M.K. (draft), 19 Oct. 1861, Elmina.

[4] M. K. to M. B. Z., 5 Oct. 1861, B.Z. 2999; Bentinck to Russell, 4 Nov. 1861, London, F.O. 97/250.

[5] Andrews to Newcastle, 6 and 8 Feb. 1862, Cape Coast, C.O. 96/57; Andrews to Nagtglas, 25 Feb., 7 and 22 March 1862, Cape Coast, G. 727; ibid., Nagtglas to Andrews (copies), 3 and 18 March 1862, Elmina; ibid., Nagtglas to M.K. (draft), 2 April 1862.

[6] Andrews to Newcastle, 8 April 1862, Cape Coast, C.O. 96/57.

[7] C.O. to F.O., 7 Dec. 1861, F.O. 97/250; Russell to Bentinck, 14 Dec. 1861, N.L. 198.

D

was inclined to set his face against *any* exchange. 'We should', he declared

give up well-affected people, against their own wishes, & obtain Forts which we shouldn't know what to do with and new 'subjects' who would probably be troublesome.[1]

By the middle of 1862 the Dutch Colonial Ministry, too, was coming round to the view that, even if Britain were to take the initiative, it might be better to decline to negotiate until proofs of the Dutch right to Impohaw and other territories in dispute had been assembled.[2]

Thus matters stood for the next three years. To all Dutch protests concerning continuing 'encroachments' on the Coast the British government turned a deaf ear, as it did to a Dutch proposal for a mixed boundary commission to investigate rival claims on the spot. Indeed, when in 1864 the Legislative Council at Cape Coast was worried about the way in which the proximity of the Dutch might affect the operation of a new measure for licensing the sale of spirits, Governor Richard Pine told them plainly that in enforcing such measures they need 'not be very particular as to nice questions of Dutch territory'.[3] Neither government, however, was allowed to forget the need for an eventual settlement. The importance of this was forcefully pointed out in instructions given to Governor Elias, who succeeded Nagtglas in 1862,[4] and there was good reason for this concern at The Hague. Voices were beginning to be raised in the States-General, querying the utility of retaining these burdensome and profitless settlements, and at the end of 1863 the Colonial Minister, Fransen van de Putte, was forced to pacify these critics with an assurance that if ever an opportunity arose of disposing of the Dutch Gold Coast on favourable terms it would be fully considered.[5] In the following year the critics had ammunition ready to hand, for there had been circulated among members of the States-General an anonymous pamphlet entitled 'What must the Netherlands do with her Settlements on the

---

[1] Min. by Chichester Fortescue of 26 Nov. 1861 on F.O. to C.O., 7 Nov. 1861, C.O. 96/56.
[2] M. K. to M. B. Z., 10 June 1862, B.Z. 2999.
[3] Ibid., M. K. to M. B. Z., 22 Dec. 1863; ibid., Russell to Bentinck (copy), 3 Feb. 1864; ibid., Cardwell to Bentinck, 3 Aug. 1864; ibid., Bentinck to M. B. Z., 5 Aug. 1864; Minutes of Leg. Council, 19 Sept. 1864, ADM. 5/1.
[4] M. K. to Elias, 12 Sept. 1863, Hague, G. 718.
[5] *Hand. S.G.*, 1863–4, I, pp. 85, 87.

Coast of Guinea?'[1] The author of this work was none other than
Nagtglas himself, who, having completed his service, had retired on
pension in 1862 at the age of forty-seven, and was now living at The
Hague.[2] In his pamphlet he expatiated upon the miserable state of
the Dutch settlements, and severely criticized the dilatory and evasive
answers given by the ministry to questions about their policy for the
Coast. Only a satisfactory territorial exchange with Britain, he continued, to be followed by the imposition of import duties, could
make the Dutch Gold Coast worthy or even capable of retention :
'either this must take place, or we must make room for our neighbours the English'. The boundary he now proposed was one that
would include Wasaw in the Dutch protectorate, but *not* the adjoin-
ing territory of Denkyira (unlike his original proposal of a line due
north from the Sweet River).[3] If this and other 'absolutely necessary
changes' could not be brought about, he added, 'then the only
alternative is to dispose of our settlements. The English will not be
slow to come forward as purchasers, and as they paid 10,000 *l.* for
the two Danish forts, we might surely exact the tenfold amount for
our territories.' Finally he added his support of a suggestion already
made in a Dutch newspaper for a commission of inquiry to deter-
mine the fate of the settlements. Like Gramberg, the sometime
official and planter, who three years earlier had written that unless
Holland took some interest in her settlements she might as well sell
them,[4] Nagtglas probably had little intention at this time of seriously advocating their abandonment. If he, or Gramberg, appeared
to do so, it was with the aim of impressing upon public opinion as
dramatically as possible the urgent need for a positive policy on
the Guinea Coast; and their efforts to this end were by no means
in vain.

The growth of concern at this time in Holland about the condition
of the Dutch Gold Coast may well have been due to a feeling of
humiliation engendered by the events of 1863. In that year, after

[1] See p. 1, n. 3.
[2] See the 'Nominatieve staat van verleende Pensionen', in the estimates for 1864
(G. 792).
[3] This was the boundary already proposed by Pine in a Memo. of 20 May 1859 on
F.O. to C.O., 23 April 1859, C.O. 96/46.
[4] Gramberg, *Schetsen*, p. 346.

their long period of quiescence, the Ashantis invaded the coastal regions, where they met with little real opposition. If the policy of ineffectual 'neutrality' adopted by the Dutch authorities in these troubles gave little cause for patriotic rejoicing in Holland, the inability of the British authorities and the unwillingness of the British Government to offer effective resistance to the Ashanti incursion drew the attention of Britons to the unsatisfactory nature of *their* position on the Gold Coast. The long-standing aversion to these expensive and troublesome settlements now came to a head. To many in Britain, not merely or even primarily Cobdenite free-traders intent on 'retrenchment',[1] it seemed that the time had come for the narrowing of responsibilities if not for actual abandonment.[2] The events of 1863, they argued, showed clearly that the Coast was deriving no benefits from the presence of Britain, and moreover that the alarmingly vague British 'protectorate' there was thought by the 'protected' to involve obligations which Britain neither could nor would honour.[3] The expression of such feelings in Parliament, and the likelihood of the appointment of a select Committee, made the government even more reluctant to open negotiations which might tie their hands to any future line of policy.[4]

On 21 February 1865 the Commons duly agreed to appoint a Select Committee to consider the state of the British West African Settlements, following a debate in which strong doubts were once more expressed as to the utility or desirability of the Gold Coast establishments.[5] The Committee received a report from Ord on a mission

---

[1] On this point, Dr. Dike's chapter 'Background to the Parliamentary Select Committee of 1865' in *Trade and Politics in the Niger Delta, 1830–1885* (Oxford, 1956), should be read in the light of J. D. Hargreaves' important review article in *Sierra Leone Studies*, n.s. No. 6 (June 1956): though it is certainly true, as Dr. Dike points out (p. 167), that concern about the mounting cost of the Gold Coast settlements to the imperial treasury played a major part in the genesis of the Select Committee. Cobden himself had declared in 1859 that 'if France took the whole of Africa' she would do no harm to 'us or anybody else save herself' (quoted in A. T. Wyatt, *Britain in the Tropics, 1527–1910* (London, 1911), p. 421).

[2] A Colonial Office memorandum of 1874 says that 'from this period a general desire became evident on the part of all statesmen to narrow as much as possible the obligations and responsibilities of this country on the Coast' (Conf. Print, African No. 49, March 1874).

[3] Cf. J. H. Rose, A. P. Newton, and E. A. Benians, Ed., *Cambridge History of the British Empire*, ii (Cambridge, 1940), p. 673.

[4] Cardwell to Bentinck, 3 Aug. 1864, B.Z. 2999; *Hansard*, 3rd ser., clxxv, cols. 545–52, 1728–9, 1839–41, 1950–2023; clxxvi, cols. 1658–81.

[5] Ibid., clxxvii, cols. 535–59; Conf. Print, African No. 49, pp. 15–16.

of inquiry that he had lately made on behalf of the Colonial Office, heard a number of witnesses, the chief of whom was Ord himself, and reported in the middle of 1865. At first sight their Resolutions strongly recommended a policy of strict 'non-extension' in West Africa, with a view to ultimate withdrawal from some at least of Britain's responsibilities in that area. They were widely interpreted in this sense both at home—by the Committee's own chairman, Adderley, for example[1]—and on the Coast, where educated Africans took them as a pledge of speedy self-government.[2] But they also contained the admission (inserted on the motion of the Colonial Secretary) that it might, 'in peculiar cases', be necessary to extend the existing settlements for the sake of their 'more efficient and economical administration'.[3] The Resolutions, in fact, were not only 'vague and inconclusive', as a Colonial Office official complained some years later,[4] but also dangerously ambiguous. While seeming to many to foreshadow withdrawal or even abandonment, they could be, and in the event were, interpreted to sanction the acquisition of territory. A policy which was capable of such diverse interpretation was not a policy at all but a blank cheque.

The evidence presented to the Committee and printed as an appendix to its report was full of complaints of the attitude and actions of the Dutch on the Coast, and in particular of their failure to agree to a joint tariff. The general tenor of the opinions expressed on this point was, in the words of ex-Governor Sir Benjamin Pine, that 'the best thing would be to get them out altogether; if we could not get them out altogether, then to put them on one side, they to take one part of the coast and we the other'; though Ord added a note of caution about the indisposition of the protected natives 'to quit our protection'. Several witnesses urged the desirability of getting rid of the Dutch, and Ord stated that the question of selling the Dutch Gold Coast had been mooted in the States-General,[5] adding that in

---

[1] Sir C. B. Adderley, *Review of 'The Colonial Policy of Lord J. Russell's Administration', by Earl Grey, 1853; and of subsequent colonial history* (London, 1869), pp. 206–10.
[2] Claridge, op. cit., i, pp. 538–9.
[3] P.P. 1865, v (412), p. iii. For the divisions of opinion within the committee see Hargreaves, op. cit.
[4] Conf. Print, African No. 50, p. 16.
[5] This I take to refer to Fransen van de Putte's assurance in 1863; see above, p. 36.

his opinion a proposal of this sort from Britain might be entertained at The Hague, and that the expenditure of £20,000 to this end would not be a bad speculation.[1]

The publication of the Select Committee's report gave rise to an interchange with the Dutch which was eventually to result in the agreement which had for so long been sought in vain. On 25 July the Colonial Secretary, Cardwell, sent a copy of the Committee's Resolutions to the Dutch envoy Bentinck, adding that 'If at any time you should wish to enter upon the subject with me, I shall always be most ready to meet you'.[2] There was little inclination at The Hague to attach much importance to this extremely vague profession, but on 8 September, in a long-delayed interview with Bentinck at which he once more rejected the Dutch proposal of a mixed boundary commission, Cardwell made plain his desire to resume negotiation for the tariff agreement[3] on which the Committee's witnesses had laid such stress. Such an agreement no doubt seemed more necessary than ever to the Colonial Office, if the retention of the settlements despite the Committee's recommendations was to be justified. Here at last, then, was the initiative that had been lacking for five long years. For a while it looked as though things would move speedily: the ex-Governors Nagtglas and Elias were asked to make ready to journey to London to confer with Ord, and meanwhile they prepared a note on the previous negotiations, in which they advised their government not to agree to a tariff without an exchange and not to agree to an exchange without Wasaw.[4] Before they could set out, however, it was learned that Ord, who does not seem to have been informed that his continued presence in London was desired, had returned to his post of Governor of the Bermudas.[5] In his place Cardwell offered to set up a small committee in the Colonial Office to meet Nagtglas and Elias. The Dutch accepted, but with no great enthusiasm; they were doubtless well aware that in the past

[1] P.P. 1865, v (412), pp. 52–3, 102, 115, 129, 139, 290, 299; 318, 335–6.
[2] Cardwell to Bentinck (copy), 25 July 1865, B.Z. 2999.
[3] Ibid., Bentinck to M. B. Z., 27 July and 9 Sept. 1865; ibid., M. K. to M. B. Z., 12 Aug. 1865; Cardwell to Bentinck, 8 Sept. 1865, N.L. 198.
[4] M. K. to M. B. Z., 28 Sept. 1865, B.Z. 2999; ibid., Nagtglas and Elias to M. K., 3 Oct. 1865, Hague.
[5] Ibid., Bentinck to M. B. Z., 3 Oct. 1865.

Ord had been much more willing than the officials of Downing Street to barter away Wasaw.[1]

The Dutch Government had good reason to welcome the more forthcoming attitude now apparent in London, for in Holland, as in England, discontent was mounting over the condition of the Gold Coast. In the deliberations of the States-General on the budget proposals for 1866, the opinion was expressed that it was desirable to hand the settlements over to another power, or, if this seemed impracticable, to abandon them altogether. In reply van de Putte was able to ask members to await the outcome of the current negotiations.[2] But these negotiations, which had seemed imminent in October 1865, were in fact to be postponed for more than a year. This curious hiatus seems to have been due in the first place to unexpected difficulties in dispatching Nagtglas and Elias on their mission,[3] and was presumably prolonged by the unstable political situation which in both countries produced changes of government during the course of 1866.[4] But it is not easy to escape the impression that the Dutch were hanging back, perhaps in order to see whether Britain would accept the views of Adderley and his friends and abandon the Gold Coast altogether.[5] In any case they may well have thought it in their interest to wait until Ord was once more available.

If little more was heard from The Hague for the time being, pressure for an exchange was now being brought to bear on the Colonial Office from another quarter. From Cape Coast Governor[6] Conran was now sending home strong recommendations for an exchange along the lines long advocated by Nagtglas. His first dispatch

[1] Ibid., Cardwell to Bentinck (copy), 7 Oct. 1865, Balmoral; ibid., M. B. Z. to M. K. (draft), 20 Oct. 1865. It was at this time that the Dutch Colonial Minister hinted to the British envoy at The Hague that if Britain would give way in the dispute about differential duties imposed by the Dutch in Sumatra, Holland might 'throw into the bargain' the Dutch Gold Coast (Milbanke to F.O., 31 Oct. 1865, Hague, F.O. 37/450). Nothing came of this remark, but it has some interest in view of the later 'link' between the cession of Dutch Guinea and the settlement of the Sumatra question.

[2] Hand. S.G., 1865-6, I, p. 60.

[3] Including an attack of rheumatism suffered by Nagtglas: M. B. Z. to Bentinck (draft), 17 March 1866, B.Z. 2999.

[4] In Holland there were *two* new governments during the course of the year.

[5] For the circulation in Holland of rumours to this effect see Hand. S.G., 1865-6, Bijlagen, p. 402.

[6] Demoted to 'administrator' in April 1866, as a result of the subordination of the West African settlements to a central government at Sierra Leone (in accordance with the 1865 Committee's recommendations).

to this effect, written in February 1866, evoked a non-committal response from the Colonial Office,[1] but in September he returned to this subject in a dispatch which deserves quotation at some length, because it sets out the considerations which were bringing about a vital change in the British attitude to the Dutch exchange proposals.[2] The difficulties of administration 'in the absence of properly defined instructions from the Home Authorities', he complained, were increased by

those daily arising between people under Dutch protection and our own . . . the time has arrived for the definite settlement of many subjects, with which the Dutch local government have not the least cause to trouble themselves beyond addressing the British Administrator merely and the complaint must be adjusted . . . at our expense and trouble as they keep not a single Policeman, and but a few men under Arms (natives of the place) in the shape of Troops officered by Civilians in Uniform for the defence of Elmina . . . and as every other Settlement of theirs on the Coast seems to be similarly situated and circumstanced, it is plain that we are not only protecting the Natives of the Gold Coast but actually protecting the Dutch from the Natives as well . . .

After more in this vein Conran made the following declaration:

The conduct of the Appolonia and Wassaw people for a long time, but especially for the last year or two has been so bad and disobedient to our rule that in place of its being a hardship in placing them under Dutch protection, owing to their great distance from here and their proximity to Axim, a Dutch Settlement, I consider it would prove a blessing.

Since the natives showed no gratitude to Britain for all they owed her there was little reason, implied Conran, for Britain to feel much obligation towards them. He therefore favoured a boundary line running from the Sweet River (and, incidentally, the transfer of the administrative centre to Accra). Such an arrangement would force the Dutch to participate in 'the common defence of the country which has hitherto devolved upon us', facilitate the cutting off of supplies from Ashanti in the event of war, and enable each power to raise a

---

[1] Conran to Cardwell, 5 Feb. 1866, Cape Coast, P.P. 1867, xlix (198), p. 50; ibid., p. 92, Cardwell to Blackall, 21 March 1866.
[2] Conran to Blackall (confidential—copy), 6 Sept. 1866, Cape Coast, ADM. 1/687. It seems unlikely that this particular dispatch (to the Governor-in-Chief at Sierra Leone) was ever seen by the Colonial Office. It is not to be found in the volume of Gold Coast dispatches for Sept.-Dec. 1866 (C.O. 96/72).

revenue of not less than £12,000 a year by means of import duties. Surely, Conran concluded, since the prospect of effective *self*-government in these territories was so remote, it was 'better to try half courses than to throw up the Protectorate altogether', adding that the Dutch Governor Idsinga was in complete agreement with his proposals.

There is some irony in the fact that the 'bad and disobedient' conduct, which in Conran's view justified going over the heads of the natives to effect an exchange, resulted in part from the Select Committee's advocacy of ultimate withdrawal, which had had a strongly unsettling influence in both the settlements and the 'protectorate' (where British prestige was already at a low ebb as a result of the events of 1863–4).[1] Thus the Committee unwittingly contributed to the effecting of an exchange which in turn proved the prelude, not to withdrawal, but to the considerable extension and consolidation of British authority.

With Conran following in the footsteps of Ord and Andrews as a convert to the abandonment of Wasaw, the steadfast resistance at the Colonial Office to such a course seems to have broken down by the time that the long-delayed semi-official conference took place. It should not, of course, be forgotten that such abandonment could be represented as conforming to the now fashionable ideal of withdrawal from West African responsibilities! In November 1866 the new Dutch Government, probably anticipating further trouble about the Guinea Coast when the States-General took the budget for 1867 into consideration,[2] indicated its willingness to proceed with the conference as originally planned in the previous year.[3] Carnarvon, Colonial Secretary in the new Derby-Disraeli administration, concurred,[4] and at the turn of the year Nagtglas travelled to London alone (Elias being no longer available), armed with detailed instructions. He was to begin by broaching the subject of an exchange, linking this with the introduction of a joint tariff should this be necessary to make it more acceptable to the British, in which case he was

---

[1] Claridge, op. cit., i, pp. 539–45; *Cambridge History of the British Empire*, ii, pp. 673–4.
[2] And rightly so: see *Hand. S.G.*, 1866–7, II, pp. 402, 728.
[3] M. B. Z. to Bentinck (draft), 22 Nov. 1866, B.Z. 2999.
[4] Ibid., Bentinck to M. B. Z., 30 Nov. 1866; ibid., Carnarvon to Bentinck (copy), 15 Dec. 1866, Newbury.

to urge that steps be taken to obtain French participation in such a scheme.[1]

Between 4 and 12 January Nagtglas and the Dutch envoy Bentinck conferred with a British committee of two. Of these one was Elliott, an Assistant Under-Secretary from the Colonial Office, the other Ord, again in London on his way to assume his new position of Governor of the Straits Settlements.[2] In these discussions an informal agreement was reached which, as Nagtglas pointed out to his government, represented a considerable concession on the part of Britain, and which, he thought, would allow the Dutch to attract a great part of the Ashanti trade back to their possessions. Above all, the British negotiators had agreed to an exchange of territory with the boundary line running north from the mouth of the Sweet River. In return, the Dutch had agreed to a uniform customs system, consisting of high duties on the import of alcohol, tobacco, firearms and gunpowder, and a three per cent. *ad valorem* duty on everything else. They did not insist upon the need for French participation, in view of the abortive efforts already made to this end in 1857 by Ord;[3] on the other hand, the British did not press their request for the joint levying of anchorage dues. The conference ended with the drawing up of a draft treaty along the lines agreed, to serve as a basis for future formal negotiations, and Nagtglas hurried back to The Hague to report progress.[4]

It was not to be supposed that these proposals, which represented a victory for the Dutch point of view, and which bear witness to the influence now enjoyed by Ord at the Colonial Office, would encounter any substantial objection from the Dutch Government.[5] In London, however, though Carnarvon was ready enough to back Ord

[1] Ibid., M. B. Z. and M. K. to Nagtglas (draft), (Dec. 1866).

[2] Whether this was pure coincidence, or whether the conference was timed to occur during Ord's stay in London I do not know. The 1867 negotiations and their preliminaries seem to be very scantily documented in the relevant Dutch and British archives (though it is certainly not true, as stated in a Colonial Office memorandum of 1874 (Conf. Print, African No. 52) that 'no record of the origins or proceedings' of the conferences between Elliott, Ord, Bentinck and Nagtglas 'can . . . be traced').

[3] See above, p. 20, n. 4; and cf. P.P. 1865, v (412), pp. 44, 52.

[4] Nagtglas to M. B. Z. and M. K., 20 Jan. 1867, Hague, B.Z. 3000 (enc. 'Heads of a proposed agreement').

[5] M. B. Z. to Bentinck (draft), 23 Jan. 1867, Algemeen Rijksarchief/Verzameling van Zuylen van Nijevelt, Aanwinst 1946 (Collectie 105), No. 101.

and Elliott and proceed to the convention,[1] there was some hesitation at the Foreign Office, where a memorandum was drawn up pointing out that the draft agreement conceded the very demand—namely the abandonment of Wasaw—which had caused Britain to break off the previous negotiation in 1861.[2] In reply Carnarvon stated that the proposed boundary line was based in part on Ord's opinion of the Wasaws, adding that the withdrawal of British protection from these people involved no breach of faith, since 'we merely leave them to themselves—we do not transfer them to the Dutch'.[3] Given this interpretation the draft treaty now seemed acceptable to Stanley, the Foreign Secretary, and the way was clear for the formal conclusion of a Convention. By 21 February Stanley and Carnarvon as plenipotentiaries on the one side, and Bentinck and Nagtglas on the other, had reached complete agreement on its terms, and on 5 March the long-awaited treaty was duly signed at the Foreign Office. Much to the satisfaction of the Dutch, this treaty followed the draft agreement in giving them everything they wished, even to an article stipulating that the boundary settlement would not be upset by any subsequent abandonment of the customs arrangements.[4]

The main objections to the treaty had nothing to do with the exchange, and were raised in Holland, where approval by the States-General was a constitutional necessity. The preliminary examination of the convention by the Second Chamber was not the occasion of any fundamental criticism, though members demanded and obtained assurances on two points which were to be of some importance for the future: first, that the treaty would not preclude the possibility of ceding the settlements to another power, and secondly, that all territory behind the windward Coast as far as the Ashanti frontier would in fact be 'Dutch'.[5] But by the time the measure was debated, on 29 June, the Rotterdam house of H. Muller, van Ryckevorsel's successor, had presented an address strongly criticizing the proposed

---

[1] F.O. to C.O. (draft), 12 Jan. 1867, F.O. 37/466; ibid., C.O. to F.O., 17 Jan. 1867.
[2] Ibid., Memo. by H. P. A. (nderson) on C.O. to F.O., 17 Jan. 1867.
[3] Ibid., Carnarvon to Stanley (copy), 31 Jan. 1867.
[4] Ibid., Stanley to Bentinck (drafts), 4 and 14 Feb. 1867; ibid., Bentinck to Stanley, 5 and 11 Feb. 1867; Bentinck to M. B. Z., 21 Feb. and 5 March 1867, B.Z. 3000.
[5] *Hand. S.G.*, 1866–7, Bijlagen, pp. 952–3, 991. These assurances were based on Nagtglas's opinions: Nagtglas to M. B. Z., 2 June 1867, Hague, B.Z. 3000. On the claim that the interior districts were being 'ceded' to Holland, see also below, p. 47.

system of valuing imports for customs duty. In particular it attacked the permission given to customs officers to confiscate goods on payment of their declared value plus ten per cent.[1]

The spectre of opposition in the legislature worked up by commercial interests, which had been so dreaded by previous Dutch Governments whenever exchange and tariff agreements had been mooted, had thus once more been raised. But 1867 was not 1860. The influence of traders on the Coast had been weakened by the abolition of private trading by officials,[2] and in any case the opportunities for a commercial 'lobby' at home were less now that opinion had been roused about the condition of the Dutch settlements. Above all, the government could now fairly claim to have got the better of the bargain. Muller's objections, based on technical considerations which need not be explored here, were in fact speedily combated by the ministry.[3] They formed the burden of the criticism heard in the Second Chamber's debate, but the Foreign Minister did not hesitate to declare that Muller, like van Ryckevorsel before him, was interested only in keeping the Gold Coast trade free of duty; and after the former Colonial Minister Rochussen had supported the measure it was approved by thirty votes to twenty-three. The question of valuation arose again in the debate in the First Chamber on 3 July, which was, however, mainly remarkable for the intervention of Cremers, a former Foreign Minister, who, unabashed by aspersions on his patriotism, insisted that the time had come to get rid of the Gold Coast for good. No other voice was heard in support of this assertion, and the measure was approved by the convincing vote of twenty-six to one—the single dissentient being yet another former minister, van de Putte.[4]

Two days later ratifications were duly exchanged, and it was agreed that the treaty should take effect on 1 January 1868, a delay which gave time for some leisurely negotiations to clear up disputed or doubtful points in the projected customs system. Thus, without making any attempt to consult the peoples concerned, Great Britain

[1] H. Muller and Co. to Second Chamber (copy), 19 June 1867, Rotterdam, B.Z. 3000.
[2] Herman, op. cit., ii, p. 70.
[3] M. B. Z. and M. K. to Chairman of Second Chamber (copy), 26 June 1867, B.Z. 3000.
[4] Hand. S.G., 1866–7, I, pp. 188–96; II, pp. 1348–55; Milbanke-Huskisson to Stanley, 5 July 1867, Hague, F.O. 37/442.

and the Netherlands agreed to barter them, as was truly said a few years later, 'like so many bullocks'.[1] Technically, of course, Carnarvon was perfectly correct in claiming that the interior tribes were not to be 'transferred' but 'merely' abandoned; indeed they *could* not be 'transferred' unless the pretty startling assumption was made that they were under British sovereignty. Article I of the treaty laid down an exchange of 'forts, possessions, and rights of sovereignty or jurisdiction', with a boundary running 'as far as the boundary of the present Ashanti kingdom', which at first sight might seem to imply that the 'protectorate' *was* included in the exchange; but Carnarvon's legally impeccable point was that, strictly speaking, Britain had no 'rights' over the protectorate, so there was nothing to transfer. The Dutch themselves were brought to acknowledge this in the following year and to renounce their absurd claim that the treaty had automatically made the British 'protectorate' Dutch.[2] But, even had they understood it, this fine distinction could carry little weight with people who, in effect, found themselves living in a Dutch 'sphere of influence'. In any case, Carnarvon's logic-chopping had no bearing on the case of the British settlements on the windward Coast. Nevertheless, once the treaty was signed little apprehension seems to have been felt of serious trouble from this or any other direction. None, perhaps, was to be expected from a Foreign Secretary who, two years earlier, had told the Commons that the life of one British naval officer, 'measured by any rational standards of comparison, is worth more than the merely animal existence of a whole African tribe'.[3] Governor Boers at Elmina thought it possible that there might be some trouble along the coast, but that the Wasaws were longing to come under Dutch protection.[4] From Cape Coast Acting Administrator Ussher foresaw some 'purely local' resistance at Dutch Accra, but he too was not greatly worried.[5] Only from Nagtglas, himself in large measure the author of the treaty, came a

---

[1] *African Times,* 24 Oct. 1870.
[2] Stanley to Harris, 27 March 1868, F.O. 238/149; M. B. Z. to Harris (copy), 2 April 1868, Hague, C.O. 96/78. Cf. A. B. Ellis, *History of the Gold Coast of West Africa* (London, 1893), p. 244: 'The British also relinquished to the Dutch the protectorate over Wasaw, Denkera and Apollonia'. This, like some of Ellis's other errors, has been widely copied.
[3] *Hansard,* 3rd ser., clxxvii, cols. 535–59.
[4] Boers to M. K. (draft), 5 Sept. 1867, Elmina, G. 722.
[5] Ussher to Blackall, 5 Dec. 1867, Cape Coast, ADM. 1/688.

real note of warning. From his retirement he vainly counselled his government that trouble with the Wasaws, Denkyiras and Apollonias was inevitable, and that on no account should force be used to induce them to accept the Dutch flag; but even he anticipated little difficulty with the British settlements of the windward coast, not even with the Komendas.[1]

What impelled Holland and Britain to conclude an agreement which Carnarvon's successor Buckingham described as 'very desirable',[2] but which in the event proved a monstrous blunder? There was no question of a hasty, ill-considered decision; each side had had twenty years to think out the issues involved. Nor was this a case in which governments at home unwillingly deferred to the interested, partial views of merchants or missionaries. The Dutch, indeed, had gone *against* the views of their merchants, and in 1870 the heads of one of the two major British trading concerns on the Coast were able to declare that the treaty 'was made and carried into effect without any notice or advice from the local traders'.[3] It is true that the *African Times*, mouthpiece of the British merchants, welcomed the news of the treaty; but it added that it would have preferred to see the outright purchase of the Dutch settlements![4] As for the British Methodist missionaries, far from advocating the exchange, they were perturbed that the Dutch would 'interfere with the full working of our machinery' in the settlements that would be handed over to them.[5]

It is clear, in fact, that both governments were acting in what they fondly believed to be the best interests of the Gold Coast as well as their own. They wanted at one and the same time to make their settlements profitable, or at least viable, to remove existing causes of friction, and to facilitate economic and social development. The fact that they acted after mature deliberation, and without undue pressure from interested parties, makes their failure to foresee the consequences all the less defensible. There is, indeed, some defence for the Dutch, who were quite correct in believing 'their' natives would

---

[1] Nagtglas to M. B. Z., 14 Oct. 1867, Hague, B.Z. 3000.
[2] Buckingham to Blackall, 22 March 1867, ADM. 1/27.
[3] F. and A. Swanzy to Granville, 28 Feb. 1870, Cannon St., C.O. 96/86.
[4] *African Times*, 23 May 1867.
[5] W. West to W. B. Boyce, 17 May 1867, Cape Coast, Methodist Missionary Society/Gen. Corres.: G.C. 1859–67.

make little difficulty about being transferred, and who could not be expected to have first-hand knowledge of the likely reactions of the 'British' natives concerned. But what defence—unless we accept a plea of ignorance—is there for the British? It is here that the bulk of the responsibility for the outcome of the exchange must lie; upon the men on the spot and the 'expert' who recommended it, and upon the home government which carried it through despite many previous warnings. It is not always possible, even for governments, to gamble on certainties; but it is usual at least to ascertain the odds *before* taking the plunge. One need not be unduly charitable to men who, through indolence or incompetence, failed to take this elementary precaution when the stakes were human lives.

3

THE COAST IN FLAMES, 1868–1870

So CONFIDENT do the British seem to have been, despite all their previous misgivings, that they would be able to hand over the places concerned without incident to the Dutch, that it was not until 10 December that the impending transfer was proclaimed at Cape Coast.[1] There had, of course, been no possibility of keeping the treaty a secret on the Coast until this announcement. As early as 6 July Ussher had reported 'that all the Eastern tribes, with the exception of a few disaffected Accras, contemplate with unmixed satisfaction the cession of Dutch Accra to the British Government'.[2] Such observation of the effect of unofficial rumours was unfortunately no substitute for the proper consultation of the peoples concerned. In any case, what mattered was the reaction of the 'British' natives on the windward coast. No one had ever suggested that those on the leeward coast (apart from 'a few Accras') would complain; so that all Ussher's impressive-sounding assurances amounted to was that nobody in the eastern districts objected to the transfer except those who might be expected to.

The proclamation of 10 December called forth a stream of indignant protests. The 'protected' tribes rejected the Dutch flag outright, while the feelings of the coastal settlements were well voiced in the warning from Dixcove that 'there will be some disturbances of bloodshed in our country'.[3] The roots of the trouble lay far back in the long-standing feuds between 'Dutch' and 'British' natives on the windward Coast, greatly aggravated, particularly since the beginning

---

[1] Circular letter from Ussher to chiefs (printed), 10 Dec. 1867, C.O. 96/77.
[2] Ussher to Blackall (copy), 6 July 1867, Accra, ADM. 1/687.
[3] See the several replies, during December, to Ussher's circular in C.O. 96/77. The Dutch had issued a similar proclamation in November, which had called forth a protest from Dutch Accra (King and chiefs of Dutch Accra to Boers (copy), 17 Nov. 1867, 'Dutch Town Accra', G. 722).

of the nineteenth century, by the Elmina-Ashanti connexion. It was indeed the Ashanti connexion which was now foremost in the minds of those 'British' tribes who saw themselves threatened with Dutch rule or 'protection'. Without the memory of previous Ashanti invasions and the apprehensions of new ones, Komendas and Elminas, Dixcoves and Bushuas *might* have learned to live together under the Dutch flag, and Wasaws and Denkyiras might well have agreed to return to Dutch protection. Thinking Dutchmen themselves had long realized the suicidal nature of these ties with Ashanti, which were gradually making the Dutch position on the Coast untenable and greatly aiding Britain in her 'encroachments'. Nagtglas, indeed, envisaged the exchange as a prelude to the severance of the Ashanti link and the forging of bonds between the Elminas and their erstwhile enemies on the Coast.[1] But the fears and hatreds bred of centuries of conflict could not be wiped out by a stroke of the pen, and the threat of subjection to Ashanti's complaisant ally Holland made the British connexion seem precious. 'It is not my delight to be called a Dutchman,' declared the King of Denkyira, 'but I will live and die with the English, as my Brother did with the English.'[2]

Despite this almost universal protest from the British settlements and 'protectorate', the Cape Coast authorities showed no hesitation in proceeding with the transfer at the appointed time. Their persistence was rewarded with disaster. The Dutch settlements in the east accepted their transfer peaceably enough, but of the western British settlements Dixcove and Sekondi submitted only with manifest reluctance, while English Komenda took up arms when the Dutch Governor Boers insisted on hoisting the Dutch flag there. Boers retaliated by destroying the town with mortar fire, but the Komendas retired to the bush and continued to defy the Dutch.[3] What made this defiance infinitely more serious was the speedy and powerful support that it received, not only from the interior tribes from whom

---

[1] Nagtglas to M. B. Z., 14 Oct. 1867, Hague, B.Z. 3000.
[2] See above, p. 50, n. 3.
[3] Blackall to Buckingham, 6 and 28 Jan. 1868, Accra and Sierra Leone, C.O. 96/76; Boers to M.K. (drafts), 21 Jan. and 5 Feb. 1868, Elmina, G. 723; Ussher to Blackall (copy), 3 Feb. 1868, Cape Coast, C.O. 96/76; Jeekel, op. cit., pp. 5, 9, 14, 62–8; J. A. B. Horton, *Letters on the Political Condition of the Gold Coast* . . . (London, 1870), letter 1.

E

British 'protection' had been withdrawn and who had set their faces against any dealings with the Dutch, but also from the Fantes of the British settlements and 'protectorate'. The long-standing distrust of this people for the Dutch and their hatred of the Elminas, both springing from the Dutch-Elmina link with their traditional foes the Ashantis, spurred them on not merely to defend the Komendas, but even to use this occasion as an opportunity for a final settlement of scores. By the beginning of April Elmina was besieged and block-aded by the army of hostile ex-'British' natives and their Fante sympathizers (now banded together in a so-called 'Fante Confederation'), and, crowded with refugees from the surrounding bush-villages, was in grave danger of being conquered not so much by force of arms as by famine. After a frontal assault on Elmina had been beaten off on 26 May by the guns of Fort Coenraadsburg the enemy camp broke up, but the blockade continued, as did the Fante attacks on the Elmina bush-villages.[1]

European authority on the Coast seemed to be collapsing. The Elminas blamed Governor Boers for all their troubles[2]—a view which found considerable sympathy at The Hague[3]—and in August wrote to the King of the Netherlands asking him either to give them proper support against their enemies or else formally to withdraw Dutch 'protection'.[4] Meanwhile, tension between Administrator Ussher and the Fantes, created in the first place by the transfer itself, had become so great as a result of Ussher's unsuccessful attempts to keep the 'British' natives neutral, and, when this had failed, to mediate between them and the Elminas, that each side broke off all relations with the other

---

[1] Ussher to Blackall (copy), 6 Feb. 1868, Cape Coast, C.O. 96/76; Boers to M.K. (drafts), 15 Feb., 3 and 16 March, 4 and 15 April, 7 May and 1 June 1868, Elmina, G. 723; Ussher to Kennedy (copies), 16 Feb., 6 and 19 March, 6 and 16 April, 7 and 18 May, and 7 June 1868, Cape Coast, C.O. 96/76; Horton, op. cit., letters 1, 2 and 3; Jeekel, op. cit., pp. 68–70; Herman, op. cit., ii, pp. 81–2, 84, 89–92. For the continuation of the blockade see Herman (p. 93) and Horton (letter 3), and cf. the account in Claridge (op. cit., i, pp. 562–74), whose total lack of sympathy with the Dutch makes his treatment of the events of this period less than trustworthy. This is in any case not the best-understood period of Gold Coast history. The most recent volume of the *Cambridge History of the British Empire* (iii, p. 87) assures us that the 'troubles of 1867–8' (*sic*) were due to 'rumours of the impending evacuation of the Dutch settlements in favour of Britain'—rumours which did not in fact reach the Coast until July 1870.
[2] Boers to M. K. (draft), 4 Oct. 1869, Elmina, G. 723.
[3] e.g. Brocx to Boers, 5 Sept. 1868, Hague, G. 729.
[4] King, etc., of Elmina to King of Netherlands (copy), 6 Aug. 1868, Elmina, G. 723.

in July.[1] On the other hand, relations between British and Dutch authorities on the Coast had rarely been as close as those between Boers and Ussher, thanks largely to Ussher's strenuous efforts to negotiate a peace, the failure of which he ascribed entirely to the 'cruelty' and 'faithlessness' of the Fantes.[2] Even after Acting Administrator Simpson took over at Cape Coast in August when Ussher went home on sick leave, this closeness persisted for a while; as late as October Boers testified his indebtedness to the powerful and kind co-operation of the British.[3] But Simpson's more conciliatory attitude towards the Fante Confederation, though it helped to heal the breach between them and the British, led to a speedy deterioration in the relations of Elmina with Cape Coast. The same was true of the vehemently insistent advocacy by the Governor-in-Chief, Sir Arthur Kennedy, of an offensive-defensive alliance, aimed against Ashanti, between Elminas and Fantes, a scheme as abhorrent to the former as it was agreeable to the latter. Soon the authorities on the Coast were bombarding their home governments with bitter complaints of each other's conduct,[4] while recriminations flew thick and fast between them.[5]

Such was the situation when, on 20 March 1869, the discredited Boers was dismissed from his post and Nagtglas accepted the appointment of Governor and Royal Commissioner. Nagtglas, principal architect of the 1867 Treaty, had been bitterly disappointed by its outcome,[6] but still hoped that it might be possible to retrieve matters by arranging a Fante-Elmina peace, on the basis, if necessary, of a defensive alliance, with the Elminas thus holding a middle position between Fantes and Ashantis.[7] Relying as he was on British co-operation in this task, Nagtglas was shocked on his arrival in May

---

[1] Ussher to Kennedy (copy), 7 Aug. 1868, Cape Coast, C.O. 96/77 (and enclosures).
[2] Ussher to Boers, 13 July 1868, Cape Coast, G. 728; Ussher to Kennedy (copy), 17 July 1868, Cape Coast, C.O. 96/76.
[3] Boers to M. K. (draft), 13 Oct. 1868, Elmina, G. 723.
[4] Boers to M. K. (drafts), 4 Sept. and 6 Nov. 1868, Elmina, G. 723; Kennedy to Buckingham, 7 Nov. 1868, Cape Coast, C.O. 96/77; Kennedy to Granville, 14 Jan. 1869, Sierra Leone, C.O. 96/79. Ussher, it is true, had also been in favour of an offensive-defensive alliance, but not as publicly nor as urgently as Kennedy.
[5] For Simpson's letters to Boers see G. 724 and 728; for Boers' letters to Simpson see ADM. 1/834.
[6] Nagtglas to M. K. (copy), 3 Sept. 1868, Hague, B.Z. 3001.
[7] Nagtglas to M. K., 3 Dec. 1868, Kol. 11. XII. 1868. Kab. Geheim litt. B. 16; Mollema, op. cit., p. 225.

to learn that Simpson had been encouraging the Fante leaders to insist on an offensive-defensive alliance, at the same time attacking the exchange treaty and even, allegedly, proclaiming that 'Elmina must go'. The British Government eventually disavowed Simpson's words, as it had already disavowed the offensive-defensive alliance project, but the damage was done.[1]

Events, in fact, were conspiring to ruin all chance of an agreed settlement. The enemies of the Dutch, already incensed by a fruitless attack on the rebellious Apollonians,[2] were not likely to be appeased by the sack of Dixcove in June by 'Dutch' natives in circumstances suggestive of collusion by the Dutch authorities.[3] On the other hand, feeling in Holland in favour of a more forceful policy on the Coast, already mounting fast,[4] was greatly strengthened when at the end of May the Komendas captured five shipwrecked Dutch sailors, killing one and holding the rest to ransom.[5] As a result a punitive force was sent out which in December 1869 and January 1870 succeeded in pursuing the elusive Komendas into the bush, killing a few of them and burning some of their villages.[6] Technically, no doubt, a successful operation, but its most concrete result was to make yet more difficult the task of conciliation. The chances of this were being still further reduced by the activities of the

---

[1] Mins. by Rogers of 16 Jan. and 17 May 1869 on F.O. to C.O., 5 Jan. and 13 May 1869, C.O. 96/82; Granville to Kennedy, 22 Jan. 1869 (copy), C.O. 402/9; 'Notes of the Proceedings at the meeting . . . at Mankessim April 22nd–28th 1869' (copy), C.O. 96/80: ibid., Lovell to Boers (copy), 15 May 1869, Cape Coast; ibid., Nagtglas to Kennedy (copy), 20 May 1869, Elmina; Granville to Kennedy, 24 May 1869, ADM. 1/27; Forster and Smith to Granville (copy), 3 June 1869, New City Chambers, C.O. 96/83; Granville to Kennedy (copy), 13 July 1869, ADM. 1/679.

[2] Simpson to Kennedy (copy), 5 June 1869, Cape Coast, C.O. 96/80.

[3] The Dixcoves had been transferred to the Dutch against their will in 1868, but the traditional enmity between them and the surrounding 'Dutch' natives continued. The copious evidence as to Dutch responsibility for this incident is conflicting and inconclusive. Compare the account in Claridge (op. cit., i, pp. 587–90) with the statements of Alvarez (C.O. 96/81, 27 June 1869) and Nagtglas (G. 724, 14 July 1869).

[4] For expressions of this feeling in the States-General see Hand. S.G., 1868–9, II, pp. 745–6, 1137–40, 1331–6, 1577–80; see also De Rarekiek der Hollandsche Huishouding, of Java, Suriname, de Goudkust en Nederland bekeken door den Oud-Bankier. Twcede Vertooning (Alkmaar, 1869), pp. 21–3.

[5] For this incident and its consequences see W. J. van der Werff, Guinea. Eene Bladzijde uit Nederland's Maritime Gedenkboeken ('s-Gravenhage, 1881), passim; for the reaction in Holland see Hand. S.G. 1868–9, I, p. 364, II, pp. 1605, 1614–18.

[6] F. A. van Braam Houckgeest, De Expeditie naar de Kust van Guinea in het Jaar 1869 (Nieuwediep, 1870), passim; G. Fabius, 'De Gebeurtenissen in Guinea gedurende de Laatste drie Jaren, waarin dit Gebied in nederlandsch Bezit was, 1869–1872', Bijdragen voor Vaderlandsche Geschiedenis en Oudheidkunde, VIIIe reeks, dl. IV (1942), pp. 2–17.

Ashanti ambassador Akyeampon. Entering the Dutch settlements from the west on the pretext of escorting a number of Elmina messengers returning from Kumasi, Aykeampon had marched towards Elmina in November and December 1869 with an armed force which murdered or enslaved all Fantes, or others suspected of hostility to the Dutch, that it could lay its hands on. After committing these atrocities, Aykeampon and his followers, whom the Dutch authorities dared not eject, remained in Elmina for more than two years, bedevilling Fante-Elmina relations by their very presence.[1] Their real object, according to the missionaries held captive at Kumasi at this time, was to watch for a favourable opportunity for a renewed assault on the 'British' coastal tribes (to be led by Akyeampon himself at the head of a combined Elmina-Ashanti force). According to the same authority, there was no connexion between this marauding reconnaissance and an appeal for help that had been sent to Kumasi by the King of Elmina during the siege of 1868.[2] Simpson, however, claimed to have proof positive that later in 1868 a *further* appeal had been made with the direct or tacit approval of Boers.[3] By this time Simpson was ready to believe almost anything against the Dutch, as too was Kennedy, who had little doubt that Akyeampon's descent was in response to this alleged invitation;[4] but these suspicions were certainly lent a little colour when, in the middle of 1870, Akyeampon himself told the astonished Nagtglas that he had been summoned to Elmina by the government to give them his assistance.[5] True or not, this story of an 'invitation' (vehemently denied by Boers himself)[6] did nothing to promote harmony between Cape Coast and Elmina.

Thus matters continued to stand on the Coast, with hostilities now for the most part confined to isolated raids and skirmishes, but with the prospects of peace as remote as ever. By March 1870 Nagtglas feared that this situation might last for months or even years, and

---

[1] The best account of Akyeampon's activities is to be found in the documents printed as Appendices 1 K to 1 X to the '1874 Report'. See also Horton, op. cit., letter VIII.

[2] F. A. Ramseyer and J. Kühne, *Four Years in Ashantee* (London, 1878: 2nd ed.), p. 203.

[3] Simpson to Boers, 6 April 1869, Cape Coast, G. 728.

[4] Kennedy to Granville (confidential), 8 Feb. 1870, C.O. 96/84.

[5] Nagtglas to M. K. (draft), 4 June 1870, G. 725.

[6] Boers to Simpson, 8 April 1869, Elmina, ADM. 1/834.

thought the best thing would be to 'leave them entirely to themselves . . . only protecting the seaside trade, and to drive them back from the forts when attacked'.[1] Similarly Ussher, now back at his post, was 'inclined to give up the Elmina-Fante question as a hopeless business' since the Fantes would 'listen to *nothing* but offensive and defensive alliance against the Ashantee', and confined himself 'to keeping order as well as possible along the Coast'.[2] Towards the middle of July, however, the outlook was suddenly transformed by the arrival of private letters, soon to be confirmed by Dutch and English newspapers, announcing the impeding cession of the Dutch settlements to Britain.[3]

[1] Memorandum from Nagtglas to Kennedy (copy), 6 March 1870, Elmina, C.O. 96/84.
[2] Ussher to Nagtglas, 14 April 1870, Cape Coast, G. 728.
[3] Nagtglas to M. K. (draft), 4 Aug. 1870, Elmina, G. 725; Same to same (copy), 28 Aug. 1870, Elmina, B.Z. 3002.

4

THE TREATY OF CESSION—I

NEGOTIATION AND ASHANTI INTERVENTION

THE idea of giving up the Gold Coast settlements, and in particular of ceding them to Britain, was no novelty in Holland.[1] In recent years a few members of the States-General had persistently queried their value and demanded their abandonment,[2] and a Dutch Colonial Minister had actually hinted to the British envoy that this might form part of an Anglo-Dutch colonial 'bargain'.[3] The outcome of the 1868 exchanges had emboldened the advocates of abandonment,[4] and with reason, for the settlements were now more of a burden on the mother country than ever. The new tariff was certainly producing a significant revenue, but the expenses of maintaining Dutch authority were now so great that the subsidy from the home government had to be increased.[5] Moreover, it began to appear that the operation of the tariff was rapidly driving away the already exiguous Dutch trade. Muller, seeing more advantage in the trade with Mozambique and the Congo, was soon sending only one ship a year to the Coast.[6] The cause of abandonment received further encouragement when the Fock-van Bosse ministry took office in June 1868, and with it de Waal as Colonial Minister. De Waal was known to favour a policy of rigorous economy in colonial expenditure and of concentration of

---

[1] See above, p. 24.
[2] See above, pp. 36, 41.
[3] See above, p. 41, n. 1.
[4] *Hand. S.G.*, 1868–9, I, p. 364; 1868–9, II, p. 1488; 1868–9, Bijlagen, pp. 1333–4.
[5] '1874 Report', section I B; 'Begrootingen van ontvangsten en uitgaven', G. 792.
[6] van der Aa, op. cit., Ch. V; Herman, op. cit., p. 106. Muller's seem to have given up their establishment at Elmina altogether about the time of the cession, after which there was no Dutch firm operating on the Coast until 1921 (*Ghana, 6 Maart 1957* (Afrika Instituut, Rotterdam), p. 41).

resources and effort upon the development of Java and Sumatra.[1] He was said (by a critic) to have declared at one time that if ever he were Minister, one of his first actions would be to cede the Dutch Gold Coast to Britain,[2] though he himself was later to claim that he had known next to nothing about affairs on the Coast before he took office.[3] Certainly he now made little secret in the States-General of his desire to be rid of the settlements should a suitable opportunity arise.[4]

On the face of it, it seemed unlikely that Britain would look very kindly upon such an offer. We have seen that the idea of purchasing the Dutch Gold Coast had in earlier years been contemplated not only by the coastal authorities, weary of the difficulties and dangers of divided jurisdiction, and by merchants interested in expanding their trade, but also by the Colonial Office itself.[5] But this had been before the events of 1863-4 and the subsequent deliberations of the Select Committee, which had declared that 'all further extension of territory or assumption of Government, or new treaties offering any protection to any native tribes, would be inexpedient'. There were, it is true, some loopholes written into the Select Committee's report,[6] which was just as well in view of the realities of the West African situation, but hitherto the Colonial Office had shown little inclination to take advantage of these. Thus, in the debates on the exchange treaty in 1867, the Dutch ministry could quite truthfully inform the advocates of cession that the British had displayed no interest in it.[7]

At Cape Coast, it is true, Acting Administrator Ussher was not slow to conclude that the removal of the Dutch might be the best way of clearing up the troubles resulting from the transfer. As early as 6 March he reported that 'their departure would be hailed with joy and our rule is the only one desired'. A month later he was recommending his superiors to consider purchasing the Dutch Gold Coast,

---

[1] Mollema, op. cit., p. 226.
[2] J. P. Schoemaker, *Laatste bladzijde onzer Nederlandsche West Afrikaansche Historie . . .* (c. 1900) (reference by courtesy of Miss Mollema).
[3] E. de Waal, *Onze Indische Financiën (Nieuwe Reeks Aantekeningen)*, dl. I ('s-Gravenhage, 1876), p. 68.
[4] *Hand. S.G.*, 1868–9, I, pp. 113–4; 1868–9, Bijlagen, p. 670.
[5] See above, pp. 18, 24–5.
[6] See above, p. 39.
[7] *Hand. S.G.*, 1866–7, Bijlagen, p. 991. Cf. Nagtglas to M. K. (draft), 4 Nov. 1870, G. 725.

not merely as a remedy for present ills, but also with a view to future commercial benefits and to forestalling its purchase by the French.[1] In Sierra Leone, Kennedy, the new Governor-in-Chief, was at first decidedly averse to the idea of extending the Protectorate, which would, he feared, result in a collision with Ashanti, though he agreed with Ussher as to 'the desire of the French Government to acquire territory and trading posts on this Coast'.[2] By June, however, he had come round to the view that the acquisition of Elmina was the key to the pacification and future welfare of the Coast,[3] and by the beginning of 1869 he was ready to set forth its advantages in detail. The Gold Coast would be rendered self-supporting and prosperous; higher duties could be levied upon arms and liquor going into the interior, thus achieving fiscal and moral benefits at the same time; withdrawal of troops would soon be possible; and so strongly did the peoples of the Protectorate desire to be rid of the Dutch that they would subscribe handsomely to the purchase-money. Above all, this was the 'one way of escaping from the labyrinth in which a series of mistakes and miscalculations has involved both Governments'.[4]

Such arguments made little impression on the Conservative administrations which governed Britain for most of 1868. Pressure for 'ultimate withdrawal' was still strong, and was felt particularly keenly at the Colonial Office, where the Parliamentary Under-Secretary was now none other than Adderley, chairman of the 1865 Committee. Adderley took the view that such settlements as those in West Africa were held 'for special purposes' by the Crown, which might, 'if these objects cease to exist, abandon, cede, or exchange at any time, only fulfilling engagements made, and securing interests created . . .'. He could not see what useful object was now being served by the maintenance of British authority on the Gold Coast, where it had been

partially beneficial in checking barbarous practices, human sacrifices,

---

[1] Ussher to Kennedy (copies), 6 March and 6 April 1868, Cape Coast, C.O. 96/76.
[2] Ibid., Kennedy to Buckingham, 16 April 1868, Sierra Leone.
[3] Ibid., same to same, 16 June 1868, Sierra Leone.
[4] Kennedy to Granville, 11 Jan. 1869, Sierra Leone, C.O. 96/79. J. A. B. Horton, a Sierra Leonean military surgeon, who also held civil posts on the Coast, publicly advocated purchase in his *West African Countries and Peoples* (London, 1868), p. 256 —and later in Letter IX of his *Letters on . . . the Gold Coast* (London, 1870).

and endless internal feuds, but much more abused as a basis on which native intrigues, and rotten governments have been sustained.[1]

Far from wishing to purchase Elmina, he repeatedly urged that the Dutch should be offered the British settlements.[2] December 1868 saw the advent of a Liberal administration under Gladstone, but, on the surface at least, there was little change in the British attitude towards Kennedy's proposals. Adderley, it is true, gave place to Monsell, who was 'convinced that if we remain at the Gold Coast, we ought to have Elmina';[3] but the new Colonial Secretary, Granville, told Kennedy plainly that the government could not 'entertain any idea of extended British occupation in that quarter'.[4] At The Hague, meanwhile, de Waal was now beginning in the strictest confidence to press upon his colleague, the Foreign Minister Roest van Limburg, the desirability of relinquishing the totally unprofitable and now untenable Gold Coast to either France or Britain. Roest van Limburg, though sympathetic, insisted that the king's authority was necessary before any approach could be made to the powers concerned, but the British envoy Harris, after an interview with de Waal in February 1869, was able to report 'that the Dutch would be glad to get rid of their settlements on the Gold Coast if they could find a purchaser'.[5]

De Waal's request to the king for authority to negotiate the abandonment or cession of the Gold Coast settlements was made on 17 April 1869. Everything, he declared, seemed to point to this: the financial burden of the settlements; the uncertainty of success and costliness of execution of the plans put forward for their development; the insignificance of their trade; and, above all, the impossible position in which the Dutch now found themselves, with the choice of endless hostilities with the Fantes or the imposition of

---

[1] Sir C. B. Adderley, op. cit., pp. 195, 206–10.
[2] Minute by Adderley of 4 March 1868 on Ord to Buckingham, 16 Jan. 1868, Penang, C.O. 273/17; Minute by Adderley of 26 Sept. 1868 on Ord to Buckingham (confidential), 3 Aug. 1868, Singapore, C.O. 273/21.
[3] Min. by Monsell of 1 March 1869 on F.O. to C.O., 23 Feb. 1869, C.O. 96/82.
[4] Granville to Kennedy, 9 Feb. 1869, ADM. 1/27. See also Conf. Print, African No. 49.
[5] M. K. to M. B. Z., 4 and 11 Dec. 1869, B.Z. 3002; ibid., M. B. Z. to M. K. (draft), 9 and 16 Dec. 1868; Harris to Clarendon, 11 Feb. 1869, Hague, F.O. 37/468. Admiral Edward Alfred John Harris (1808–88) had held a variety of consular and diplomatic posts before his appointment to The Hague in 1867.

an offensive-defensive Fante alliance upon the Elminas, which, in turn, would mean war with Ashanti. If the British wanted the settlements they should be given them for nothing more than the cost of the stores that they took over; the French, too, might well be interested.[1] These arguments made no impression on the Council of State, to which they were referred, and by which they were rejected on several grounds: the exact situation on the Coast was not yet clear; it would be dishonourable to take the initiative by *offering* territory to a foreign power; the cession of *any* colony was undesirable unless it formed part of a general settlement which contained compensating advantages, since it was bound to injure the position of Holland both as a colonial and as a European power; and, finally, this would not be a fit way of repaying the Elminas for their outstanding loyalty to the Dutch flag for more than two centuries.[2]

This first rebuff left de Waal undismayed. He had the support of his colleagues, and Harris seemed sympathetic in private conversation,[3] even if unwilling, without instructions, to respond when Roest van Limburg, 'as if in jest', told him that Britain should take over the Dutch settlements.[4] The greatest obstacle to de Waal's plans was the king, whose views were believed to have been reflected by the Council of State and who, as Harris remarked, was 'very sensitive about losing territory';[5] but this did not deter the Colonial Minister. While declaring in the States-General that no decision to give up the Coast could be taken for the time being,[6] he questioned Nagtglas about the willingness of the Elminas to accept the British flag. Nagtglas, taking the hint, sounded Simpson privately on the matter, but was told that the British Government had absolutely no desire to take over the Dutch settlements.[7] Subsequent conversations both with Kennedy and with a visiting French naval commander were no more promising.[8]

[1] M. K. to King, 17 April 1869, Kol. 17. IV. 1869. Kab. Geheim. Litt. D. 6.
[2] Minister of State to king, 1 June 1869, Kol. 1. VI. 1869. Zeer Geheim. Litt. A. 3.
[3] Roest van Limburg to M. B. Z., 10 June 1871, Baden Baden, Afst. IV.
[4] Van Lansberge to M. B. Z., 10 June 1871, Brussels, Afst. IV.
[5] Harris to Clarendon, 29 Sept. 1869, Hague, F.O. 37/469.
[6] *Hand. S.G.*, 1868–9, II, pp. 1577–80.
[7] M. K. to Nagtglas, 20 July 1869, G. 730; Nagtglas to M. K. (draft), 18 Aug. 1869, G. 724.
[8] Nagtglas to M. K. (drafts), 25 Jan. and 3 March 1870, G. 725; Kennedy to Granville, 23 March 1870, Sierra Leone, C.O. 96/84; '1874 Report', Section I B.

The private exchanges with Harris came to a head on 30 September, when de Waal met the British envoy by chance while walking in the 'Bois' and entered into conversation with him about the Dutch Gold Coast settlements. 'He said he anticipated more trouble there', reported Harris in a private letter of 1 October to the Foreign Secretary, Clarendon, 'and would be only too glad if we would take them off their hands merely remunerating his Gov^t for the value of the stores which they would leave there.' The king, said de Waal, 'did not appear to entertain any great repugnance' to this proposal, though there might be

some anger on the part of the public unless they previously vindicated the honour of the Dutch flag and gave those native tribes who assailed it a licking.

He could not yet make an official proposition, but asked Harris to inform his government privately of the conversation.[1]

Serious historians have long ceased to think of mid-Victorian British colonial policy in terms of a Liberal 'Little Englander'— Conservative 'Jingoist' dichotomy, so that it is unnecessary here to labour the point that de Waal's hint was to get a much more favourable reception from the 'retrenching' ministry of Mr. Gladstone than it could possibly have hoped for from that of his 'imperialist' predecessor, who, indeed, only three years earlier had adjured Lord Derby to 'leave the Canadians to defend themselves; recall the African squadrons; give up the settlements on the West Coast of Africa'.[2] We should note, however, the light thrown by the nature of this reception upon what might be called the *éminence grise* theory of policy-making. It is fashionable to emphasize that

The Frenchman stated that far from being interested in Elmina France would be only too glad to hand over Grand Bassam, Assini and Gabon, without compensation, to the Dutch! Whether the expectations voiced in both London and The Hague of French interest in the Dutch Gold Coast were based on anything more than conjecture I do not know; but to judge from France's neglect at this time of her existing posts on the Ivory Coast they do not seem to have had much foundation in reality.

[1] Harris to Clarendon (private), 1 Oct. 1869, Hague, MS. Clar. Dep. C. 484. See also the 'statement' by Harris (copy), 29 May 1871, Afst. IV; Harris to Granville, 1 June 1871, Hague, F.O. 37/491. De Waal's version of this conversation agrees with Harris's though he adds that it was Harris who asked to be allowed to inform the Foreign Secretary of it (De Waal, op. cit.), p. 69.

[2] For this quotation and for a discussion of 'imperialism' in politics at this time see C. A. Bodelsen, *Studies in Mid-Victorian Imperialism* (Copenhagen, 1924), pp. 121 *et sqq.*

colonial policy in this period and earlier was largely the work of permanent officials rather than of shadowy or, as in the case of Granville, not over-energetic ministers. There is obviously a good deal of truth in this, especially in the case of such able and forceful men as James Fitzjames Stephens and Granville's own Permanent Under-Secretary, Sir Frederic Rogers. But Rogers, though he had by no means approved of Adderley's ideas,[1] was certainly no enthusiast for expansion, in West Africa or anywhere else,[2] and it was neither Rogers nor any other permanent official who initiated the virtual reversal of British policy which followed the fateful interview in the Bois—it was the Colonial Secretary, Granville.

Although 'he took his duties lightly', rarely drafting a dispatch himself, Granville, thanks to his intimacy with Gladstone, enjoyed considerable freedom of initiative.[3] This he chose to exercise when the news from The Hague reached him in a note from the Foreign Secretary Clarendon, who thought 'that Parlt. wd. prefer to sell our own to buying others . . .'.[4] The Colonial Secretary was out of London, away from the Colonial Office at his home at Walmer Castle, when he received this note, to which he replied by return in these words:

If the Colony can pay for it, which I believe Kennedy thinks it can, it would be well worth buying Elmina. Whether we remain on that Coast, or retire from it, it is equally desired for Trade and Peace to get rid of the Dutch.[5]

This, from the man who only eight months earlier had refused to consider the extension of the West African settlements, was a real volte-face. On the other hand, the events of those eight months on the Coast had powerfully reinforced the arguments of Kennedy and Ussher, which had also not very surprisingly received the support of the Fante chiefs and of F. and A. Swanzy, one of the most important British firms engaged in the Gold Coast trade.[6] It had been

---

[1] Minute by Rogers of 20 Jan. 1869, on Ord to Buckingham (confidential), 9 Dec. 1869, Penang, C.O. 273/22.
[2] See the revealing passage from his letter of 28 May 1877 to Sir H. Taylor, quoted in *Cambridge History of the British Empire,* iii (Cambridge, 1959), p. 60.
[3] P. Knaplund, *Gladstone and Britain's Imperial Policy* (London, 1927), pp. 99–100.
[4] Clarendon to G(ranville) (private), 5 Oct. 1869, Watford, P.R.O. 30/29/55.
[5] G(ranville) to Clarendon (private), 7 Oct. 1869, Walmer Castle, F.O. 361/1.
[6] Simpson to Kennedy (copy), 15 June 1869, Cape Coast, C.O. 96/80; A. Swanzy to Granville, 31 Aug. 1869, London, C.O. 96/83.

easy enough to trot out the gospel of non-extension when the question of cession was purely hypothetical; but now that it was actually being raised, albeit informally, by the Dutch Government, the whole matter took on a very different complexion for the Colonial Secretary.

Granville's next step was to consult Kennedy, who was home on leave at this time. It was a foregone conclusion that Kennedy's opinion, delivered in a letter of 14 October, would be highly enthusiastic. Once more he urged the commercial, fiscal, and administrative advantages of acquiring the Dutch settlements, the favourable disposition of all natives, 'the small tribe of "Elminas" excepted', to Britain, and the need to forestall the French. The cost of the Dutch stores, which he thought could not be more than £1,000, could be met from the colonial revenue. He urged the need for speed in carrying out this transfer, which, he said, 'would be most popular and profitable to the trading community', though he added some words of caution as to the necessity of obtaining the acquiescence of the Elminas (otherwise Britain might 'fall into the same mistake the Dutch are now suffering from') and also of ascertaining the reaction of the Ashantis.[1] Granville forwarded Kennedy's letter to Clarendon, repeating his own conviction that it would 'be an advantage to get rid of the Dutch',[2] and Clarendon himself had a long talk with Kennedy on 20 October.[3]

Thus advised, Clarendon on 21 October replied to Harris's letter of 1 October in a tone of cautious encouragement. He was not, he explained, authorized to express any desire on the part of Britain to acquire the Dutch settlements, but Harris should try to ascertain without delay the wishes and intentions of the Dutch Government in that matter, though 'of course exhibiting no eagerness on our part for a decision'. It was easy to understand why the Dutch wished to be rid of this '*damnosa possessio*', but our attitude towards any proposal 'would much depend on the terms'. There was 'no care in this country for our African possessions', and there was little prospect of

[1] Kennedy to Rogers (private), 14 Oct. 1869, London, MS. Clar. Dep. C. 500; see also same to same (private), 4 Nov. 1869, London, C.O. 96/83.
[2] G(ranville) to Clarendon (private), 16 Oct. 1869, Walmer Castle, MS. Clar. Dep. C. 500.
[3] C(larendon) to Granville (private), 21 Oct. 1869, Watford, P.R.O. 30/29/55.

getting a vote through Parliament for extending the settlements—indeed, 'an announcement of intention to get rid of them would be popular'—but if de Waal stuck to his suggestion that only the stores left behind should be paid for 'a negotiation might be possible'.[1] The implication here, of course, was that the value of the stores could be met from the colonial revenue and that any recourse to the Commons would thereby be obviated.

London had thus thrown the ball back to The Hague, where Harris, after talking things over with de Waal and Roest van Limburg, saw 'no obstacle unless party spirit should rouse opposition to it which I think unlikely'. It would be necessary to refer the question to the king again before any further steps could be taken, but de Waal 'anticipated no objection' from this quarter and had written off to Nagtglas for a report on the value of the stores.[2]

But de Waal was wrong. 16 November 1869 saw the opening of the Suez Canal, a development which in the long run would give added force to de Waal's argument that Dutch colonial interests should be concentrated in the East.[3] On 17 November, however, fell the anniversary of the proclamation of the House of Orange in 1813, and the king, elated by 'the display of loyal feeling' which resulted, and unwilling to 'cede any territory at such a moment', once more refused his consent to the opening of negotiations for cession.[4] Clarendon, who had already agreed with Granville that there was little point in extending Kennedy's leave 'while the Dutch are making up their minds as to how much they can squeeze out of us',[5] now commented that 'that stupid pig the King will not part with his costly and useless African possessions'.[6] Granville professed

---

[1] Clarendon to Harris (private—copy), 21 Oct. 1869, MS. Clar. Dep. C. 476.
[2] Harris to Clarendon (private), 29 Oct. 1869, Hague, MS. Clar. Dept. C. 484.
[3] e.g. van Bijlandt to M. B. Z., 21 July 1871, London, Rijks Geschiedkundige Publicatien: J. Wolteringen (ed.), *Bescheiden betreffende de Buitenlandse Politiek van Nederland*, 2de periode, 1ste deel, pp. 165-6.
[4] Harris to Clarendon (private), 26 Nov. 1869, Hague, MS. Clar. Dep. C. 484.
[5] Granville to Clarendon (private), 15 Nov. 1869, Walmer Castle, MS. Clar. Dep. C. 500; C(larendon) to Granville, 15 Nov. 1869, P.R.O. 30/29/55.
[6] Ibid., same to same, 30 Nov. 1869. For a rather more restrained critique of the king see the opinions of Lord Napier quoted by J. C. Boogman in 'De Britse Gezant Lord Napier over de Nederlandse Volksvertegenwoordiging (in 1860)', *Bijdragen en Mededeelingen van het Historische Genootschap*, 71ste dl., p. 205 n. In Napier's view William III was 'apt to be excited by conversation, new company, and convivial indulgence. . . . There is nothing consistent or dignified in His Majesty's behaviour. . . . (He is) most respected when least known'.

himself 'not surprised at the King of Holland declining to part with Elmina, as he probably does not know where it is . . .'. 'I am rather sorry', he added,

as we ought to leave the place unless we can make a good job of it, and abandoning it (for which this is not an opportune moment for other reasons) is almost impossible unless the Dutch would go too. They are in our way whether we go or stay.[1]

De Waal was not unduly discouraged. The king, he told Harris, might be induced to change his mind by the end of the year, since 'on its having been mentioned to him on a previous occasion he did not look on it unfavourably'.[2] For the moment, however, de Waal was not well placed for taking a further initiative. His critics in the States-General had got wind of his abortive proposal and were doing their best to make capital from it.[3] Harris thought that this might 'have the effect of testing public opinion on the subject of a cession', and hoped that the success of the Komenda expedition would make many Dutchmen feel that an honourable abandonment was now possible.[4] In the middle of January 1870 de Waal confirmed that this was so, but explained that because there was still strong opposition in some quarters the time was not yet ripe for a further approach to the king.[5] This news was not well received by Harris, who was beginning to have doubts of de Waal's good faith. Since the new constitution of 1848, he told Clarendon,

the changes of ministries have been so frequent that no Minister of the Colonies can count on remaining in office a sufficient time to mature or carry out any consistent policy. Mr. de Waal though more liberal & obliging than most of his predecessors, is still rather slippery.

This growing distrust led Harris to refer to de Waal's unofficial proposals in a public dispatch of 14 January—the first official intimation of this affair to be received in London. He took this step, he explained, 'in order that it might not be said hereafter that the

---

[1] Granville to Clarendon, 1 Dec. 1869, Walmer, MS. Clar. Dep. C. 500.
[2] Harris to Clarendon (private), 26 Nov. 1869, Hague, MS. Clar. Dep. C. 484.
[3] This 'leak' was the work of van Sypesteyn, who, though a member of the Second Chamber, nominally retained his post of *Chef de Bureau* in the Colonial Ministry. *Hand. S.G.,* 1869–70, II, pp. 334, 827; Harris to Clarendon (private), 24 Dec. 1870, Hague, MS. Clar. Dep. C. 484.
[4] Ibid., Harris to Clarendon (private), 24 Dec. 1869, Hague.
[5] Harris to Clarendon (most confidential), 14 Jan. 1870, Hague, F.O. 37/479.

matter originated from any intrigues on our part'. Events were to show the wisdom of this precaution.[1]

The Colonial Office took less and less trouble to hide its impatience at the continuing delay. In January, Sir George Barrow, the chief clerk, thought there was 'some hope of the Dutch relinquishing their settlements',[2] but by March, Granville, alarmed by the news of Akyeampon's outrages, was pressing for a speedy decision.[3] Near the beginning of March King William once more refused his consent to the opening of negotiations, though 'not in such decided terms as before',[4] but the Colonial Office, itself urged on by merchant opinion expressed through Fitzgerald, editor of the *African Times*,[5] continued to call for 'some answer from the Netherlands Govt. as to the relinquishment of Elmina . . .'.[6] Harris, however, strongly deprecated any attempt to put pressure on the Dutch, and in this he was backed by the Foreign Office, which pointed out that opposition to cession, especially on the part of the king, 'would probably be rather strengthened than weakened by pressure from H.M. Govt. . . .'.[7] De Waal continued to assure Harris that the king would eventually give way, although the patriotic emotion which the return of the Komenda expedition stirred in the royal breast was something of a setback to the Colonial Minister's plans.[8] Harris, who feared that a display of eagerness for the cession might not only arouse 'national sensitiveness' but also increase 'the price we may have to pay', accepted de Waal's assurances. 'The King', he told Clarendon,

is not easy to deal with in a case of this kind, but as his ministers are unanimous for the cession and several of those of the opposition who have his ear have come round to the same opinion, I doubt not he will eventually give way.[9]

Harris could speak with some assurance of the views of de Waal

[1] Harris to Clarendon (private), 14 Jan. 1870, Hague, MS. Clar. Dep. C. 484; same to same (most confidential), 14 Jan. 1870, Hague, F.O. 37/479.
[2] Minute by Barrow of 20 Jan. 1870, on F.O. to C.O., 19 Jan. 1870, C.O. 96/86.
[3] C.O. to F.O. (copy), 15 March 1870, Hague, F.O. 238/157.
[4] Harris to Clarendon (confidential), 18 March 1870, Hague, F.O. 37/479.
[5] J. Fitzgerald to Granville, 19 and 28 April 1870, London, C.O. 96/86.
[6] C.O. to F.O. (copy), 30 April, 1870, F.O. 238/157.
[7] F.O. to C.O. (confidential), 5 May 1870, F.O. 238/157.
[8] Harris to Clarendon (confidential), 12 May 1870, Hague, F.O. 37/479 (dated 1860 in error).
[9] Harris to Clarendon (private), 13 May 1870, Hague, MS. Clar. Dep. C. 484.

F

and his colleagues, for he was being brought into close and frequent touch with the Dutch ministers by the negotiations now proceeding at The Hague for two Anglo-Dutch conventions—one for the revision of existing agreements concerning the East Indian island of Sumatra, the other for the recruitment in British India of coolies to work in the plantations of Dutch Guiana (Surinam).

On 21 May 1870, de Waal, at last confident of success,[1] made his formal application to the king. Now that the Komendas had been punished, he declared, it was time to reconsider the cession project, since only by the unification of the Coast under one power could peace be restored there. Holland could not in justice *force* the Elminas to come to terms with the Fantes, but she *could* hand them over to the English, especially in view of their obstructive attitude to Nagtglas's attempts at pacification. As for compensation, Britain was willing, as a result of the negotiations already undertaken, to abandon her objections to Dutch expansion in Siak (in Sumatra), and to allow the recruiting of labourers for Surinam in British India. But the best reason of all for reopening this question was that the British Government itself had now confidentially proposed that it should take over the Dutch Gold Coast! This proposal, declared de Waal, had been made by Harris in October 1869, and renewed by him more recently.[2] In a subsequent communication to the king de Waal agreed with the Council of State that in negotiating the cession, Holland should seek to obtain from Britain release from earlier understandings that might stand in the way of further Dutch expansion in the East Indies, particularly in Sumatra. He also suggested that she should ask a round sum—say a million guilders—for stores and fixtures handed over.[3] On 24 June he received formal permission to negotiate along these lines with the proviso that there was to be no question of 'selling' the settlements.[4]

It is not difficult to understand why de Waal was so anxious to establish that Britain had taken the lead in proposing the cession of

---

[1] Harris to Clarendon, 3 June 1870, Hague, F.O. 37/479.
[2] In May 1870, according to a later version of this story: 'Nota voor de Minister-raad', 31 Jan. 1871, Afst. IV.
[3] M.K. to King, 21 May and 16 June 1870, B.Z. 3002.
[4] Directeur v.h. Kabinet des Konings to M. B. Z. and M. K., 24 June 1870, B.Z. 3002.

the Dutch Gold Coast. If this were so he could of course more easily defend himself against the criticism that he was showing an unbecoming eagerness to give away Dutch territory; but the thesis of a British initiative had another, more fundamental advantage. Politically-minded Dutchmen in the nineteenth century were well aware that their status as a second-class power (in Europe, at least) rendered them peculiarly dependent upon Britain. They knew that, as an American scholar has recently put it, 'in the last analysis' they 'depended for their security upon British sea-power', and that 'this was true not only for the homeland but also for the vast colonial empire in South-east Asia'.[1] Never was it more true than in the years when they found themselves standing between Bismarck's Prussia and the Second Empire, a situation in which, as Harris remarked in 1868, they naturally tended to turn 'an appealing look to England'.[2] At this time, moreover, the danger of a third power seeking a foothold in Sumatra by taking advantage of the growing anarchy in Acheh and the Dutch vassal states there gave British co-operation and goodwill in the East a peculiar importance in Dutch eyes.[3] Small wonder, then, that de Waal should make much of the alleged request of Britain for the sole possession of the Gold Coast. He knew that this argument would bring forth from many Dutchmen the reaction which is reflected in words written by the Dutch envoy in London some two years later:

. . . le désir bien évident de l'Angleterre d'obtenir la côte de Guinée eut un désir dont il vaut la peine de tenir compte, comme venant de la part d'une puissance ami, qui, le cas échéant, peut nous être si utile.[4]

The only weakness of de Waal's argument was that it did not correspond with the facts. It is clear that the British 'proposal' by which he set so much store was nothing more than the reply to his own initiative.[5] As the committee of *rapporteurs* of the Second

---

[1] Vandenbosch, op. cit., p. 4.
[2] Harris to Stanley, 7 May 1868, Hague, F.O. 37/487.
[3] Vandenbosch, op. cit., pp. 193–4.
[4] Van Bijlandt to M. B. Z., 21 July 1871, London, Wolteringen, op. cit., 165–6.
[5] This can be demonstrated by evidence from Dutch sources, leaving aside Harris's own clear statements: see van Lansberge to M. B. Z., 10 June 1871, Brussels, Afst. IV. Roest van Limburg's successor Gericke seems also to have been satisfied that the first initiative came from Holland (Harris to Granville, 1 June 1871, Hague, F.O. 37/491). See also Mollema, op. cit., p. 228.

Chamber was to remark a year later, the official Dutch account of these events, which represented Britain as taking the initiative, was simply not true.[1] It is indeed difficult to acquit de Waal of a certain disingenuousness in this matter. It is true enough that throughout 1869, in connexion with the Siak and Surinam negotiations, he and Harris were engaged in confidential discussions which covered the whole field of Anglo-Dutch relations, discussions during which agreement seems to have been reached on the desirability of the Gold Coast's coming under one power, with the tacit understanding (on the Dutch side, at least) that the power referred to was Britain.[2] But to claim, as de Waal was later to do, that the initiative for a formal negotiation came not from his approach to Harris in the Bois, but from Harris's subsequent communication of Clarendon's interest in this approach,[3] is to put the whole transaction in a false light. It is not, in any case, easy to see why he should have regarded the British response as being invested with a formality which his initial approach did not possess. On this point, indeed, he was himself far from consistent. Thus on 2 July he wrote to Nagtglas that formal proposals had been received from Britain. This was fully in line with the version of events he had given to the king; but only four days earlier he had advised Roest van Limburg to go ahead and open negotiations *without waiting for a formal proposal*!

Acting on this advice the Foreign Minister informed Harris verbally of the royal consent to negotiations, at the same time requesting that any resulting convention should be signed at the same time as the Surinam and Siak treaties, and presented for the approval of the States-General along with them. On 11 July he followed this up with a letter which, according to Harris, was the first *official* proposal of negotiation to be made by either side. In this he repeated his government's readiness to cede the settlements, but now added certain conditions, the most important of which was the broadening of the Surinam and Siak agreements. With regard to the latter, Britain was now asked expressly to recognize the right of the Dutch

---

[1] *Hand. S.G.,* 1870–1, Bijlagen, pp. 1858–60.

[2] Harris to Granville, 1 June 1871, Hague, F.O. 37/491; Roest van Limburg to M. B. Z., 10 June 1871, Baden Baden, Afst. IV.

[3] De Waal, op. cit., pp. 69–70; 'Dit voorstel om over 't denkbeeld te onderhandelen bracht de zaak van het particuliere terrein af.'

to an almost unlimited extension of their dominion in the East Indies.[1]

This Siak agreement, the fate of which was henceforth to be bound up with that of de Waal's plans for the Gold Coast, was an attempt to remedy the causes of dissatisfaction in both Britain and Holland about the state of affairs in the East Indian island of Sumatra.[2] The Dutch had a strong position here, but were precluded from extending their authority over the whole of the island by the terms of a treaty made with Britain in 1824. This obstruction to the expansion of their eastern empire was doubly annoying to the Dutch because it seemed increasingly likely that while they stood by some other power— perhaps Britain herself—might walk into 'free' Sumatra. A fine pretext for such intervention was to hand in the piratical actions of the inhabitants of the kingdom of Acheh. The Dutch themselves suffered from these, but their undertaking (in the 1824 treaty) not to restrict Achinese independence prevented them from taking effective counter-measures. On the other hand, British traders in eastern Sumatra watched with alarm the way in which, despite the 1824 treaty, de facto Dutch administrative control was gradually being established in this area (as for example through a treaty made with the kingdom of Siak in 1858). Their great fear was that the Dutch might become powerful enough to squeeze out British trade by imposing the differential tariff system which obtained in the Dutch East Indies. Their complaints did not go unheeded at home; but when, after 1866, the Dutch started to liberalize their commercial policy in the Indies by reducing the tariff differentials, the attitude of the British Government towards the extension of Dutch sovereignty in Sumatra began to change. With the tariff threat removed, this extension, enabling the Dutch to put an end to the anarchical state of affairs in Acheh and in those 'vassal' territories where they exercised influence, but were at present prevented from obtaining effective control, might well be of positive advantage to British trade.

This, then, was the background against which Harris and de Waal

---

[1] M. K. to M. B. Z., 28 June 1870, B.Z. 3002; Harris to Clarendon, 1 July 1870, Hague, F.O. 37/479; M. K. to Nagtglas, 2 July 1870, G. 730; M. B. Z. to Harris (copy), 11 July 1870, F.O. 37/479.
[2] This paragraph and that which follows are derived from E. S. de Klerck, De Atjeh-Oorlog ('s-Gravenhage, 1912), passim, and Vandenbosch, op cit., pp. 191–4.

had carried on the negotiation of the Siak treaty. From the Dutch point of view the result of their efforts was something of a disappointment. Britain withdrew all objection to the extension of Dutch sovereignty over Siak; in return Holland guaranteed that British subjects would trade on the same terms as Dutch, not only in Siak, but in any future Dutch acquisitions in the interior of Sumatra. De Waal had failed to extract from Harris what Holland really wanted, namely Britain's consent to the extension of her sovereignty over the whole of Sumatra, and particularly over the troublesome kingdom of Acheh. Now, in July 1870, the Dutch ministers hoped that the projected Gold Coast negotiations would provide them with another chance to realize their aims in the East.

First reactions at the Colonial Office to the news that the king had finally authorized negotiation were ones of deep satisfaction. Rogers, who had already realized that the acquisition of Elmina would be a useful 'kind of set off' for the contemplated cession of the Gambia to France, 'for those who require such an apology',[1] began to think out the details. The sum suggested by de Waal as payment for stores should be reduced, he thought, and 'we shd before going to the Cabinet be able to show by figures the possibility of making the Gold Coast pay this sum'. Britain should also consider 'whether we intend to take over these settlements as part of the Protectorate merely . . . or as sovereignty like Cape Town [sic]'.[2]

Such speculations and preparations were somewhat rudely arrested by the news of Roest van Limburg's proposals of 11 July. By the time that this arrived in London, Granville had moved from the Colonial to the Foreign Office, following the sudden death of Clarendon on 27 June. Ten months later de Waal's successor van Bosse was to declare that Clarendon's death had been a grievous blow to Dutch interests,[3] and he may have been right. His later career at the Foreign Office was not to earn 'Pussy' Granville the reputation of a hard bargainer, but one of his first acts as Foreign Secretary

---

[1] Minute by Rogers of 13 June 1870 on F.O. to C.O., 9 June 1870, C.O. 96/86. Negotiations were in progress for such a cession (with some compensation for Britain north of Sierra Leone), but were suspended owing to the outbreak of the Franco-Prussian war.

[2] Minutes by Barrow of 7 July and Rogers of 9 July on F.O. to C.O., 5 July 1870, C.O. 96/86.

[3] M. K. to M. B. Z., 26 May 1871, Afst. IV.

was to demonstrate to the Dutch the weakness of the position in which their undisguised haste to be rid of their settlements had put them. His resolution was no doubt strengthened by the conviction, now gaining ground at both the Foreign and Colonial Offices, that 'the Dutch must relinquish their Settlements on the G. Coast nolens, volens', so that it would not be wise to negotiate for their acquisition 'except on the terms of the cession being unconditional'.[1] He therefore informed Harris in a strongly worded dispatch that he had no intention of reopening the negotiations, already successfully concluded, concerning Siak and Surinam, adding that 'if further conditions are required, Her Majesty's Government would prefer that the question of the Gold Coast should be deferred'.[2]

The moral of this was plain enough; as Harris was said to have remarked to a Dutch official,

you people seem to forget that you offered the Coast to us and that we are doing you a service by taking it, for which you should be thankful instead of trying to obtain further advantages.[3]

De Waal's hope of 'compensation' in the East Indies had been dashed, and in September he had to reconcile himself to signing the Siak treaty as it stood, with the addition only of an 'explanation' by Harris about Acheh which did little or nothing to meet Dutch desires.[4] This fiasco meant that the whole tone of the forthcoming negotiations had been set, as Miss Mollema remarks, in a fashion most unfavourable to the Dutch,[5] who now had the choice of capitulating to the British terms or losing this opportunity of ridding themselves of the Gold Coast.

The Dutch ministers hastened to capitulate. They even assured Harris that they had not meant that the completed negotiations should be reopened; all they wanted was that all the treaties should go to the Second Chamber together, linked if possible by a

---

[1] F.O. to C.O., 13 July 1870, C.O. 96/86, with minute of 21 July by Barrow. Cf. the leader in the *Nieuwe Amsterdamsche Courant*, 14 July 1870, advocating abandonment *either* to Britain *or* to the natives.

[2] Granville to Harris, 14 July 1870 (dated 4 July in error) in 'Memorandum upon the Sumatra and Gold Coast Treaties between England and Holland', by H. P. Anderson, 5 Jan. 1874 (printed for use of F.O.), F.O. 37/534.

[3] Van Lansberge to M. B. Z., 10 June 1871, Brussels, Afst. IV.

[4] De Klerck, *De Atjeh-Oorlog*, p. 455.

[5] Mollema, op. cit., pp. 228–9. In his recollections of the negotiations (op. cit., pp. 70–1) de Waal, perhaps significantly, makes no mention of this episode.

preliminary note or preamble which applied to all three.[1] What was implied here, though not explicitly stated, was that if the three treaties were linked together in the guise of a general readjustment of Anglo-Dutch colonial relations, the popularity of the Surinam treaty might serve to carry the other two through. By itself the Siak treaty was certain to be unpopular, since it formally granted the British rights of trade and navigation equal to those of the Dutch in all future Dutch acquisitions in Sumatra, while the cession of the Gold Coast was bound to come under fire as a stain on the national honour.[2]

Without even waiting for a reply to this proposal the Dutch ministers produced a draft treaty to serve as a basis for negotiation: negotiation in which they proved eager to agree with almost every British proposal. The British would not hear of the recruitment of soldiers by the Dutch on the Coast once the settlements had been ceded, they would not give an unconditional guarantee to protect former 'Dutch' natives if the 'British' natives tried to pay off old scores, nor could they accept the Dutch proposals for calculating the indemnity for stores and fixtures—and in every case the Dutch agreed. Granville made it clear that in his view England was doing the Dutch a favour—and the Dutch envoy in London agreed! On one point only, but that a vital one, did the Dutch stand firm. When Granville, taking up the earlier Dutch suggestion of a 'link' between the various colonial agreements, demanded that the Siak and Surinam treaties should 'stand or fall together' (that is, if one were not approved by the States-General then neither should be ratified), the Dutch insisted that the Gold Coast treaty also be included in this arrangement. For once it was the turn of Britain to agree.[3]

---

[1] Harris to Granville, 25 July 1870, Hague, F.O. 37/479; M. B. Z. to Harris (copy), 12 Aug. 1870, F.O. 37/480. Privately de Waal was alarmed by Granville's seeming coolness and irritated by Harris's pressure for the separate signature of the Siak and Surinam treaties: M. K. to M. B. Z., 26 May 1871, Afst. IV; perhaps these factors helped to make him 'more reasonable', as Harris put it (Harris to Granville (private), 19 Aug. 1870, Hague, P.R.O. 30/29/103).

[2] Harris to Granville, 30 September 1870, Hague, F.O. 37/480; 'Memorandum upon the Sumatra and Gold Coast Treaties . . .', 5 Jan. 1874, F.O. 37/534.

[3] Harris to Granville, 16 Aug. (enclosing draft Convention), 23 and 30 Sept. 1870, Hague, F.O. 37/480; Gericke to M. B. Z., 9 Sept. 1870, London, Kol. 20. IX. 1870. Kab. Geheim. Litt. R. 12/No. 33; Granville to Harris (draft), 12 Sept. 1870, F.O. 37/478; Harris to M. B. Z. (copy), 20 Sept. 1870, F.O. 37/480; ibid., M. B. Z. to Harris (copy), 28 Sept. 1870; Granville to Harris, 24 Oct. 1870, F.O. 238/158.

As will be seen later, the 'link' thus forged between the various treaties was to be the subject of bitter controversy in the following year, when the practical limitation that it put on the freedom of action of the States-General was much resented by the members of that body. In later years de Waal attempted to show that he had not intended anything of the sort. He recalled Granville's demand that the Siak and Surinam treaties should 'stand or fall together', adding that there was no objection to be made to this, but that 'in order politely to remind that (*i.e.* British) government of the course of the negotiations, and arising from this, the intrinsic value of each of the treaties', Harris was informed that the Dutch would like 'a similar solidarity' to be established between the Siak and Guinea treaties. He was, he added, surprised when Granville, when agreeing to this in October, added that all three treaties must now stand or fall together. This, de Waal explained, had not been his intention at all; what he had wanted was rather 'to replace the link between the Siak and Surinam treaties with a simple agreement for simultaneous discussion of the three treaties (*i.e.* by the States-General)'.[1] This is difficult to swallow. If he really meant nothing more than this, why did the Colonial Minister ask for 'a similar solidarity' when he knew, by his own account, that the British interpretation of this was that the treaties concerned must 'stand or fall together'? His version of these events might command more respect if it did not omit all mention of the *original* Dutch proposal for a 'link' between all three treaties.[2]

While this negotiation went on, the Colonial Office had to consider how the indemnity to be paid for the Dutch stores and fixtures was to be raised. From the first, Kimberley, the new Colonial Secretary, insisted that the sum should be determined by valuation and that 'it would be out of the question to ask Parliament to provide the money'. It was therefore necessary to make sure that the Gold Coast itself could foot the bill, since recourse to Parliament might

---

[1] De Waal, op. cit., pp. 71-2.

[2] E. S. de Klerck, who in his survey of these negotiations in his *History of the Netherlands East Indies*, Vol. ii (Rotterdam, 1938) follows de Waal's account closely, says that this 'most unexpected condition' was imposed by Britain after the ratification of the treaty, in February 1871 (p. 339); see also the same author's *De Atjeh-Oorlog*, pp. 307 *et sqq.*

well put paid to the whole project,[1] and on 20 September Kimberley sent Kennedy a confidential request for his assurances on this
point.[2] By the end of September, however, Harris was emphasizing
the desirability of concluding speedily 'without the delay for reference to the Coast respecting the indemnity', especially since Swanzy's
agent Cleaver had recently told him that 'if the whole Coast were
in our hands the revenue there would be doubled'.[3] Anxious that 'so
unusually favourable an opportunity . . . should not be lost',[4] Granville decided to wait no longer before laying the whole question
before the Prime Minister. In a letter to Gladstone of 8 October,
after declaring that the cession

will put an end to the deadlock in which things were—and which made
it impossible for us to govern the Colony thoroughly or to withdraw
from it,

the Foreign Secretary got down to brass tacks. 'There will', he declared,

be no difficulty in charging the revenues for the sum required to pay for
existing stores. It is estimated that the Colony could do it without difficulty, but the Dutch Government have a right to look for security to us,
& I presume with no objection on your part to this being done.[5]

If Granville thought, by emphasizing the financial question, to divert
his chief from the larger principles involved, he met with no success.
On 11 October Gladstone sent a slightly chilly reply. 'They have',
he wrote,

sent me a mass of papers without any precis or guide from the C.O. on
the proposed cession of territory by the Dutch on the Gold Coast, but
they do not as far as I can find contain the only thing material for me
which is a statement of the reasons, why contrary to our general policy
we are in this quarter (apparently) to extend our responsibilities. I am
therefore quite unable at present to give any opinion.[6]

---

[1] Minute by Kimberley of 4 Aug. 1870 on memo. by Barrow, 18 July 1870, C.O.
96/86; ibid., minutes by Kimberley of 30 Aug. and 1 Sept. 1870, and minute by
Herbert of 31 Aug. 1870, on F.O. to C.O., 22 Aug. 1870.
[2] Kimberley to Kennedy (confidential-copy), 20 Sept. 1870, C.O. 402/12.
[3] Harris to Granville (private), 30 Sept. 1870, Hague, P.R.O. 30/29/103.
[4] F.O. to C.O., 3 Oct. 1870, C.O. 96/86.
[5] Granville to Gladstone, 8 Oct. 1870, Walmer Castle, A. Ramm (Ed.), op. cit., i,
pp. 140-1.
[6] Ibid., p. 144, Gladstone to Granville, 11 Oct. 1870.

Granville had 'presumed' too far, and for a moment it seemed that the whole negotiation might be brought to nothing by Gladstone's adherence to his 'general policy'. Kimberley hastily undertook the task of overcoming his leader's scruples. He sent him a memorandum describing the disordered state of affairs on the Coast, together with a tactful letter which emphasized that

it is by no means a case of extending our responsibilities, to which I should be most adverse, but of relieving us from a serious embarrassment in the only way in which that relief can be effectively obtained.

He pointed out that the British guarantee of the payment of the indemnity would be merely a matter of form, and that another 'very beneficial' treaty, concerning Sumatra, was dependent upon the successful conclusion of this one.[1] Gladstone was completely satisfied with this explanation. He was not sure that the Dutch were *entitled* to ask the home government for a guarantee of payment, but, he added, 'the matter is not worth vexing them or stopping a good cluster of arrangements, & if Lowe does not object I do not'.[2] Lowe, the Chancellor of the Exchequer, did not object, and on 18 October, only ten days after Granville's application to Gladstone, Kimberley was able to note, no doubt with some relief, that 'the Gold Coast Convention may go on'.[3]

By the end of October negotiation was completed and both sides were ready to sign a convention, but now an unexpected difficulty arose. The Dutch Government had lost the confidence of the States-General, and its days were numbered. Roest van Limburg had already tendered his resignation and maintained that in view of this it would be unconstitutional for him to sign the treaty. Despite all de Waal's persuasions he would not join in asking for royal authority to sign, so that for the moment affairs were at a standstill.[4]

In taking this stand, as Miss Mollema remarks, Roest van Limburg was probably influenced by the vocal criticism now beginning

[1] Kimberley to Gladstone (private), 14 Oct. 1870, Kimberley House, B.M./Add. MS. 44224.
[2] Gladstone to Kimberley (copy), 16 Oct. 1870, Add. MSS. 44539.
[3] Minute by Kimberley of 18 October 1870 on F.O. to C.O., 3 Oct. 1870, C.O. 96/86.
[4] M. B. Z. to M. K., 28 Oct. 1870, Kol. 29. X. 1870. Zeer geheim. Litt. X. 14; M. K. to M. B. Z., 29 Oct. 1870, B.Z. 3002; ibid., M. B. Z. to M. K. (draft), 31 Oct. 1870; Harris to Granville, 4 and 11 Nov. 1870, Hague, F.O. 37/480.

to be heard both in Holland and on the Coast of the rumoured project of cession. If de Waal's support of this project was strengthened by the fact that Nagtglas, despairing of any effective co-operation on the part of the Cape Coast authorities, was himself now advocating it,[1] Roest van Limburg may well have been disturbed by Nagtglas's reports of the hostile reaction on the Coast to the rumours from Holland. Most serious of all was the petition to King William III by the king and chiefs of Elmina who condemned the actions of English and Fantes alike, and declared that they would remain faithful to the Dutch flag as long as there was a Dutchman left in Holland;[2] well might de Waal rebuke Nagtglas for forwarding this address, the first of several of this tenor.[3] Try though he might to argue that its truculent tone confirmed the desirability of cession, and even that it was the duty of the Dutch Government to do what it thought best regardless of the views of the Elminas,[4] he well knew how difficult it would be to gain approval for a measure which—if the Elmina protest was to be believed—seemed likelier to intensify the troubles on the Coast than to end them.[5]

Nagtglas, however, attached little importance to this protest. It was possible, he wrote, that a few Elminas might view the departure of the Dutch with regret, but the majority of them would be quite unconcerned. In any case, he added, what did the inclinations of 12,000 Elminas count for against those of the remaining 100,000 inhabitants of the Coast? A sorely disappointed man, he now gave his full backing to de Waal's policy. Her Gold Coast settlements, he declared, had not the slightest value for Holland; in particular, Dutch trade with them was negligible, involving only two firms (one of which was said to be going into liquidation), and with insignificant amounts of gin and gunpowder as the sole Dutch imports.

---

[1] Nagtglas to M. K. (draft), 31 July 1870, Elmina, G. 725; same to same (copy), 2 Sept. 1870, Elmina, B.Z. 3002.

[2] ibid., Nagtglas to officials (circular—copy), 24 Aug. 1870, Elmina; ibid., Nagtglas to M. K. (copy), 28 Aug. 1870, Elmina (enclosing King, etc., of Elmina to William III (copy), n.d.).

[3] M. K. to Nagtglas, 3 Oct. 1870, Hague, G. 730.

[4] M. B. Z. and M. K. to king, 29 Oct. 1870, Algemeen Rijksarchief/Kabinet des Konings (=Kab.) 1871 (B¹). This is the request for authority to conclude the treaty that was drafted by De Waal, but never sent because of Roest van Limburg's refusal to sign it.

[5] M. K. to M. B. Z., 13 Oct. 1870, B.Z. 3002.

The real trouble with the settlements, he was convinced, was in the Dutch themselves. He remarked bitterly that 'Holland has enough money but not enough vitality to maintain herself with success in these parts'.[1]

The reactions of the 'Dutch' natives to the rumours of impending cession were now being closely watched by the British authorities. Kennedy, convinced that the Dutch were 'naturally anxious to escape from a position which their own mismanagement has rendered untenable', reflected that it was 'all the more necessary that we should resume the Protectorate of the quondam British settlements (sic) under condition to assure peace'.[2] To this end he sounded Nagtglas early in October on several points connected with the anticipated cession, including the willingness of the Elminas to accept British protection, and the existence of any treaty engagements with Ashanti inconsistent with such protection. Nagtglas, though claiming to know nothing officially of the proposed cession, assured Kennedy that the Elminas would not resist it, since he would persuade them to accept it, that 'there exists no treaty, nor any official engagement between Elmina and Ashantee', and that 'the King of Ashantee has no recognized claim upon the Territory of the people of Elmina'. Ussher, on the other hand, while agreeing that the Elminas would give no trouble once the forts were in British possession, was of the opinion that the King of Ashanti had definite claims on Elmina.[3]

Ussher's warning had little effect upon Kennedy, who, regarding the cession as 'one of the most important and I feel convinced one of the most successful steps which has ever been taken to promote commerce and civilization in West Africa', seized upon Nagtglas's vague talk of 'preparing' the Elminas as a pretext for making his own overtures to them. This course of action was authorized by the Colonial Office, which rather curiously took a Dutch appeal for greater co-operation in pacifying the Coast as authority for a direct approach to the Elminas, assuring them of effective protection after

---

[1] Nagtglas to M. K. (draft, v. secret), 4 Nov. 1870, Elmina, G. 725.
[2] Kennedy to Kimberley, 19 Oct. 1870, Sierra Leone, C.O. 96/85.
[3] Kennedy to Nagtglas, 9 Oct. 1870, Sierra Leone, P.P. 1872, lxx [C. 670], pp. 1–2; ibid., p. 3, Ussher to Kennedy, 17 Oct. 1870, Cape Coast; ibid., pp. 3–4, Nagtglas to Kennedy, 25 Oct. 1870, Elmina; same to same (draft), 25 Oct. 1870, G. 725.

the cession.[1] Few actions could have been more calculated to inflame the already apprehensive Elminas, but once more a fatal blindness to African sensibilities seemed to have descended on Downing Street. There was indeed more than a hint of downright callousness in the attitude of Sir George Barrow, who, when there was talk of 'preparing the minds' of the natives, noted that 'the Elminas . . . are the only Natives whose minds need be prepared—& they will have little option when the Dutch depart'.[2] In the event the unfortunate Ussher, having carried out his orders by issuing proclamations to both Fantes and Elminas concerning the impending cession and the consequent need for them to settle their differences, found himself not only criticized by Nagtglas, but also disavowed by his superiors. The latter were not so much concerned by the hostility which Ussher's proclamation had stirred up in Elmina, nor yet by his reference, which gave much offence to the Dutch, to the 'sale and purchase' of the settlements,[3] as by his categorical assurance that the Elminas would receive complete protection against all attacks—an assurance which the British had never given, and were in no position to give, to any tribe on the Coast.[4]

The extremely hostile reception given by the Elminas to both Dutch and British attempts to 'prepare' them for the cession— though somewhat discounted by Nagtglas, who, like Ussher, tended to attribute it largely to the machinations of Akyeampon[5]—made the

[1] M. B. Z. to envoy in London (draft), 17 Oct. 1870, B.Z. 3002; Kimberley to Kennedy (copy), 27 Oct. 1870, C.O. 402/12; Kennedy to Kimberley, 3 Nov. 1870, P.P. 1872, lxx [C. 670], pp. 2–3; (Kennedy) to (Ussher), 21 Nov. 1870, Ghana National Archives/Accessions [ACC.] 368/51.

[2] Minute by Barrow of 24 Oct. 1870, on F.O. to C.O. (confidential), 20 Oct. 1870, C.O. 96/86.

[3] Although, as Kimberley admitted, this was 'not only most injudicious but also erroneous, as no payment is to be made to the Dutch for the cession' (Minute by Kimberley of 7 Feb. 1871 on F.O. to C.O., 3 Feb. 1871, C.O. 96/90).

[4] Ussher to Kennedy, 4 Dec. 1870, Cape Coast, P.P. 1872, lxx [C. 670], pp. 7–10 (with enclosures); Nagtglas to Ussher (copy), 4 Dec. 1870, G. 728; ibid., Ussher to Nagtglas, 4 Dec. 1870; Nagtglas to officials (circular letter—draft), 6 Dec. 1870, G. 725; Kennedy to Kimberley, 12 Dec. 1870, Sierra Leone, C.O. 96/85; Nagtglas to M. K., 16 Dec. 1870, Elmina, Afst. IV: ibid., M. K. to M. B. Z., 8 and 25 Jan. 1871; Kimberley to Kennedy, 25 Jan. 1871, ADM. 1/29; Ussher to Nagtglas (copy), 15 Feb. 1871, Accra, Afst. IV; Ussher to Kennedy (copy), 16 Feb. 1871, Accra, C.O. 96/87. For some repercussions in the Second Chamber of Ussher's proclamations see Hand. S.G., 1870–1, II, pp. 919, 925.

[5] Nagtglas to M. K. (draft), 4 Nov. 1870, G. 725; Same to same (copies), 3, 5 and 16 Dec. 1870, Afst. IV: Nagtglas to Ussher (copies), 4 and 20 Dec. 1870, G. 728; Bartels to Ussher (with enclosure), 21 Dec. 1870, Cape Coast, P.P. 1872, lxx [C. 670],

new Thorbecke ministry at The Hague eager to adopt Nagtglas's advice and carry out the cession before the situation on the Coast got any worse.[1] Nor was it only on the Coast that they found good reason for haste. At home criticism of the proposed cession, taking advantage of the delay occasioned by the ministerial crisis, had been increasingly heard in the States-General and in the press.[2] The most influential protest at this time was made by the distinguished scholar J. K. J. de Jonge, who combined in one pamphlet a serious study of the origins of the Dutch settlements with a denunciation of what seemed to him the imminent betrayal of a glorious past.[3]

The anxiety of the Dutch Government to conclude the bargain was increased still further by the apparent cooling of British enthusiasm.[4] The latter was the direct result of the news that in mid-December a letter had arrived at Cape Coast from King Kofi Karikari of Ashanti protesting against the proposed transfer of Elmina. 'The fort of that place', declared the king,

> have from time immemorial paid annual tribute to my ancestors to the present time by right of arms, when we conquered Intim Gackidi, King of Denkera. Intim Gackidi having purchased goods to the amount of nine thousand pounds from the Dutch, and not paying for them before we conquered Intim Gackidi, the Dutch demanded of my father Osae Tutu I, for the payment, who paid it full the nine thousand pounds, and the Dutch delivered the Elmina to him as his own, and from that time tribute has been paid to us to this present time. I hope therefore your Excellency will not include Elmina in the change, for it is mine by right.[5]

pp. 14–16; 'Protest' by Elminas, 4 Jan. 1871, Kol. 3. II. 1871. Zeer Geheim. Litt. S. 1/No. 3; Nagtglas to M. K. (draft), 15 Jan. 1871, G. 726; Ussher to Kennedy (copy), 17 Jan. 1871, C.O. 96/87; M. K. to M. B. Z., 18 Jan. 1871, Afst. IV.

[1] Nagtglas to M. K. (copies), 4 Jan. and 26 Feb. 1871, Afst. IV; Harris to Granville, 11 and 24 Jan. 1871, C.O. 37/490; M. B. Z. to M. K., 9 Feb. 1871, Kol. 11. II. 1871. Zeer geheim. Litt. O. 2; M. B. Z. and M. K. to King (copy), 11 Feb. 1871, Afst. IV.

[2] *Hand. S.G.*, 1870–1, II, pp. 199–200, 250–1, 289–90; Harris to Granville, 17 Dec. 1870, Hague, F.O. 37/480; same to same, 5 and 30 Jan. 1871, Hague, F.O. 37/490; *Het Vaderland* (leader), 20 Jan. 1871; *Arnhemsche Courant* (article), 11 Feb. 1871; *Nieuwe Rotterdamsche Courant* (letter), 14 Feb. 1871. Some items favourable to the cession may be found in *Arnhemsche Courant* (report), 21 Jan. 1871; *De Nederlandsche Spectator* (review), 4 Feb. 1871, and (leader), 8 April 1871; *Het Noorden* (leader), 15 Feb. 1871.

[3] J. K. J. de Jonge, *De Oorsprong van Neerland's Bezittingen op de Kust van Guinea* (Hague, 1871).

[4] M. B. Z. to M. K., 10 Feb. 1871, Kol. 11. II. 1871. Zeer geheim. Litt. O. 2.

[5] Kofi Karikari to Ussher, 24 Nov. 1870, Kumasi, P.P. 1872, lxx [C. 670], p. 13. For a discussion of the rival interpretations of the significance of the 'Elmina note' see above, pp. 7–11.

Ussher, who had anticipated some such claim, immediately referred the letter to Nagtglas. The latter declared himself 'extremely surprised', and insisted that the annual payment was a 'present' paid 'in name of subsistence', and that the Ashantis had never had any rights over the Elmina forts. The king's letter, he suggested, was merely an attempt on his part to ward off an event which he feared might damage his trade.[1] Ussher was not convinced. He could not help seeing a connexion between the Ashanti claim and the reluctance of Nagtglas to remove Akyeampon from Elmina by force, a point about which the British authorities were becoming increasingly restive.[2] Kennedy concurred, and in a confidential letter to Nagtglas of 30 December he laid down the lines which Britain was to follow in this matter in the weeks to come. 'It rests', he wrote,

with the Netherlands Government to place their title to the ownership of St. George d'Elmina beyond a doubt before the Convention can be acted upon; and I think that the first step in asserting your rights should be the expulsion of the Ashantee chief Atjiempon from Dutch territory.

His presence there was 'calculated to give colour to the king's claim', and without his expulsion the convention could not possibly be executed.[3] In London, where Granville had already decided that the removal of Akyeampon was one essential prerequisite of cession,[4] Kennedy's dispatches soon produced the conviction that the renunciation of the Ashanti claim was another, and the Dutch were duly informed of this.[5]

On 25 February the long-awaited signing of the convention took place at The Hague, but in view of the reservations now being made by Britain, Harris's self-congratulation seemed somewhat

[1] Ussher to Nagtglas, 15 Dec. 1870, P.P. 1872, lxx [C. 670], pp. 12–13; ibid., pp. 13–14, Nagtglas to Ussher, 20 Dec. 1870; Nagtglas to M. K. (draft), 21 Dec. 1870, G. 725.
[2] Ussher to Kennedy, 16 Dec. 1870, P.P. 1872, lxx [C. 670], p. 12; same to same (copy), 19 Dec. 1870, C.O. 96/87.
[3] Kennedy to Nagtglas, 30 Dec. 1870, Sierra Leone, G. 728.
[4] Granville to Harris (draft), 5 Jan. 1871, F.O. 37/489.
[5] Kennedy to Kimberley, 2 and 25 Jan. 1871, C.O. 96/97; same to same, 11 Jan. 1871, P.P. 1872, lxx [C. 670], p. 17; C.O. to F.O. (copy), 3 Feb. 1871, C.O. 402/13; Granville to Harris (draft), 11 Feb. 1871, F.O. 37/489; same to same, 14 Feb. 1871, F.O. 238/161; minute by Knatchbull-Hugessen of 15 Feb. 1871 on F.O. to C.O., 11 Feb. 1871, C.O. 96/90; Harris to Granville, 18 Feb. 1871, Hague, F.O. 37/490; Kimberley to Kennedy, 28 Feb. 1871, P.P. 1872, lxx [C. 670], p. 37.

premature.[1] Knatchbull-Hugessen, the new Parliamentary Under-Secretary at the Colonial Office, commented that

the actual transfer ought not to take place—nor the matter indeed be considered as finally settled until the Dutch have set matters right with the Ashantee King & got rid of his savage relation from Elmina,

and Kimberley concurred.[2] In vain did the Dutch ministers impute the blame for Akyeampon's continued stay to Ussher's refusal to guarantee him safe passage through the British protectorate; on this point the British remained adamant, though they relaxed their pressure for a while when news came that on 14 April Nagtglas had placed the Ashanti ambassador under arrest. This, however, was as far as Nagtglas, no doubt recalling the disfavour into which his predecessor had fallen by his recourse to forceful measures, was prepared to go without specific orders from The Hague.[3]

The prospect of becoming embroiled with Ashanti as a result of the cession was in fact inspiring second thoughts in London, where even Knatchbull-Hugessen, who was far from being an apostle of 'non-extension', declared that it would not break his heart if the States-General turned down the convention.[4] More ominous still was the way in which the arch-advocate of cession, Kennedy, a past master (as both Simpson and Ussher knew to their cost) at disavowing responsibility for unsuccessful policies, was beginning to suggest that the Dutch settlements might prove 'an expensive and troublesome acquisition'.[5] An attempt was made in the Commons to make the execution of the treaty subject to parliamentary approval, and the Earl of Derby, who as Lord Stanley had signed the

---

[1] 'You will have been pleased to know that I had at last been enabled to sign the third (i.e. Guinea) Convention. . . . Patience and temper are put to the test in negotiating with Dutchmen' (Harris to Granville (private), 8 March 1871, Hague, P.R.O. 30/29/103).
[2] Minutes by Knatchbull-Hugessen of 4 March 1871 and Kimberley, n.d., on F.O. to C.O., 1 March 1871, C.O. 96/90.
[3] M. K. to Nagtglas, 21 Jan. 1871, G. 730; M. K. to M. B. Z., 21 Feb. and 20 March 1871, Afst. IV; Harris to Granville, 27 Feb., 1 and 28 March, 1871, F.O. 37/490; Granville to Harris (draft), 9 March 1871, F.O. 37/489; Harris to M. B. Z. (copies), 13 and 23 March 1871, F.O. 37/490; ibid., M. B. Z. to Harris (copy), 24 March 1871; M. B. Z. to envoy in London (draft), 29 March 1871, Afst. IV; ibid., Nagtglas to M. K., 16 April 1871.
[4] C.O. to F.O. (copies), 28 Feb. and 23 March 1871, C.O. 402/13; minute by Knatchbull-Hugessen of 21 March 1871 on F.O. to C.O., 18 March 1871, C.O. 96/90.
[5] Kennedy to Kimberley, 24 Feb. 1871, C.O. 96/87.

G

1867 Treaty and was now Conservative leader in the Lords, told the Dutch envoy that Holland had the best of the bargain and that he would sooner that Britain had given up *her* possessions on the Coast.[1]

The Dutch, too, shrank from any suggestion of conflict with Ashanti. Hence their indignant embarrassment when Britain asked that they should obtain the renunciation of the Ashanti claim to Elmina.[2] On 11 March, however, Kimberley declared himself satisfied with the evidence presented to him of the Dutch title. This evidence was based on the explanation already furnished by Nagtglas to Ussher of the origins and nature of the *kostbrief*, which represented this troublesome document as a mere record of an agreement to pay an annual free gift for the encouragement of trade. Convinced by this of the 'unquestionable' right of the Dutch to dispose of their possessions as they thought fit,[3] Kimberley paid no heed to the lone voice of Ussher, who continued to point out that, justified or not, the Ashanti claim had been put forward in all seriousness and sincerity.[4] Confident that

it cannot . . . be impossible to make the Ashantees and Fantees clearly understand the real nature and object of the Stipend,

the Colonial Secretary actually proposed (against Ussher's advice) to take over and continue this payment after the cession in the interests of peace and trade.[5] No more was heard of the demand that the Dutch should induce the Ashantis to renounce their claim, and from the British point of view the only remaining obstacle to a

---

[1] Van Lansberge to M. B. Z., 24 March 1871, London, Afst. IV; *The Times,* 28 March 1871.
[2] M. K. to Nagtglas, 21 Jan. and 21 Feb. 1871, G. 730; Harris to Granville (copy), 2 Feb. 1871, F.O. 37/490; M. K. to M. B. Z., 21 Feb. 1871, Afst. IV.
[3] F.O. to C.O. (with enclosures), 4 March 1871, P.P. 1872, lxx [C. 670], pp. 41–2; ibid., pp. 37–8, Kimberley to Kennedy (No. 4), 11 March 1871; minute by Rogers of 20 March 1871, on F.O. to C.O., 18 March 1871, C.O. 96/90.
[4] Ussher to Kennedy (copy), 14 April 1871, C.O. 96/88.
[5] Kimberley to Kennedy, 16 May 1871, ADM. 1/29. The Dutch themselves had no intention of honouring the *kostbrief* once they had left the Coast. At first Nagtglas advocated the payment of a lump sum in compensation (thus reverting to the scheme of 'capitalizing' the *kostgeld,* which he had propounded before he knew of the proposed cession), but the Ashanti attitude in the matters of the claim to Elmina and Akyeampon led him to substitute a proposal for the simple payment of arrears (Nagtglas to M. K. (secret—draft), 7 Sept. 1869, G. 724; M. K. to Nagtglas, 11 Feb. 1871, Hague, G. 730; Nagtglas to M. K. (draft), 14 March 1871, G. 726). This payment (calculated to the end of 1872, and amounting to 5,280 guilders) was duly made, though not till 1876 (Hamel to M. B. Z., 5 July 1876, Elmina, Afst. V).

speedy cession appeared to be the continued presence of Akyeampon
and his followers at Elmina. Failure to remove them forthwith,
London pointed out, was bound to be interpreted as tacit admission
of the unwarranted Ashanti claims. This Nagtglas firmly denied. He
felt, perhaps not unreasonably, that the British were using these
claims as a lever to force him to expel Akyeampon—he even suspected that their ultimate object was to stir up trouble between the
Dutch and the Elminas, thus paving the way for a renewed Fante
onslaught. In fact the Ashanti pretensions, even though his rejection
of them had been accepted in London, had materially worsened the
already very difficult position of the harassed Nagtglas, pressed by
his government simultaneously to deal with Akyeampon, pacify the
Elminas, co-operate with the British and placate the Ashantis.

Thus, when in the middle of May he was visited by Ashanti
ambassadors demanding the release of Akyeampon, Nagtglas did
not fail to upbraid them with their king's claims to Elmina. To his
complaints, the chief ambassador, Effifrah, replied that the famous
letter to Ussher could not have been a proper expression of their
king's meaning. The whole thing, he said, was a misunderstanding,
if not, as he hinted, a deliberate attempt to stir up bad blood between
Dutch and Ashantis on the part of the writer of the letter, Ossoo
Ansah. Ansah, who was himself a member of this embassy, was an
Ashanti prince who had been taken to Cape Coast as a hostage under
the terms of Maclean's treaty with Ashanti in 1831, had subsequently been educated in England, and on his return to Africa had
settled down in Cape Coast on a Foreign Office pension as a firm
friend of the British authorities. In 1867 he had gone to Kumasi
with Ussher's blessing to work for a lasting peace between Fante
and Ashanti, and while there he had been entrusted with the com-
position of the letter to Ussher. Encouraged and apparently convinced by Effifrah's arguments, Nagtglas lost no time both in releasing Akyeampon, on 20 May, and also (as suggested by the
ambassadors themselves) in sending off to Kumasi one Henry Plange,
a government clerk, to request a formal withdrawal of the claim to
Elmina. Ansah, meanwhile, seeing the determination of Effifrah,
backed by the Elminas, to disavow the letter, decided to delay his
own return to Kumasi in order to see 'whether the king really will

beg pardon in order to receive the payment [*i.e.* the *kostgeld*]'. To his friends Ramseyer and Kühne, the missionaries held captive at Kumasi, he wrote, 'I know my countrymen well enough to be sure that it is advisable to be careful . . .'.[1]

Here for a time the matter rested, with the Methodist missionaries at Cape Coast, who had given a grateful welcome to the news of the intended cession,[2] bemoaning the fact that 'recent reports give very little hope that the Dutch settlements are to be transferred at all'.[3] At the beginning of June, Nagtglas, who had long been demanding his recall, decided that his health would not allow him to remain longer on the Coast, and sailed for Holland. Two weeks later his successor, the Governor *ad interim* Hugenholz, imprisoned Akyeampon once more, owing to the latter's failure to leave Elmina within thirty days of his release as he had promised. Two weeks after this Ussher received a further letter, dated 20 May, from the King of Ashanti, repeating the claim to Elmina, and not, of course, written by Ossoo Ansah, who was still in Cape Coast.[4] Ussher's suspicion that Nagtglas had been duped by the Ashanti ambassadors was thus amply confirmed; but, as Ansah had seen, the question remained whether the ambassadors themselves, who had returned to Kumasi with Plange, could or would induce their king to withdraw his claim.

Nagtglas's last few months on the Coast had been a sad end to his career. Undoubtedly sincere in his repudiation of the Ashanti claim, he was less than frank in discussing the *kostbrief*, since he knew better than anyone that the Ashantis, in the past at least, had tended to interpret this document somewhat differently from the Dutch. However much he may have disagreed with their interpretation, and however 'surprised' he may have been that they thought

---

[1] '1874 Report', Appendices Iv, Iw, IIId, IIIe and IIIf; Nagtglas to M.K. (drafts), 21 March, 9 May and 1 June 1871, G. 726; Nagtglas to Ussher, 20 May 1871, Elmina, P.P. 1872, lxx [C. 670], pp. 19–20; Nagtglas to Kennedy, 1 June 1871, Elmina, C.O. 96/88; Nagtglas to M. K., 27 May 1871, Afst. IV; Ossoo Ansah to Ramseyer and Kühne, 21 June 1871, Ramseyer and Kühne, op. cit., pp. 312–17; Petition from John Ossoo Ansah, 11 July 1872, *Further Correspondence respecting the Ashantee Invasion* (No. 2) (P.P. 1874, xlvi [C. 891], pp. 161–2.

[2] Grimmer to Boyce, 17 Oct. and 5 Dec. 1870, Cape Coast, M.M.S./Gen. Corres. G.C. 1868–76.

[3] ibid., same to same, 25 May and 2 Aug. 1871, Cape Coast.

[4] Nagtglas to M.K. (draft), 7 June 1871, G. 726; Hugenholz to M. K. (copy), 21 June 1871, Afst. IV; Ussher to Kennedy, 6 July 1871, Accra, P.P. 1872, lxx [C. 670], p. 22.

fit to put it forward so as to obstruct the cession, it cannot have been utterly new to him. He had, moreover, allowed himself to be deceived into setting Akyeampon at large. He left the Coast a tired and grievously disappointed man, all his plans for the Dutch settlements brought to nothing. He was now reviled both by the Elminas and by the enemies of the cession at home. Nothing could have been more unfair. He was sometimes misguided, particularly with regard to the exchange, and the close of his career certainly saw some lapses both of judgement and of candour; but, though he may have lacked the imagination and enterprise of a Maclean, he was an able, shrewd and humane administrator who thought long and deeply of the needs of the Dutch Gold Coast. Had more of his predecessors possessed his qualities he might not have found himself under the disagreeable necessity of preparing for its abandonment.[1]

After the signing of the treaty of cession on 25 February the Dutch ministers prepared to seek the approval of the States-General. Delay was dangerous, for every week that passed saw the opposition in press and pamphlets growing more and more vocal.[2] Harris was increasingly alarmed by these outbursts. On 7 February, though recognizing that 'we may have a stout opposition in the Chambers', he had had 'little doubt of a majority', but as the weeks went by his confidence diminished. He observed that the 'Government Press' made no attempt to repel the attacks by 'daily articles appearing in the paper, in pamphlets &c hostile to the Convention', and he found the Foreign Minister Gericke 'deficient in nerve to face opposition'. In fact, he reported, as a result of all this commotion the king was beginning to have second thoughts, and Gericke and his colleagues were inclined to regard the treaty 'as a rather unwelcome legacy from their predecessors although fully recognising its expediency and advantage'.[3] At the same time the ministry was not

---

[1] After his retirement Nagtglas continued to advise the Dutch government on West African affairs. He was still alive, and apparently active, in 1877 ((Hamel) to (M. B. Z.) (draft), 17 Nov. 1877, Hague, N.C. Elmina 6).

[2] e.g. H. Muller Szn., *De Afstand der Kust van Guinea aan Engeland* (reprinted from *Nieuwe Rotterdamsche Courant,* May 1871); C. M. Kan, *Nederland en de Kust van Guinea* (Utrecht, 1871).

[3] Harris to Granville (private), 7 and 17 Feb., 21 April 1871, Hague, P.R.O. 30/29/103; same to same, 1 and 28 March 1871, Hague, F.O. 37/490; same to same, 26 April 1871, Hague, F.O. 37/491. The only pamphlet that I have seen that defends the cession is Robidé van der Aa, op. cit.

unaware that, while it was generally assumed in Holland that Britain was eager to take over the Dutch settlements, the British Government in fact now seemed alarmingly indifferent to the fate of the treaty. As for public opinion in Britain about the cession, according to the Dutch envoy in London this ranged from hostile to cool.[1] Under other circumstances the doubts now evident on both sides of the political wisdom of the treaty might perhaps have led to its being quietly shelved; but this was scarcely possible in view of the 'link' that had been forged between it and the Siak and Surinam treaties, the former of which the British were as eager to see ratified as were the Dutch the latter.

The popularity in Holland of the Surinam agreement was, however, more than a little offset by the growing conviction that in the three colonial treaties as a whole Britain was getting very much the best of the bargain. This was the burden of the report made by the Council of State on the proposal to seek the States-General's approval of these treaties.[2] The Council stated emphatically that in its view the Siak and Surinam treaties were totally inadequate as compensation for what was being surrendered in the Gold Coast treaty. After castigating those who had conducted the negotiations for their weakness and complaisance, the Council demanded a further approach to Britain with a view to a considerable extension of the Siak treaty.[3] One can only wonder whether this demand represented a deliberate attempt to kill the Gold Coast treaty; certainly, as Gericke and his colleague at the Colonial Ministry, van Bosse, pointed out in reply, there was every reason to believe that an attempt to impose conditions already decisively rejected by the British Government might well put paid to the whole cession project. Holland, as they had to admit, was in a thoroughly weak bargaining position, a fact which they explained in general terms by reference to the relative power of Britain and Holland. They made no reference to the cause of weakness particular to this bargain—the transparent eagerness that de

[1] Van Lansberge to M. B. Z., 29 April 1871, London, Afst. IV; ibid., M. K. to M. B. Z., 5 May 1871; van Lansberge to M. B. Z., 11 May 1871, London, Kol. 22. VI. 1871. Openbaar Verbaal. Litt. AA. No. 3.
[2] Under the Dutch constitution no bill could be put before the States-General without first being referred to the king and the Council of State.
[3] Minister of State to king, 4 April 1871, Kab. 1871 (A²).

Waal and his colleagues had shown to rid themselves of the Dutch settlements as swiftly as possible.[1]

Contrary to the advice of the Council of State, the bills approving the Gold Coast and Siak conventions were laid before the Second Chamber of the States-General on 23 April, together with a lengthy *Memorie van toelichting* (explanatory memorandum) from the ministers.[2] The latter, in so far as the Gold Coast treaty was concerned, rehearsed the by now well-worn arguments in favour of cession—the benefit to the natives of a single authority, the need to concentrate Dutch energies, the financial drain on Holland, the insignificance of Dutch trade with the settlements—adding that the previous ministry had been led to consider this question both by representations made in the States-General and by the receipt of a proposal from Britain.[3] As was customary, it fell to a committee of 'reporters' (*commissie van rapporteurs*) to draw up a preliminary report (*voorlopig verslag*) on the bills, on the basis of observations made by the five 'sections' (*adfelingen*) of the Chamber. The 'sections' submitted the two treaties to very detailed scrutiny, and were unanimous in expressing disappointment with the Siak treaty. The committee summed this up well by declaring that at first it had been imagined that this treaty was an 'equivalent' for the cession, but that this seemed unlikely since it had been found to be at least as advantageous for Britain as for Holland. As regards both the principle and the details of the Gold Coast treaty there was no such unanimity. There was a good deal of criticism of the injury to Dutch honour and prestige—as one Dutch historian shrewdly remarks, even the most worthless possessions seem valuable where there is a question of parting with them[4]—but there was also plenty of support for the necessity of the cession. But a most ominous measure of agreement was manifested in requesting further information concerning the history of the treaties. What was the nature of the connexion between them? Were the Siak and Surinam treaties (the latter had yet to be

---

[1] M. B. Z. to M. K. to king, 19 April 1871, Kab. 1871 (T²).
[2] For a succinct account of the legislative procedure of the States-General see Vandenbosch, op. cit., p. 17.
[3] *Hand. S.G.*, 1870–1, Bijlagen, pp. 1625–39.
[4] W. J. van Welderen, Baron Ringers, *Schets Eener Parlementaire Gerschiedensis van Nederland, 1849 tot 1891* (Hague, 1918), p. 417.

put before the States-General) in fact to be regarded as an 'equivalent' for the cession of the Coast? How did the treaties originate? Did the British proposal come out of the blue or as the result of a Dutch hint? Such questions were pressed by the committee, which further demanded the publication of all relevant documents on the grounds that there was much concerning the history of the treaties that remained doubtful and obscure.[1]

With an aim that would have been uncanny had it not been directed by a member with an inside knowledge of the affairs of the Colonial Ministry,[2] the government's critics were working towards the exposure of the two facts which could do most damage to the ministry's chance of success: first, that, contrary to what had been publicly stated, the initial proposal for the cession—and, what was more to the point, the whole impetus towards it—had come from the Dutch side; and secondly, that, contrary to what was soon to be asserted,[3] the 'link' between the Gold Coast treaty and the others had been forged at Dutch instigation, and could therefore be construed, with considerable justice, as an attempt to call in British aid to induce the States-General to swallow the Guinea pill for the sake of the Surinam sugar. Small wonder that the ministers were thrown into confusion when Harris, disturbed by newspaper articles dilating on the rapacity that Britain had shown in proposing the cession, demanded that this 'inaccuracy' in the explanatory memorandum be publicly corrected. At first Gericke seemed inclined to comply, but van Bosse hastened to warn him of the political dangers of acknowledging the Dutch initiative. Consequently Gericke temporized by writing to Roest van Limburg, de Waal and van Lansberge[4] for their accounts of the negotiations, though in private he told Harris that he was satisfied that Harris's version was correct. De Waal, alas, does not seem to have replied, but the answers received from his

---

[1] *Hand. S.G.,* 1870–1, Bijlagen, pp. 1783–94.

[2] Van Sypesteyn: see above, p. 66, n. 3.

[3] See below, pp. 91–2. The version of the negotiations in which Britain proposed both the cession *and* the 'link' had been put before the Cabinet in January ('Nota voor den Ministerraad', 31 Jan. 1871, Afst. IV).

[4] Ambassador in Brussels. Previously in London, and before that Roest van Limburg's deputy at the Foreign ministry, where he had played a major part in negotiating the three colonial treaties. As Governor-General of the Dutch East Indies from 1874 to 1881 he found himself in charge of the long Acheh war which arose out of the Sumatra treaty.

ex-colleagues gave little support to the story, which he had originated, of a British initiative.[1]

On 22 June Gericke and van Bosse presented their formal reply
to the queries of the *commissie van rapporteurs*. The section of this
reply dealing with the history of the treaty was carefully worded,
but the ministers' embarrassment could scarcely be concealed. There
had, it was explained, been an 'involuntary misunderstanding'. First,
there had been private and informal discussions between de Waal
and Harris, which had culminated in a confidential inquiry from
the latter about the conditions on which Holland might consider
ceding her settlements to Britain; this had led de Waal to look
seriously into the matter and could be regarded as the question to
which the note of 11 July 1870 had been the answer. De Waal had
regarded the informal inquiry, Britain the formal note, as the start-
ing-point of the negotiations; hence an honest difference of opinion
as to which side had first 'proposed' the cession.[2] This was scarcely
the explanation that Harris had demanded, but he gave in to
Gericke's 'earnest request' 'not to push the question further at the
moment' and so embarrass the ministry in its dealings with its
critics.[3] He does not seem to have noticed that in their latest statement the ministers had also declared that the 'link' between the Gold
Coast and Siak treaties had been forged at the British request. The
commissie van rapporteurs, however, was not so easily satisfied. In
its final report (*eindverslag*)—somewhat to Harris's satisfaction—it
tore the ministers' explanation to shreds, demonstrating the untrust-
worthiness of de Waal's version of events, and flatly contradicting
the lame attempts that had been made to uphold the myth of British
initiative as regards both the cession itself and the 'link'. Now that
the ministers had belatedly agreed to make all the relevant papers
available, it could be demonstrated conclusively that the Chamber
had been misled about the facts of the negotiation, while its freedom

---

[1] Harris to M. B. Z. (copy), 22 May 1871, F.O. 37/491; ibid., Harris to Granville,
26 May and 1 June 1871, Hague; M. B. Z. to Harris (draft: not sent), (May 1871),
Afst. IV; ibid., M. K. to M. B. Z., 26 May 1871; M. B. Z. to Harris (copy), 31 May
1871, F.O. 37/491; Roest van Limburg to M. B. Z., 10 June 1871, Baden Baden, Afst.
IV; ibid., van Lansberge to M. B. Z., 10 June 1871, Brussels.

[2] *Hand. S.G.*, 1870–1, Bijlagen, pp. 1815–25; see also M. B. Z. to Harris, 23 June
1871, Afst. IV.

[3] Harris to Granville, 26 June 1871, F.O. 37/491; Granville to Harris, 30 June 1871,
F.O. 238/161.

to deal with each treaty on its merits had been obstructed by the 'link'.[1]

In the lengthy and at times violent debate on the treaties, which took place on 5, 6 and 7 July, the ministers abandoned the hopeless task of defending the now discredited version of the negotiations that they had inherited from de Waal. Van Bosse fell back upon a plea of ignorance; he was not, he admitted, in a position to provide full information concerning the origins of the treaty. Gericke, too, while claiming that de Waal had had the best intentions in negotiating the 'link', could not say how the latter had come into existence. The ministers, he declared, were themselves not fully informed—a truly remarkable admission. At the same time both ministers vigorously asserted the desirability of a speedy cession, and on 7 July, despite several impassioned denunciations by its critics, the Gold Coast treaty was approved by the Second Chamber by 34 votes to 30. The Siak treaty, however, was rejected by the more convincing majority of 36 to 28. If the 'link' was to be maintained, this rejection automatically involved the shelving of the treaty that had just been approved.[2]

The significance of the votes of 7 July should not be overlooked. They dispose of the idea that the cession was part of a colonial bargain between Britain and the Netherlands, an idea that had been put abroad by de Waal and perpetuated by his successors in the hope that it would make the treaty more palatable at home. We have already seen that there had been no connexion between the *negotiation* of the Siak and Surinam treaties and that of the Gold Coast treaty. The notorious 'link', which gave colour (as de Waal intended it to) to the idea of a 'bargain', had been forged only after the first two treaties had been signed. It is now apparent that the approval of the cession by the Second Chamber was not primarily due to the existence of this 'link'. If the latter was not strong enough to save the Siak treaty it can scarcely be credited with winning approval for the much-maligned Gold Coast treaty.

Although Harris might with some justice remark that both treaties

---

[1] *Hand. S.G.*, 1870–1, Bijlagen, pp. 1858–60; Harris to Granville, 4 July 1871, F.O. 37/491.
[2] *Hand. S.G.*, 1870–1, II, pp. 1087–1146. Voting was not on party lines; *v.* van Welderen, op. cit., p. 418.

might have been approved 'if the present Government had assumed a bolder front at first in support' of them, the ministry now showed no desire to use the setback in the States-General as a pretext for shelving them. It was in fact casting about for a way to save them, and as a result the officials of the Colonial Ministry found themselves unusually busy. 'I dine on Guinea and sup off Siak,' grumbled one of them in a private note, adding (with a sly glance at the Surinam treaty) that he would be very happy to see the States-General emigrate as coolies.[1] On the day after the rejection of the Siak treaty Gericke discussed with Harris the possibility of undoing the 'link' between this and the other treaties, which, he thought, would win approval without much difficulty.[2] Harris easily obtained his government's consent to this, only to be told by Gericke, to his considerable annoyance, that he was mistaken in thinking that any official request of this nature had been made.[3] The Dutch Government, in fact, had had second thoughts about risking the rejection of the Gold Coast treaty by putting it before the First Chamber 'during the present excited state of feeling', and by a narrow majority it succeeded in obtaining from that Chamber permission to hold up the bill for the time being.[4]

It was hope as well as fear that made the Dutch reluctant to dispense with the 'link': a hope, born of conversations in London and The Hague, that the British Government, in order to help the Dutch to overcome their difficulties, might be willing to discuss further concessions for the Dutch in the East Indies. If these could be obtained, as Gericke and van Bosse pointed out to the king, then the

[1] Van Alphen to Schimmelpenninck v.d. Oye, 8 July 1871, Wolteringen, op. cit., p. 148.
[2] Harris to Granville, 8 July 1871 (two letters), F.O. 37/491. For the unpopularity of the 'link' in Holland, see the cartoon entitled 'Traktaten met Engeland' in the generally pro-government *Nederlandsche Spectator*, 8 July 1871.
[3] Note by Gericke, 14 July 1871, Wolteringen, op. cit., p. 154; ibid., p. 155, Harris to M. B. Z. (private), 16 July 1871; ibid., pp. 155–6, M. B. Z. to Harris (private), 16 July 1871; Harris to Granville (private), 18 July 1871, Hague, P.R.O. 30/29/103; Granville to Harris, 19 July 1871, F.O. 238/161; van Bijlandt to M. B. Z. (copy), 24 July 1871, Kol. 4. XI. 1871. Geheim Litt. S. 18; Harris to M. B. Z. (copy), 24 July 1871, F.O. 37/491; ibid., M. B. Z. to Harris (copy), 29 July 1871. On Gericke's side it should be noted that there is no mention of this request in his record of the interview with Harris: note by Gericke, 8 July 1871, Wolteringen, op. cit., pp. 146–7.
[4] Harris to Granville, 14 and 19 July 1871, F.O. 37/491; M. B. Z. to van Bijlandt (copy), 19 July 1871, Kol. 4. XI. 1871. Geheim. Litt. S. 18; *Hand. S.G.*, 1870–1, I, pp. 226–30.

ill-fated Siak convention could be transformed into a Sumatra treaty which would be welcomed by the States-General and might actually assist the passage of the Gold Coast treaty through the First Chamber. Here, then, was a decisive argument both for preserving the 'link' and for holding up the Gold Coast treaty until the Siak treaty had been revised.[1]

Why was the British Government now ready to consider the very concessions that it had so peremptorily refused to de Waal? Partly, as Miss Mollema points out, because it had no desire to lose the benefits that would accrue under the Siak treaty;[2] but this was not all. The period of hesitation in Downing Street, which Kofi Karikari's intervention had induced, was over. While maintaining its demand that Akyeampon be removed before the execution of the treaty, the Colonial Office, under the influence of Kennedy, once more thought it 'very desirable that we should now get rid of the Dutch from the Gold Coast'.[3] Kennedy himself, now in London, had abandoned his misgivings and was particularly insistent upon the need for a *speedy* cession, which alone could prevent a more formidable outbreak of violence than any yet seen. He told Sir George Barrow that he was apprehensive of serious consequences if the cession should not take place after all.[4] From this point of view it was not enough to sit back, as Granville had seemed inclined to do immediately after the rejection of the Siak treaty, and wait for the Dutch to be forced to abandon the Coast.[5] The long struggle between the eagerness of Cape Coast and the caution of Downing Street was over; the former, now strongly supported by the go-between

---

[1] M. B. Z. and M. K. to king, 4 August 1871, Wolteringen, op. cit., pp. 170–4.
[2] Mollema, op. cit., p. 236.
[3] Minute by Holland of 12 Sept. 1871, on F.O. to C.O., 4 Sept. 1871, C.O. 96/90.
[4] Kennedy to Kimberley, 7 Aug. 1871, London (with minutes by Barrow of 8 Aug. and by Knatchbull-Hugessen of 10 Aug. 1871), C.O. 96/91; ibid., Kennedy to C.O., 6 Sept. 1871. It is futile to seek for much consistency in Kennedy's views, which were forever oscillating between fear of a collision with Ashanti and desire to get rid of the Dutch. This apparently unconscious vacillation was typical of Kennedy and gave him the best of both worlds, since he was able to claim the credit for his subordinates' successful policies while disavowing their mistakes. Perhaps it was an almost inevitable result of his intermediary position between London and Cape Coast. Kimberley's high opinion of Kennedy was not, incidentally, wholly shared by Rogers, who in 1873 thought that the most vulnerable part of the Gladstone government's record on the Coast was what 'Kennedy did or allowed the Fantees to do' to the Elminas (Blachford to Kimberley, 30 Sept. 1873, Blachford, Kimberley Papers PC/A/52).
[5] Van Lansberge to M. B. Z. (copy), 15 July 1871, (London), Kol. 4. XI. 1871. Geheim. Litt. S. 18.

Kennedy, had finally won the day. Kennedy's urgency, well reflected in an anonymous letter to *The Times*, which in violent terms accused the Dutch of 'playing over again the old surliness of the dog in the manger',[1] seems to have banished all thought of the Ashanti claim to Elmina. From the British side, the new negotiations were undertaken to save the Gold Coast as well as the Siak treaty.

Van Bijlandt, the Dutch envoy in London, was assiduous in keeping his government informed of these developments. On 11 July he put the position succinctly:

En somme, et dit en peu de mots, mon impression est qu'une reprise des négociations sur des nouvelles bases ne sera pas impossible, et cela d'autant plus qu'il ne paraît que l'on tient beaucoup ici à la ratification et exécution du traité adopté concernant la cession de la Côte de Guinée; de sorte que le principe de connexité, tellement blâmé par quelque membres de la Chambre, finirait par nous être utile dans cette circonstance. Car autrement, sans autre traité, où serait pour nous la compensation pour la cession?

On the same day that he wrote this van Bijlandt had a conversation with Granville which confirmed him in these impressions. Without the 'link' Holland could expect no concessions from Britain; with it she held a trump card, since 'le but principal' of the British Government was to have sole possession of the whole Guinea Coast.[2]

It is not easy to say with any certainty what part economic considerations, in particular the prospect of commercial advantage, may have played in stimulating this determination of Britain to carry through the cession, or indeed what part they had played in influencing the attitude of the British Government throughout the negotiations. It is quite clear that ever since the events of 1868–9, if not before, interested British merchants had been strongly in favour of the acquisition of the Dutch settlements, and we have noted in passing some instances of their activity in pressing their views upon the government. It is far less clear that these representations had any significant influence upon the formulation of policy; certainly there is little in the correspondence of the responsible ministers and officials

---

[1] *The Times*, 1 Sept. 1871.
[2] Van Bijlandt to M. B. Z., 11, 12, and 21 July 1871, Wolteringen, op. cit., pp. 150–3, 165–6.

to suggest it, or to indicate that the considerable expansion of British trade with West Africa in general and the Gold Coast in particular, the boom in West African palm-oil, or any similar consideration, had much weight in Whitehall, or for that matter at Cape Coast Castle, where a deep distrust of the mercantile community was normally an article of faith. On the whole, then, it does not seem possible to clothe the dry bones of this piece of diplomatic history with the alluring flesh of economic forces, which certainly existed, but were not of great importance. Nor is it necessarily to be assumed, with Dr. Dike,[1] that the merchants were *on principle* 'demanding more protection' for the sake of the trade that would follow the flag; their motive in advocating the annexation of the Dutch settlements seems rather to have been a simple desire to clear away the obstacles to trade arising from 'mixed possession' and in particular from the unrest after 1868. Their rooted dislike of official interference was scarcely compatible with an enthusiasm for British territorial expansion, unless this seemed necessary in order to cure political ills which were obstructing commercial intercourse.

The negotiations went smoothly. London accepted, though only after some heart-searching, the Dutch request for a free hand in the whole of Sumatra, and this was incorporated in a new treaty signed on 2 November.[2] Gericke also took this opportunity to recall a demand which had been heard during the debate in the Second Chamber, namely that if ever Britain decided to recruit emigrant labour for her colonies from the Gold Coast, the Dutch should have the same right. Granville agreed to incorporate a declaration to this effect in a protocol to the treaty. The sole purpose of this otherwise meaningless gesture (recruitment of this sort, as Nagtglas pointed out, was practically impossible among West African negroes, and in any case it was unthinkable that any foreseeable British Government would give the necessary lead) was to smooth the treaty's passage through the First Chamber.[3] Only in reply to a Dutch proposal for

---

[1] Dike, op. cit., pp. 180–1.
[2] 'Memorandum upon the Sumatra and Gold Coast Treaties. . . .', 5 Jan. 1874, F.O. 37/534; Mollema, op. cit., p. 236.
[3] Nagtglas to M.K. (copy), 18 Aug. 1871, Rotterdam, Afst. IV; M. B. Z. to Harris (copy), 29 Aug. 1871, F.O. 37/491; Harris to Granville, 20 Sept. 1871, F.O. 37/492; Granville to Harris, 23 Sept. 1871, F.O. 238/161.

a modification of the Surinam treaty did Britain prove unaccommodating.[1]

Reinforced by these concessions, the Dutch Government once more submitted the treaties for the approval of the States-General at the opening of its new session. Now that the Siak treaty had been replaced by one more acceptable to Dutch opinion, it was the Gold Coast convention which was the most vulnerable to attack. Harris reported that the press was now almost unanimous in denouncing it, so that, as Gericke remarked, it could pass only 'through the sober judgment of members resisting the pressure upon them'.[2] Indeed, while the Surinam and Sumatra treaties passed easily and speedily through the Second Chamber, strenuous efforts were made to obstruct the Gold Coast treaty by arguing that it, too, should pass through that Chamber once more.[3] Rejecting this claim, the ministry presented all three treaties to the First Chamber on 16 December.[4] Five days later Harris wrote that opposition to all three treaties had considerably diminished, an assertion which seemed to be borne out by the provisional report on the Gold Coast treaty produced on the following day by the *commissie van rapporteurs* of the First Chamber. From this it was clear that most of the members were in principle in favour of cession, even though many of them were puzzled and disturbed by Britain's willingness to accept such a burdensome inheritance. Even some of those hostile to the treaty were yet reluctant to oppose the bill in case its rejection meant throwing away the advantages to be gained under the new Sumatra treaty.[5] The apparent goodwill of the Chamber to the treaty was still further emphasized when the *commissie* expressed its complete satisfaction with the ministers' reply to its report.[6] Gericke nevertheless had good reasons for his continuing anxiety about the fate of this treaty.[7] Unpleasant news was arriving from Elmina, and the opponents of the cession were already showing their determination to exploit it to the full.

[1] 'Memorandum upon the Sumatra and Gold Coast Treaties. . . .', 5 Jan. 1874, F.O. 37/534.
[3] Harris to Granville, 20 Sept. 1871, F.O. 37/492.
[2] *Hand. S.G.*, 1871–2, II, pp. 635–9.
[4] *Hand. S.G.*, 1871–2, I, p. 59.
[5] Ibid., pp. 94–6; Harris to Granville, 21 Dec. 1871, F.O. 37/492.
[6] *Hand. S.G.*, 1871–2, I, pp. 132–5.
[7] For which see Harris to Granville, 22 Dec. 1871, F.O. 37/492.

THE TREATY OF CESSION—II
APOLOGY AND EXECUTION

I

FOR more than five months after Nagtglas's departure Elmina was governed by a succession of three governors *ad interim*, two of these being the captains of Dutch warships on the Guinea station. This was a quiet time in Elmina, with Akyeampon secure in the castle and with the authorities still able to assure the natives that no final decision about the cession had yet been taken. The king and chiefs were still loud in their protestations that they would never give up the Dutch flag—that this surprised van Bosse shows that he had as little acquaintance with the affairs of the Coast as with the history of the treaty—but were somewhat reassured in November by the news that a successor to Nagtglas had at last been appointed.[1] The most important happening during this period was the long-awaited return, on 26 October, of the messenger Plange with the King of Ashanti's reply to Nagtglas's rejection of the claim to Elmina.

In effect the documents brought by Plange amounted to a renunciation of this claim. In a 'Certificate of Apologie', dated 19 August and written in English by Plange, the king asserted that his letter to Ussher of 24 November 1870 had been 'totally misrepresented on the part of the parties entrusted with the writing and dictating'. 'I only meant,' he declared, 'board wages or salary and not "tribute by right of arms" from the Dutch Government.' He held to the story of the nine thousand pounds paid in settlement of the King of Denkyira's liabilities, but explained that this was 'to

---

[1] Hugenholz to M. K. (drafts), 8 Aug. and 8 Sept. 1871, G. 726; Wirix to M. K. (copy), 26 Sept. 1871, Afst. V; Le Jeune to M. K. (draft), 31 Oct. 1871, G. 726; same to same (copy), 13 Nov. 1871, Afst. V; ibid., M. K. to M. B. Z., 16 Dec. 1871.

ensure good will or feeling, toward the Dutch Government on the Gold-Coast Settlement in Elmina Fort, but not for purchasing the said Elmina Castle or Fort'. In conclusion he insisted that the letter to Ussher had been a 'vague, formal or nominal expression, the sentiments of which I therefore must now write that the whole is a *mistake*'. In a covering letter (in Dutch) addressed to Nagtglas he declared that 'if anyone says I considered Elmina my rightful property, it is a *lie*'.[1]

The 'Certificate' brought to Elmina by Plange is one of the most celebrated documents of Gold Coast history. It owes its fame to two generally accepted beliefs: first, that it was instrumental in inducing Britain to go through with the treaty of cession; and secondly, that it was not 'genuine', in the sense that Plange was guilty either of outright forgery, or of the sort of 'total misrepresentation' of which the 'Certificate' itself accused Ansah.[2] Before going further with our story it will be as well to look more closely at the origins of, and the evidence for, these highly questionable beliefs. */ o o o / o*

The assertion that Britain had declined to go through with the cession until the Dutch had obtained the renunciation of the Ashanti claim to Elmina was first made by Knatchbull-Hugessen in May 1873. Hard pressed in the Commons by the critics of a policy which, it was suggested, had provoked the Ashanti invasion, the Colonial Under-Secretary declared that the printed correspondence relative to the cession showed that Britain had refused to take over the Dutch forts until the King of Ashanti had withdrawn his claim.[3] A year later Knatchbull-Hugessen, now out of office and defending the late government against further criticism of its Gold Coast policy, was to elaborate this story. In a speech by no means free of error and inexactitude[4] he stated that Kimberley had been determined not to take over the Dutch settlements unless the natives were willing to change their flag and the Ashanti claims were settled by the Dutch.

---

[1] '1874 Report', Appendices IIIg and IIIh; Wirix to M. K. (copy), 28 Oct. 1871, Afst. V. To my considerable regret I have been unable to find the original 'Certificate'.
[2] e.g. Claridge, op. cit., i, pp. 610–13; Ellis, op. cit., pp. 270–3.
[3] *Hansard,* 3rd ser., ccxv, cols. 1807–13.
[4] e.g. The statements that in 1869 the Ashantis destroyed Dixcove (the Ahantas were in fact responsible), and that Kennedy ('one of the best Governors we had ever had in our West African Settlements') had *always* strongly urged the taking over of the Dutch possessions.

H

Thus, he declared, though the treaty had been signed in February 1871, it had not been ratified for another year, the interval being 'employed in ascertaining the feelings of the Natives and the position of the Ashantees with regard to Elmina'.[1] This explanation of the long delay in ratifying the treaty was also adopted by the official historian of the Ashanti War,[2] and by 1875 it had found its way into the information supplied in the Colonial Office List.[3]

In view of the consequences of the cession it was natural enough that Knatchbull-Hugessen should wish to convince himself and others that his government had taken all possible precautions to prevent them. As far as I know his version of events has never been queried. It certainly cannot be disputed that the Colonial Office (as will be seen later) *did* ask for and get assurances about 'the feelings of the Natives' before proceeding with the transfer (though *not*, as Knatchbull-Hugessen implied, before ratifying the treaty!),[4] but the point at issue here is what connexion, if any, 'the position of the Ashantees with regard to Elmina' had with the year's delay before ratification. A superficial study of the course of events might lead one to suppose a very close connexion. It is undeniable that, as we have seen, in February 1871 Britain asked the Dutch to induce the Ashantis to withdraw their claims on Elmina,[5] that Nagtglas subsequently sought and obtained such withdrawal (in the shape of the 'Certificate'), and that ratification and execution of the treaty followed. On closer investigation, however, one discovers strong if largely negative evidence that these events were *not* linked in a chain of cause and effect such as Knatchbull-Hugessen suggested.

To begin with, the Dutch never acceded to the British request, in reply to which Harris was handed a note which contained the following declaration:

vouloir que le Gouvernement Néerlandais se charge d'obtenir une renonciation aux prétensions extravagantes de l'un ou le l'autre chef de nègres au fondement desquelles le Gouvernement Anglais n'ajoute et

---

[1] *Hansard*, 3rd ser., ccxviii, cols. 1592–1663.
[2] H. Brackenbury, *The Ashanti War*. . . . (Edinburgh and London, 1874), i, pp. 31–4.
[3] *Colonial Office List*, 1875, pp. 55–8.
[4] See below, p. 102.
[5] See above, pp. 82–4.

ne peut ajouter foi, cela est un désir qui paraît difficilement admissible.[1]

This was an argument which became more or less unanswerable once Britain had admitted that the Dutch title to Elmina was 'unquestionable',[2] and, in fact, as has already been seen, once Kimberley had made this admission in March 1871 the British demand seems to have been quietly dropped.[3] On 20 March Rogers, minuting a letter from the Foreign Office on the question of what attitude the Cape Coast authorities should take if as a result of the negotiations for cession the Dutch were to collide with Ashanti, wrote as follows:

I wd state that Lord K is satisfied as to the invalidity of the King of Ashantee's title to Elmina *& requires no more assurance on that subject.*[4]

Perhaps the most striking evidence of the practical insignificance of the 'Certificate' as far as the cession is concerned is provided by the lack of interest taken in it at the time. The Dutch at Elmina waited for well over a month before bothering to notify Cape Coast of its arrival.[5] Possibly this was overlooked owing to the handing over of authority to the new Governor, Ferguson, but even so we can scarcely recognize here the traditional picture of the anxious Dutch seizing on the 'Certificate' to overcome the objections of the reluctant British. Moreover, when the news of the Ashanti 'apology' eventually reached London not a single member of the Colonial Office thought it called for any comment whatsoever![6] One cannot assert categorically that without the 'Certificate' the British Government *might* not

[1] M. K. to M. B. Z. (v. secret), 21 Feb. 1871, Hague, Afst. IV; Note to Harris (extract—copy), 28 Feb. 1871, F.O. 37/490. With prophetic insight this note went on to point out that the renunciation which Britain required could later be disavowed by Ashanti just as easily as the current claim had been put forward.

[2] See above, p. 84.

[3] Of course Nagtglas knew of the British demand; but he also knew of the refusal of his superiors to entertain it, so that his approaches to the ambassadors and to the king cannot be considered as its direct outcome (M. K. to Nagtglas (v. secret), 21 Feb. 1871, Hague, G. 730).

[4] Min. by Rogers of 20 March 1871 on F.O. to C.O., 18 March 1871, C.O. 96/90 (my italics). Rogers' advice was not taken, but only, it would seem, because it was not strictly relevant to the subject under discussion. Neither Kimberley nor Knatchbull-Hugessen saw fit to query his statement.

[5] Ferguson to Salmon, 3 Dec. 1871, Elmina, P.P. 1872, lxx [C. 670], p. 34. The way in which Claridge (op. cit., i, p. 610) slurs over this matter gives a salutary insight into his methods.

[6] See the minutes on F.O. to C.O. (confidential), 27 Dec. 1871, C.O. 96/90.

have had second thoughts about the cession in the early months of 1872, but it seems reasonably certain that it was not the Ashanti claim but the attitude of the States-General which held up the ratification of the treaty for so long. As far as London was concerned the claim had fallen into oblivion long before the 'Certificate' arrived, and in this sense Kimberley might well confess in after years

that knowing nothing of the affairs of the Gold Coast I did not take sufficient precautions against a quarrel with Ashanti arising out of the Treaty,[1]

an admission strikingly out of line with Knatchbull-Hugessen's attempts to shield the administration behind the 'Certificate'. On the whole this document, like the so-called 'Bond' of 1844, would seem to have played a part in Gold Coast historiography that is out of all proportion to its actual importance.

The 'genuineness' of the 'Certificate' is a far more complex (if less important) matter than its historical significance, not least because of the extreme difficulty in assessing the true import of 'letters' which were in fact the attempts of usually semi-literate scribes to put into writing the traditionally Delphic utterances of an illiterate court. The first suggestion that the document was not all that it appeared seems to have been made in a letter of 14 January 1874 to the *Standard* newspaper from T. G. Bowles, a young but rising journalist.[2] This suggested that it was 'a purely "got-up" and illusory document', adding:

There are three distinct and unmistakeable claims to Elmina addressed directly to the English government, and extending over the whole of the material period of time. Who can hesitate to put these against the interpolated copy of a Dutch translation of an Ashantee explanation, said to have been obtained by such a person as Mr. Plange is represented on both sides to be?[3]

During the parliamentary inquests on the causes of the Ashanti War,

---

[1] E. Drus (Ed.), *Journal of Events during the Gladstone Ministry 1868–1874, by John, First Earl of Kimberley* (Camden Miscellany, Vol. xxi, London, 1958), pp. 41–2.
[2] Thomas Gibson Bowles, 1842–1922. Founder of *Vanity Fair* and subsequently a Conservative M.P.
[3] *Standard*, 15 Jan. 1874. It is not easy to see why a document written in English is called a 'Dutch translation'.

in April and May 1874, members were swift to elaborate these reflec-
tions on a document which Knatchbull-Hugessen was pleading in
justification of the late government's policy. One M.P. thought that
the 'Certificate'

would require some explanation as being quite contradictory both to the
words and the acts of both parties all through the previous negotiations
and by the light of which it looked ludicrous.[1]

Others, too, thought it of little worth. It was not 'at all a clear
renunciation'; 'board wages and salary' was 'a very wide and general
term'; Plange was 'a questionable channel', and the document

was wrung at the last moment from the King by the Dutch, and was
contrary to his constant, persistent and emphatic declarations of an
opposite kind during the whole course of the negotiations.

It had certainly not been sufficient grounds for accepting the transfer,
but the Dutch had been 'too sharp for us'.[2]

These allegations were noted by Brackenbury in his official history
of the Ashanti War, but without comment.[3] It was left to Colonel
A. B. Ellis, in his *History of the Gold Coast* published in 1893, to
incorporate them into a fully-fledged denunciation of the 'Certificate' as a forgery.[4] Ellis's book, in its time a valuable piece of pioneering work, has exercised an altogether excessive and somewhat
baneful influence upon subsequent writers. Claridge, in particular,
whose very uneven *History* is still the standard authority for British
activity on the Gold Coast, leaned on it heavily, swallowing its
prejudices and reproducing its errors. With some slight reservations
he took over the 'forgery' theory.[5] Ellis himself had 'no doubt' about
this. The Dutch authorities, he suggested, had doubtless impressed
Plange with the importance of obtaining a renunciation 'and he had
thought it to the advantage of his own interests not to disappoint
them'. The King of Ashanti, on the other hand, 'had shown that he
knew nothing of the existence' of the 'Certificate' by writing two

1 *Hansard*, 3rd ser., ccxviii, cols. 1204–25.
2 Ibid., cols. 1592–1663.
3 Ellis, op. cit., i, p. 273.
4 Brackenbury, op. cit., i, pp. 33–4.
5 Claridge, op. cit., i, pp. 610–13.

letters (of 19 August and 1 September 1871) to Acting Administrator Salmon making claims 'utterly irreconcilable with the alleged renunciation . . .'. What clinched Ellis's rejection of the document was the following argument:

It was in the handwriting of Mr. Plange, and the missionaries [*i.e.* Ramseyer and Kühne], whom the King always asked to read and translate any document before he affixed his mark to it, had never seen or even heard of this particular one. On the contrary, they believed and said that Plange had altogether failed to obtain any renunciation.

Claridge accepted this, though he rather characteristically tried to get the best of both worlds by adding that if the king *did* put his mark to this document he can have had no suspicion of its contents.

Unfortunately for Ellis's case, his central argument is not borne out by a study of the published memoirs of the captive missionaries. These certainly do not mention the renunciation, but neither do they supply grounds for assuming that the king *always* consulted the missionaries about his correspondence. More important still, they nowhere suggest that 'Plange had failed to obtain any renunciation'! It is possible, of course, that Ellis got his information from the lips of the missionaries themselves, but in this case it is very strange indeed that the editor of their memoirs—and there is no reason to doubt that this edition of 1875 had their approval—specifically states that

The king had thought fit to recall the letter which had been written by Prince Ansa to Mr. Ussher as having contained vague and clumsy expression, and this recall had been given in writing to Mr. Plange.[1]

If the mere fact that in their memoirs the missionaries themselves make no mention of the 'Certificate' proves it a forgery, then the same may be argued of the letters to Salmon by which Ellis sets such store! One cannot, in fact, read too much into what is, after all, a rather scrappy compilation based on journals written in captivity.[2]

---

[1] Ramseyer and Kühne, op. cit., p. 316.
[2] Claridge himself, when he came to consider the alleged false statements of Plange in 1872, thought them 'quite possible' even though 'the missionaries . . . knew nothing' of them. 'They were not always present', he explained! (op. cit., ii, p. 7).

One thing, however, that we do learn from the missionaries is that they were *not* present at an interview which Crawford, an envoy from the authorities at Cape Coast, had with the king on 5 August 1871.[1] Had Ellis and Claridge studied a little more closely the blue-book which contains the text of the 'Certificate' they would have found printed there a letter from Crawford to Ussher describing this interview. This letter goes a fair way towards establishing the credentials of the 'Certificate'. In it Crawford reports that the king, addressing Plange, who was also present, about the letter to Ussher that Ansah had written, spoke of it as follows:

I must declare the whole sentiment of the communication to be erroneously construed, I did not mean 'tribute by right of arms', but I meant salary. It was Intim Gackedi my great-grandfather Osei Tutu conquered, and his Intim Gackedi's customary paid note was transferred to him, my great-grandfather. The Elmina people and the Ashantis are brethren; offspring of one mother we never had war with them, or had they even paid tribute to us, we are allies, friends and brethren, I never made utterance that the King of Holland is my vassal, paying me tribute; but on account of friendship, he allows me stipend from his Fort, that is the reason I disagree the exchange or Elmina cession to the English, or do not like when I hear they are molested by any nation, I did not say they paying me tribute by right of conquest.[2]

Here we have in essence the renunciation of the claim 'by right'; Karikari is explaining that his opposition to the cession is grounded rather upon his 'friendship' with the Dutch and his fear of losing their 'stipend'. Though his words do not go as far as those of the 'Certificate' they are none the less irreconcilable with the claims made in Ansah's letter. If the king, in the presence of his chiefs and counsellors, could so far forswear himself, what was to prevent him (perhaps in a more private session) from going the whole hog and authorizing Plange to write the 'Certificate'?

The conduct of Prince Ansah, both before and after Plange's mission, is difficult to account for except on the assumption that the 'Certificate' was what it purported to be. As has already been seen,[3]

---

[1] 'On August 5th, Mr. Crawford came (i.e. to the missionaries' residence) with a serious face; he had been insulted at the palace' (Ramseyer and Kühne, op. cit., p. 132).
[2] Crawford to Ussher, 7 Aug. 1871, Kumasi, P.P. 1872, lxx [C. 670], pp. 24–6.
[3] See above, pp. 85–6.

the conduct of the wily Effifrah when challenged by Nagtglas on the Ashanti claim had led Ansah to suspect that the king might 'beg pardon' for the sake of the *kostgeld*. Not doubting that he might thus be disavowed, he had prudently decided not to return to Kumasi for the time being. Thus Ansah, whose opinion cannot lightly be set aside, was in June already anticipating an apology of the kind which Plange actually brought down in October. Equally remarkable is Ansah's reaction to the 'Certificate' itself. If anyone had a direct interest in discrediting the 'Certificate', in showing that it was not an expression of the king's mind but a misrepresentation or a forgery, that person was Ansah; yet so convinced was he of its authenticity that he was willing to vouch for it—presumably after examining the marks made by the king and those who witnessed the document.[1] The ambassadors, Effifrah and Kotiko, who returned to Elmina on 20 November, also acknowledged the 'Certificate'.[2] According to Claridge (who quotes no authority) they 'had not been in Kumasi when it was alleged to have been written',[3] but even so it is not easy to understand why they, Ansah, and the kings and chiefs of Elmina should all have been either the dupes or the accomplices of Plange—which is what the forgery theory would make them.

It may also be noted that there seems to be no record of any direct disavowal of the 'Certificate' by Kofi Karikari. This is remarkable for two reasons. First, it is something that we might legitimately expect to find in the missionaries' memoirs, since it was Kühne who on 14 December translated for the king a letter from the new Dutch Governor Ferguson acknowledging receipt of the 'Certificate' and expressing satisfaction with the renunciation; but in fact there is in the account of this interview no mention of any surprise or anger exhibited by the monarch on hearing this message.[4] Secondly, when in 1873 the king was both declaring his right to Elmina and representing the misdeeds of Plange as the true cause of the Ashanti invasion of the protectorate,[5] he might surely have been expected to denounce Plange's 'forgery' to the British authorities. But he did not.

---

[1] Ellis, op. cit., p. 273.
[2] Ferguson to M. K. (secret—extract—copy), 25 Nov. 1871, Elmina, Afst. V.
[3] Claridge, op. cit., i, p. 611.
[4] Ferguson to Karikari, 28 Nov. 1871, Elmina, '1874 Report' App. IIIk; Ramseyer and Kühne, op. cit., p. 148.
[5] See below, p. 126.

So much for the circumstantial evidence. There remains to be considered what may be termed the logical case against the 'Certificate' —the argument that it is so out of line with the whole course of Ashanti policy and with more or less simultaneous Ashanti declarations that it simply *cannot* be genuine. Those who accept this reasoning must believe themselves better judges of Ashanti mentality and methods than Prince Ansah, who expected that his king would apologize for the sake of the *kostgeld*, and accepted the fact that he had done so. Once we assume, like Ansah, that Karikari would dissimulate his feelings and intentions for the sake of what was due to him—which now amounted to some £320 worth of trade goods[1]— the 'Certificate' needs no further explanation, nor need the contrast between it and Karikari's letters to Salmon cause much surprise. Both these letters, by which Ellis set so much store, asked Salmon to put right certain grievances which the Elminas had against the Fantes,[2] and Salmon understandably objected to this tacit assumption of 'protection' of the Elminas, fearing that the king's 'main object . . . is to get the Government to acknowledge in this manner his authority and jurisdiction over Elmina'.[3] *Pace* Ellis, there is nothing *explicitly* claimed in these letters which is 'utterly irreconcilable with the alleged renunciation', but it seems that in his dealings with the British, with no arrears of *kostgeld* at stake, Karikari felt a little freer to show his hand. If we take into account that Karikari was by this time certainly preparing for war with the Coast,[4] that he consequently wished both to conceal his warlike intentions and to get his hands on as much arms and ammunition as possible, then the motive behind this dissimulation becomes fairly clear.

Reading between the lines of Crawford's report we can see something almost contemptuous in the deception practised upon Plange. At the same interview at which the king solemnly disavowed his claim to 'tribute by right of arms', the king's retinue indulged in some pointed mockery of the Dutch envoy. Plange was called upon 'to translate some customary paynote' from the Dutch (probably the

---

[1] 3,840 guilders, according to Nagtglas (Nagtglas to M. K. (draft), 14 March 1871, G. 726).
[2] Karikari to Salmon, 19 Aug. and 1 Sept. 1871, Kumasi, P.P. 1872, lxx [C. 670], pp. 27–9.
[3] Ibid., p. 28, Salmon to Kennedy, 31 Oct. 1871, Cape Coast.
[4] See below, pp. 123–5.

'Elmina note' itself), and when he had done so he was told that 'he must show the reason for the said pay-note'. 'For what,' he was asked, 'they pay the King of Ashantee annually?' He replied, 'It is not inserted down here'. Crawford's account of this exchange ends with the somewhat sinister note, 'A laugh from the throne'.[1] The Ashantis were not only making a fool of Plange, but also enjoying themselves hugely in the process. The joke, however, turned out to be on Ashanti, for the newly-arrived Governor Ferguson, though satisfied with the 'apology', would not pay the outstanding *kostgeld* unless what he called the 'original' *kostbrief* was produced; so that the messengers who had accompanied Plange on his return had to go back to Kumasi empty-handed![2] Karikari's volte-face had, after all, failed to extract its financial reward.

To sum up, not only is the authenticity of the 'Certificate' supported by strong circumstantial evidence, but it *can* be reconciled with the known cause of events. It is quite possible that Plange indulged in some exaggeration of Karikari's apologetics, but it no longer seems necessary, or even permissible, to assume this, still less to use such terms as 'forgery'.[3]

2

On 25 November the Ashanti 'apology' was confirmed by the ambassadors Effifrah and Kotiko,[4] and Governor Ferguson now felt justified in releasing Akyeampon from custody. He was all the more anxious to do this in order to placate the Elminas, about whose repeatedly declared intention to resist any attempt at cession by force he felt more and more uneasy. He warned his government to expect very serious trouble when the cession took place, and himself began to make veiled preparations to secure the castle against attack from

---

[1] Crawford to Ussher, *ut supra.*
[2] Ferguson to M. K. (secret—copy), 25 Nov. 1871, Elmina, Afst. V; Ferguson to Karikari, 30 March 1872, Elmina, '1874 Report', App. IIII.
[3] I have not thought it necessary to discuss in detail the argument that Plange's 'questionable' character makes the 'Certificate' suspect. Plange was certainly not an ideal ambassador, but the only grounds for impugning his integrity that are known to me are provided by Karikari's unsupported assertion that in 1872 he delivered a false message, purporting to come from the Governor-in-Chief, and so caused the Ashanti War. For a discussion of this charge, see below, p. 126, n. 3.
[4] See above, p. 106.

the town.[1] By the end of the year he was so convinced of the inevitability of conflict that he was formulating a comic-opera plan whereby Elmina Castle would be handed over on a moonless night to British troops dressed in Dutch uniforms and giving Dutch words of command, so as to take the natives by surprise.[2] More worthy of the attention of his superiors was his dispatch of 9 December, reporting the intention of the King and chiefs of Elmina to send an emissary to Holland with a protest against the projected cession.[3]

As news of the growing excitement and unrest in Elmina reached The Hague, the Dutch ministers showed themselves increasingly concerned about the effects of these reports upon the deliberations of the First Chamber.[4] Worst of all was the news that the Elmina 'envoy', the mulatto shopkeeper David Mills Graves, was likely to arrive before the Chamber debated the treaty of cession. Gericke was convinced that Graves's mission was the result of political intrigues in Holland, and that it might have a very unfavourable influence upon the debate.[5] All this gave rise to a new series of recriminations between The Hague and London, the former claiming that the authorities at Cape Coast gave the Elminas only too much reason to believe that they would be at the mercy of the Fantes after the cession, the latter retorting by demanding the removal of Akyeampon, to whose incitement, it was said, much of the unrest was due.

Graves arrived at The Hague on 8 January, bearing petitions against the cession from the chiefs and elders of Elmina and other parts of the Dutch settlements, and immediately applied for an audience of the king. His arrival was greeted by the opponents of cession with a renewed press campaign against the treaty. In addition to their familiar arguments, they were able to make use of fresh news from the Coast, presumably obtained from Graves himself. Most effective of all was the report that there was a movement

---

[1] Minutes of meetings of Colonial Council (copies), 15 and 18 Nov. 1871, Afst. IV; ibid., Ferguson to officials (copy), 16 Nov. 1871; ibid., Ferguson to M. K. (copy), 22 Nov. 1871; same to same (copy), 25 Nov. 1871, Afst. V; Ferguson to Karikari, 28 Nov. 1871, '1874 Report', App. IIIk.

[2] Ferguson to M. K. (copy), 2 Jan. 1872, Afst. IV.

[3] Ibid., same to same (copy), 9 Dec. 1871.

[4] M. K. to M. B. Z., 16 Dec, 1871, Afst. V; Harris to Granville, 21 Dec. 1871, F.O. 37/492.

[5] Harris to Granville, 1, 5 and 6 Jan. 1872, F.O. 37/500.

amongst the Fantes to throw off British protection, especially when this was coupled with the speech alleged to have been made by Acting Admistrator Salmon to the leaders of the self-appointed Fante 'government':

Is that the thanks to Queen Victoria for the trouble she has taken to get Elmina and the other Dutch possessions for you Fantees; and now she has got Elmina for you, you are going to establish a self-government.

Why, it was asked, should the Elminas be forced to accept something that the Fantes were trying to get rid of? And was it not now evident that Britain intended to hand Elmina over to the Fantes?[1] At Gericke's urgent request Harris telegraphed his government asking for an immediate contradiction of these reports, which were in fact a somewhat garbled version of the attempt to transform the Fante Confederation from an alliance against Elmina into an organ of self-government. In reply he received the following telegram:

No statement has reached Her Majesty's Government that the Fantees have declared any wish to throw off our protection.

This denial, which Harris forthwith communicated to Gericke in a rather more emphatic form,[2] was ingenious rather than ingenuous. Perhaps technically correct, it is not easily to be reconciled with the remark by Kimberley in a dispatch of 16 January that

there is hardly room for question that some of the Articles in the Constitution of the Confederation were practically inconsistent with the jurisdiction of the British Government in the protected territory.[3]

But it had arrived opportunely for use in the States-General, although subsequent revelations of its dubious accuracy were to cause Gericke some embarrassment.[4]

[1] King, etc., of Elmina to States-General (copy), 10 Dec. 1871, F.O. 37/500; Graves to M. B. Z. and M. K., 11 Jan. 1872, Hague, Afst. IV; *Dagblad*, 12 Jan. 1872; Harris to Granville, 15 Jan. 1872, F.O. 37/500; J. E. Banck, *Alea Jacta Est. Een Laatste woord aan de Leden van de eerste kamer der Staten Generaal* ('s-Gravenhage, 1872) (reference by courtesy of Miss Mollema).
[2] Harris to Granville, 14 and 15 Jan. 1872, F.O. 37/500; Harris to M. B. Z., 15 Jan. 1872, Afst. V.
[3] Quoted by Claridge, op. cit., i, p. 620.
[4] Note by M. B. Z., n.d. (c. 25 Jan. 1872), Afst. V; ibid., Harris to M. B. Z., 25 Jan. 1872; *Hand. S.G.*, 1871-2, II, pp. 887-97.

The debate on the bill to approve the Gold Coast treaty was
opened in the First Chamber on 15 January. In a last effort to
defeat the bill the opponents of cession relied largely on an exposition of the plight of the Elminas, whose various petitions during the
previous year were read in the course of the debate. This line of
attack was not without its effect, but seems to have been largely
nullified by the continued existence of the now notorious 'link'. One
member admitted with admirable candour that he had been turned
against the cession by the Elmina addresses, but would nevertheless
still vote in favour of it for the sake of the Sumatra convention.
Several members made bitter attacks on Britain, accusing her of
taking advantage of Holland's difficulties and suggesting that the
West Indian islands and Surinam would soon go the way of the
Gold Coast. In reply the ministers praised the conduct of Britain
throughout the negotiations, questioned the professed 'loyalty' of the
Elminas, emphasized the importance of the 'link' and, on the authority of the British Government, denied the reports that were circulating about Salmon and the Fante Confederation. During this three-
day debate Graves sat in a prominent place in the gallery, but his
presence, according to Harris, was not altogether helpful to the opponents of the treaty:

Towards the end of the debate a report reached the Chamber that if
the Minority should be considerable, a demonstration in the Street would
take place on behalf of the Elmina envoy. The conservative instincts of
the First Chamber were aroused and several members who had intended
to oppose the Treaty voted in support of the Government.

The bill was duly carried in the evening of 18 January by 29 votes
to 6, and on the following day the other two treaties were approved
without opposition. The 'link' between the treaties had undoubtedly
played its part in getting the Gold Coast treaty through the Chamber
despite the almost unanimous opposition of the press. In this, and in
this alone, can one perhaps see some slight justification for the other
wise erroneous picture of the treaty as one side of an Anglo-Dutch
colonial bargain.[1]

In Harris's opinion it had been largely the 'tact and ability' of

[1] Ibid., I, pp. 179–220; Harris to Granville, 18 Jan. 1872, F.O. 37/500.

Gericke which had defeated the last 'desperate effort' of the treaty's opponents. Gericke, he added, was

> very amiable and pleasant to do business with, but a desperate fidget and liable to fits of despondency which at times have made my task not a light one.

But the worries of the past were over. The vote of the Chamber, according to Harris, would put an end to all machinations in Holland against the cession, since the Dutch, 'however tenacious their opposition to measures . . . always respect the decision of their Parliament'.[1] In making this assertion the envoy was a little too sanguine. The clamour against the treaty in the press—aptly enough described as *la moutarde après dîner* by 'one of the newspapers most violent hitherto in opposition'—did not die out, nor had the treaty's critics (prominent amongst whom was the Rotterdam merchant Muller) wholly given up hope of reviving the king's celebrated scruples about the surrender of Dutch territory and thus of preventing ratification. True, Graves, whom van Bosse described as their 'unwitting tool', met with little success in this direction at his private audience, when the king received him kindly enough, but did not make mention of the purpose of his mission; but it was arguable that Graves had forfeited the royal sympathy by his threats of violent resistance to the cession, as by an over-ingenious attempt to enlist the support of the German Emperor. Gericke, fully conscious of the delicacy of the situation, was extremely anxious that no further complications should arise on the Coast which might provide ammunition for the opposition at home. Particularly distasteful was the prospect of having to use force at the time of the cession. Nagtglas was confident that no actual exercise of force would be required, provided that 'a great show of force' was made, but in this he was more optimistic than the Dutch ministers, who seem to have feared that they would be left to pull the British chestnuts out of the fire—an apprehension that can only have been increased by indications that in London enthusiasm for the cession was once more on the wane.

---

[1] Harris to Granville, as in preceding note; same to same (private), 19 Jan. 1872, Hague, P.R.O. 30/29/103. Harris himself was made K.C.B. later in the year for his part in concluding the three colonial treaties.

Kimberley, for example, was declaring that he would gladly have seen the British settlements handed over to the Dutch.[1]

There is little doubt that this note of caution once more being sounded in London was the result of the publicity given in Holland to the threats and protestations of the Elminas. The *Pall Mall Gazette* commented that if the Elminas were as good as their word it would be impossible to execute the treaty, so that

the best course for the Dutch to pursue with the little kingdom would be either to levy a tax upon it, as the inhabitants suggest, or give it up altogether to the King.[2]

The *Daily News* gave its sympathy to

a population of 120,000 [*sic*], who have not been consulted in the matter, and who have manifested a strong indisposition to being transferred like so many head of cattle or serfs bound to the soil.[3]

Even *The Times* could find little to say for 'buying out the Dutch',[4] and in the Commons the advocates of non-extension were once more stirred to life.[5] In this atmosphere the ministers had to walk carefully. 'It would be most foolish to *force* the Treaty on the Elminas,' wrote Kimberley to Granville, 'but Sir A. Kennedy thinks by prudent management the transfer may be effected quietly.'[6] Kennedy was in London, *en route* for his new post in Hong Kong, and conferring with Pope Hennessy, who was due to succeed him at Sierra Leone and see to the execution of the treaty; but Kimberley was now too wary to stake everything on his assurances. Fearing as he did that 'the Treaty may meet with serious opposition from the Elminas', he was determined 'to avoid the disastrous mistakes of the Dutch

---

[1] Harris to Granville, 18, 20 and 24 Jan., 1 Feb. 1872, F.O. 37/500; ibid., M. B. Z. to Harris (notes—copies), n.d. (enc. in letters of 21 Jan. and 1 Feb. 1872); M. K. to M. B. Z., n.d. (Jan.), Kol. 1872; P. Hennessy to Herbert (private), 28 Jan. 1872, Hague, Kimberley Papers, PC/A/15; same to same (private), 29 Jan. 1872, Hague, C.O. 96/95; M. K. to M. B. Z., 29 Jan. 1872, Afst. V; P. Hennessy to Kimberley (private), 31 Jan. 1872, Hague, Kimberley Papers, PC/A/15; van Bijlandt to M. B. Z., 2 Feb. 1872, London, Afst. V; Harris to Granville (private), 2 Feb. 1872, Hague, P.R.O. 30/29/103; *The Times*, 6 Feb. 1872 (report from The Hague).

[2] Quoted in *The Times*, 27 Jan. 1872.

[3] 7 February 1872: quoted in *Hoofdartikelen van wijlen Professor Vreede, overgedrukt uit het Utrechtsche Dagblad, 1869–1880* (Leiden, 1906), pp. 117–19.

[4] *The Times*, 6 Feb. 1872 (leader).

[5] *Hansard*, 3rd ser., ccix, cols. 319–29.

[6] Kimberley to Granville (private), 7 Feb. 1872, P.R.O. 30/29/55.

. . . in 1868'.[1] Pope Hennessy, too, who had spent some days at The Hague conferring with Harris, Nagtglas and the Dutch ministers, stressed the need for caution. The Elmina opposition, he thought, was not entirely spontaneous:

the King of Elmina & the natives proper have been made use of by certain local officials at Elmina who imagined the Cape Coast officials were to be put over them, & by certain Dutch traders who supposed their rivals at Cape Coast would get opportunities of cutting them out of business.

However, in view of the state of opinion in Holland he was not disposed to execute the treaty until he 'received from the King & people of Elmina—or the more influential portion of them—an actual invitation to complete the transfer'.[2]

These reservations were reflected in the instructions given to Pope Hennessy on 12 February. According to these, after his arrival at Cape Coast he was to ascertain, in conjunction with Ferguson, whether the transfer was likely to lead to open violence on the part of the Elminas, who were, moreover, to be 'distinctly told that they will not be required to place themselves under British protection against their will'. On no account was force to be used to effect the transfer, which should not be proceeded with if resistance seemed likely. 'The objects', Kimberley declared,

which Her Majesty's Government have throughout had in view in negotiating this treaty are not the acquisition of territory, or the extension of British power, but the maintenance of tranquillity, and the promotion of peaceful commerce on the coast; and nothing could be further from their wish than that a treaty made with these objects should be carried into effect by violent measures.[3]

The lessons of 1868 had not, after all, been wholly lost on the Colonial Office.

On 20 January the bill for approving the Gold Coast treaty

---

[1] Min. by Kimberley of 29 Jan. 1872, attached to draft instructions to Pope Hennessy of 12 Feb. 1872, C.O. 96/95.
[2] P. Hennessy to Kimberley (private—two letters), 31 Jan. 1872, Hague, Kimberley Papers, PC/A/15.
[3] Kimberley to P. Hennessy, 12 Feb. 1872, House of Commons, *Return to an address . . . dated 5 May 1873* (P.P. 1873, xlix (266)), pp. 6–7.

received the royal assent. Every precaution was taken to prevent this news travelling to Elmina, and, indeed, it seems to have been several days before it became known in Holland. This delay encouraged the opponents of cession to make one more appeal to the king, this time in the form of a petition organized by the energetic Professor Vreede of Utrecht. The petitioners claimed that Graves's mission had revealed that several earlier protests and addresses from Elmina had been deliberately withheld from the Council of State and the Second Chamber during their deliberations on the cession. Consequently, it was argued, the whole question must be referred back to those bodies. Gericke and van Bosse defended themselves against these charges in a letter to the king of 1 February, which they concluded by proposing that the petitioners be told that, since the bill had already become law, no response could be given to their petition. A reply in this vein was issued on 8 February, by which time the royal approval of the bill had in any case become public knowledge.[1]

Undeterred, Professor Vreede continued, in the leading articles of the *Utrechtsche Dagblad*, to demand an inquiry into the conduct of the ministry and also of Nagtglas, by this time the *bête noire* of the treaty's critics. So long as the treaty, though approved, had not been formally ratified, there was always the faint hope of a last-minute royal repentance to keep the critics active. Only when they succeeded in obtaining a discussion of the whole matter in the Second Chamber, on 9 March, did they learn the closely-guarded secret that ratification of all three colonial treaties, followed by the exchange of ratifications with Britain, had taken place some three weeks earlier, on 17 February. No amount of angry oratory would now obscure the fact that the last prospect of obstructing the treaty had vanished. The association of the Netherlands with the Gold Coast was coming to an end after close on three centuries, and Africa was passing out of Dutch history.[2]

[1] M. K. to Ferguson (copy), 22 Jan. 1872, Afst. V; ibid., M. B. Z. and M. K. to king (copy), 1 Feb. 1872; ibid., Directeur v.h. Kabinet des Konings to M. B. Z. and M. K., 5 Feb. 1872; *Hoofdartikelen van wijlen Professor Vreede* . . ., pp. 104–19.
[2] M. B. Z. to M. K., 17 Feb. 1872, Kol. 22. II. 1872. Kab. Litt. G. 3/no. 7; Harris to Granville, 17 Feb. and 11 March 1872, F.O. 37/500; M. B. Z. to envoy in London (draft), 7 March 1872, Afst. V; *Hoofdartikelen van wijlen Professor Vreede* . . . , pp. 120–5.

I

3

Only the prospect of serious trouble with the Elminas could now prevent the execution of the treaty, provided of course that the long-awaited removal of Akyeampon could be effected. As soon as ratifications were exchanged, both Ferguson and Pope Hennessy were given discretionary powers to carry out the cession as and when they thought fit.[1] At the end of February the commander of the warship *Admiraal van Wassenaer*, due to sail to the Coast to assist with the transfer, was appointed Special Commissioner for carrying out the cession; but Ferguson was still authorized to go ahead without waiting for the *Wassenaer* if conditions seemed favourable.[2] In fact the only real limit upon his discretion was an injunction not to carry out a *partial* cession; as the responsible Dutch ministers explained to the king, they did not want the British taking over those peoples who welcomed them and refusing those who did not.[3]

Ferguson had meanwhile been making secret preparations. An inventory had been made of the stores to be handed over, surplus cash had been transferred to the Dutch warship *Citadel van Antwerpen*, and the archives were ready for shipping.[4] Most important of all, Ferguson's deep pessimism about the prospects of a peaceful cession was beginning to give way to a cautious optimism.[5] The news of the passage of the treaty through the First Chamber, brought back by Graves on 14 February, had caused great excitement in Elmina,[6] and now that cession seemed imminent a deep split on the question of resisting it by force was revealed amongst the inhabitants. On 24 and 25 February a majority of the 'quarters' decided not to oppose the exchange of flags, and after long discussions, in which Akyeampon tried to inflame feeling against the cession, they resolved no

[1] Kimberley to P. Hennessy, 21 Feb. 1872, P.P. 1873, xlix (266), p. 11; M. K. to Ferguson (secret), 22 Feb. 1872, Hague, G. 730.
[2] Harris to Granville, 29 Feb. 1872, Hague, F.O. 37/500; M. K. to Ferguson (secret), 10 March 1872, Fabius, op. cit., pp. 24-6.
[3] M. B. Z., M. K. and Minister of Marine to king (secret), 27 Feb. 1872, Afst. V.
[4] They were not in fact dispatched until June 1873; Bill of lading dated Elmina, 23 June 1873, N. C. Elmina 1.
[5] Ferguson to M. K. (v. secret—copy), 20 Feb. 1872, Elmina, Afst. V. For a detailed study of the military and naval aspects of the preparations for and execution of the cession see Fabius, op. cit., pp. 17-29.
[6] Except where some specific reference is given, the authority for the remainder of this paragraph and for the next is the '1874 Report', section II.

longer to recognize the authority of their king, who was wedded
to the policy of resistance. There was thus now a 'peace party', consisting of five of the quarters, together with the mulattoes, ranged
against the king, the remaining three quarters, and Akyeampon and
his followers. This 'resistance party', however, gave little evidence
of solidarity. On 4 March, at a meeting with Ferguson, *all* the
quarters voted for the removal of Akyeampon. Not even the king
showed any sympathy with the Ashanti leader, who, when he objected to leaving, was detained in the castle and promptly charged
with seditious activities. In Ferguson's opinion the spirit of resistance
was broken. He assured Ussher 'that the treaty will have a peaceable
execution, and the transfer will take place without violence or
trouble', adding that 'not a better than the present moment, could
be chosen to carry the treaty with [*sic*] effect'.[1]

This was a little too fast for Ussher, much as he sympathized with
Ferguson's urgency.[2] For one thing, he was not authorized to carry
out the cession, and Pope Hennessy, who was, was still on his way
from England via Sierra Leone. For another there was the continued
presence in Elmina of Akyeampon, harmless though Ferguson might
declare him now to be. London remained insistent that he *must* be
removed before the transfer could take place.[3] But the stay of that
turbulent ambassador on the Coast was drawing to an end. Confident of the acquiescence of the Elminas, and determined not to lose
this opportunity of carrying out the treaty, Ferguson decided to rid
himself of his troublesome guest. On 22 March Akyeampon was
tried and found guilty of sedition. Three days later a sentence of
banishment was promulgated and he and some of his followers were
put on board the warships *Citadel van Antwerpen* and *Het Loo*
without resistance. On the following day, 26 March, the *Loo*
sailed westwards to the abandoned French post of Assini, where
Akyeampon and his retinue were put on shore with a supply of pro-
visions.

Two days later Pope Hennessy, apprised by both Ferguson and
Ussher that the time was ripe, set sail from Freetown for Cape

[1] Ferguson to Ussher (confidential—copy), 5 March 1872, Elmina, C.O. 96/92.
[2] Ussher to Ferguson (confidential), 6 March 1872, Cape Coast, G. 730.
[3] Granville to Harris, 24 Feb. 1872, F.O. 238/169.

Coast,[1] where he arrived on 2 April. The stage at last was set, and the actors in their places.

On 4 April Pope Hennessy went to Elmina at Ferguson's invitation, and speedily satisfied himself (as his instructions required him to do) that the transfer was not likely to lead to violence. He had a long conference which was attended not only by the heads of the Elmina quarters, but by kings and chiefs from other parts of the Dutch settlements. To this audience he gave a general assurance that Her Majesty's favour and protection would be extended as fully to them as to the Fantes, as well as particular undertakings that Elmina town would continue to enjoy its virtual autonomy in municipal affairs, and that the Dutch policy of taking educated natives into government service would be continued. The 'satisfaction' expressed by the Elminas at this conference convinced Pope Hennessy of their goodwill, and he there and then concerted details with Ferguson of the transfer, which, they agreed, should take place in two days time, on 6 April. So confident was Pope Hennessy that there would be no trouble that he decided that the troops from Cape Coast who were to garrison the castle should not land at Elmina until the actual ceremony of cession was completed.[2]

This confidence was amply justified by the events of 6 April. The transfer of authority was carried out in public, with all due ceremony, and without a single untoward incident. The prophets of disaster were seemingly confounded. From the moment that Pope Hennessy, Ussher and their suites landed, to be greeted by Ferguson and the leading inhabitants of Elmina (not excepting David Mills Graves), to the drinking of healths in 'Champagne and Sparkling Moselle' which followed the hoisting of the English flag over the Castle, everything went smoothly. At Ferguson's request all the Elmina quarters, as well as representatives of the peoples of Shama, Sekondi and other settlements, rose in turn in the crowded 'palaver hall' and publicly announced their acquiescence in the cession. Even the King of Elmina, who now commanded the allegiance of only two of the quarters, witnessed the ceremonies without giving any

---

[1] P. Hennessy to Kimberley, 18 and 28 March, 1872, Sierra Leone, P.P. 1873, xlix (266), pp. 15–16.
[2] Ibid., p. 19, same to same, 4 April 1872, Cape Coast.

sign of protest. Among the 'mob', who were only with great diffi-culty prevented from 'filling the Castle to overflowing', feeling ap-peared to be mixed, but far from inflammatory. 'We heard', re-ported the correspondent of the *West African Herald* (the sole repre-sentative of the press at this solemn occasion)

a good deal of tall talk, and considerable abuse of the Dutch, much defiance of the Fantees, great admiration expressed at the appearance of the English Marines, delight at the Band, and wonder not unmixed with some awe at the little steam launch.[1]

The Dutch Gold Coast had thus passed to Britain, though the actual cession of the other settlements—Axim, Dixcove, Butri, Sekondi and Shama—was not completed (again without a hitch) until a few days later.[2] There now remained only the valuation by commissioners (as provided for in Article III of the treaty) of the stores and fixtures which had been handed over. This resulted some months later in the agreement of a sum of £3,790 1s. 6½d., which was paid to the Dutch Government (*plus* interest of 5 per cent. cal-culated from 5 April 1872) on 1 January 1873 by the Crown Agents acting for the Gold Coast authorities. In return for this payment Britain secured almost all the movable and immovable possessions of the former Dutch settlements. Only in the case of the archives (the transfer of which to Britain de Waal had vetoed in 1870 on the grounds that they contained too much that was not fit for foreign eyes) and of a few items of historical interest, such as the so-called baton of de Ruyter, did the Dutch exercise the option of retention which Article III had given them.[3]

The first days of British rule in Elmina were not entirely without incident. On the evening of the 6th, and also a few days later, there were fights in the town between the young men of Quarters Five and Seven, said to have been caused by the 'deposition' of the king.

---

[1] *West African Herald*, Cape Coast, 6 April 1872 (actually published 8 April); '1874 Report', section II; P. Hennessy to Kimberley (with enclosures), 6 April 1872, Elmina. P.P. 1873, xlix (266), pp. 22–30. The 'little steam launch' was the colonial steamer *Nellie*, which had brought Ussher from Cape Coast.

[2] '1874 Report', section II; P. Hennessy to Kimberley (with enclosures), 10 April 1872, Elmina, P.P. 1873, xlix (266), pp. 33–5.

[3] '1874 Report', section III; C.O. to F.O., 30 Nov. 1872, P.P. 1873, xlix (266), p. 175; Mollema, op. cit., p. 229, n.

The second of these fights was broken up by the Hausa police, the first by the onset of a violent storm which, according to the *West African Herald*, 'caused the angry partizans of the English and the Ashantees to "skedaddle pretty sudden"!'[1] More serious was a riot on 26 April in which a Dutch officer, left behind to deal with Dutch obligations and interests until the arrival of a permanent consular agent, was fatally injured. It was, however, never clearly established that the outrage, any more than the quarter fights, had any direct connexion with the cession, even if, as was far from certain, the unfortunate officer had been the intended and not merely the accidental victim of the riot.[2] On the whole, despite these upsets, the transfer could still be considered a success. When, on 25 June, Gladstone told the Commons that

Her Majesty's Government would not annex any territory, great or small, without the well-understood and expressed wish of the people to be annexed, freely and generously expressed, and authenticated by the best means the case could afford,[3]

no voice was raised to ask if the case of Elmina did not demonstrate the difficulty of applying such standards to West African conditions. Only under the impact of later events were such doubts to arise.

---

[1] '1874 Report', section II; *West African Herald*, 6 April 1872.
[2] See the depositions, etc., printed in P.P. 1873, xlix (266), pp. 38 *et sqq.*, and also the '1874 Report', section II.
[3] *Hansard*, 3rd ser., ccxii, cols. 192–219 (cited in Knaplund, op. cit., p. 133).

6

AN END AND A BEGINNING

I

WITH the successful completion of the transfer, *The Times*, ever pliable, could welcome the acquisition of our 'new colony', which, it declared, was 'likely to become the chief place on the coast of Guinea'.[1] To anyone familiar with present-day Elmina this brave prophecy will afford some wry amusement. Elmina is now little more than a picturesque backwater, bypassed literally by the coast road and figuratively by the process of spectacular growth and change that is transforming Accra, Sekondi-Takoradi and Kumasi into modern cities.[2] In one respect only does its appearance seem to have undergone substantial change since 1872: the older part of the town, which adjoined the castle walls, has completely disappeared. The warnings of the treaty's critics had not, in fact, been groundless; in January 1873 the Ashantis invaded the protectorate, and in June the British authorities found it necessary to bombard and raze the 'king's quarter' at Elmina in order to prevent a pro-Ashanti rising there. From that time forward Elmina, distrusted and neglected, ceased to have much importance in the life of the Coast. It is not surprising that to this day the memory of Dutch rule as a sort of golden age is conserved in Elmina, where the saying 'A Dutch ship has gone past Elmina' is applied, according to an Elminian author, 'to any project the character of which seems futile or irretrievable by human effort'.[3]

In 1874, following Wolseley's expedition to Kumasi, the King of Ashanti finally renounced his claim to Elmina, and the British

---

[1] *The Times*, 9 May 1872.
[2] This was written soon after Ghana obtained her independence. Since then work has been put in hand to transform Elmina into an up-to-date fishing harbour.
[3] J. S. Wartemburg, op. cit., p. 59.

Government decided to constitute the settlements into a Crown Colony and to regularize and formalize its jurisdiction in the 'protectorate', with the avowed aim of 'exercising an effective control'. It is not the purpose of this final chapter to describe in detail these developments of 1872–4, but rather to indicate their importance for the future of the Gold Coast and above all to demonstrate the links that bound them to the cession of the Dutch settlements.

2

On 15 July 1872 Henry Plange returned to Kumasi, this time as the agent of both Dutch and British, bearing gifts from the King of the Netherlands and from the British Government, together with a promise from Pope Hennessy that the annual 'stipend' hitherto paid by the Dutch would not be merely continued but doubled. It was Plange's duty also to announce the completion of the cession to the king, to which the latter replied that, though

far from being agreeable to him however as it is deemed advisable by both governments . . . he need not find fault therewith, beside he is given to understand from the despatches under reply that the stipend formerly paid to him by the Dutch Government annually will be doubled by the English Government. . . .

One of the chiefs present at this interview opined that the cession was to provide a dowry for Queen Victoria, 'owing that she is a wife of His Majesty King William, having not enough money to pay the dowry as usual custom . . .'[1]

At a private interview some three weeks later the king once more protested his 'very friendly feelings' for the British Government,[2] and on 21 September Plange reported that

---

[1] Plange to (Le Jeune), 2 Aug. 1872, Kumasi, N.C. Elmina 1; Plange to (Le Jeune?), 6 March 1874, Elmina, '1874 Report', App. Ij. Ramseyer and Kühne (op. cit., p. 176) say that 'the interpreter Nantschi explained, "The king of Holland is queen Victoria's husband; how is it he sells his possessions to his wife?" ' This audience took place on 25 July according to Plange's report, 29 July according to his recollections in 1874, and 20 July according to the missionaries.

[2] He also gave another demonstration of the Ashanti inability to comprehend the voluntary cession of territory. Was there, he asked, 'any debt due by the Dutch Government to the English Government which caused His Majesty the King of Holland to transfer his forts on the coast to the English?' With a rare access of diplomatic adroitness Plange replied, 'I am too young to answer for such a question' (Plange to (Le Jeune?), 6 March 1874, ut supra).

His Majesty is very cross with the Elminas about the expulsion of Akyeampon, but as far as the cession of the Dutch possessions to the English is concerned, he has no objection. . . .[1]

But if Plange was deceived the missionaries Ramseyer and Kühne were not. They had observed that 'the surrendering of Elmina occasioned much vexation in the palace', and they did not doubt that war was being prepared for underhand. Their explanation of events is well worth considering in detail, the more so in that it differs somewhat from what is to be found in the parliamentary apologies of Knatchbull-Hugessen. According to the missionaries the Ashantis had never considered the war of 1863-4 as ended. The avowed cause of this war was the refusal of the British authorities to deliver up to Ashanti the runaway captain Gyani, and the failure of the abortive campaign of 1863-4 to enforce this demand still rankled at Kumasi. Moreover, events since 1864 had made some sort of 'showdown' with the British seem more and more necessary. The 'exchange' of 1868, it is true, had 'caused great rejoicing in Coomassie' because their former subjects the Denkyiras had thus passed to 'the dependency of the lenient old ally of Ashantee'. The outcome of the exchange, however, was anything but welcome to the Ashantis, with their old enemies the Fantes combining with their ex-subjects of the 'protectorate' to drive their Dutch allies and their Elmina 'brethren' into the sea. Unless Ashanti was to suffer a shattering blow to her power and prestige she must deal with her enemies *and* their British 'protectors' once and for all.[2]

In this sense, then, there may have been something more than a politician's evasion in Knatchbull-Hugessen's description of the war of 1873-4 as inevitable.[3] We cannot, however, *know* that an Ashanti war would have come without the cession, while Ramseyer and Kühne themselves make it clear that the latter, if not the ultimate cause of the war, was certainly its occasion. As they point out, the Ashantis held back from a direct attack on the protectorate even when the Elminas besought them to come to their aid. The most they would do for their 'blood relations' was to send the small force

---

[1] Plange to Le Jeune, 21 Sept. 1872, Kumasi, '1874 Report', App. IIIm.
[2] Ramseyer and Kühne, op. cit., pp. 170, 201-5.
[3] *Hansard*, 3rd ser., ccxiii, cols. 1592-1663.

under Akyeampon, which was to watch for a favourable opportunity and 'prepare an attack on the British power'. They seem to have assumed that the army under Adu Boffo, which invaded Krepe in 1869, could afterwards attack the protectorate. But these plans went awry: Akyeampon's activities were curtailed by Nagtglas and his successors, and Adu Boffo was forced by heavy losses to return to Kumasi in September 1871. There was for the moment no means of preventing the cession of the Dutch settlements, so the policy of dis-simulation (already adopted, as we have seen, in a vain attempt to gain the outstanding *kostgeld*)[1] was continued for a little longer, and 'a hint from Coomassie was . . . sent to the Elmina chief to wait quietly'. But behind the protestations of friendliness and of acqui-escence war was being actively prepared.[2] Why had the Ashantis at last resolved upon the direct challenge to Britain which they had put off for so long? Let us answer this question with the missionaries' own words:

War . . . was being unceasingly desired, as the surrender of Elmina could not by any means be prevented . . . the Ashantees fully believed Elmina belonged to them, though the king wrote (through Prince Ansa) that the surrender of the fort was a grief to him, but that he would forget it.[3] To measure themselves for once with the white man was the secret desire of every Ashantee chief. That the critical hour had arrived they all acknowledged, when the news came of the surrender of Elmina. They could not allow the kingdom to be broken up bit by bit, as they considered.[4]

We can therefore say, with Ellis, who adopted the missionaries' ver-sion of events, that 'the war was due to the action of the Government in having taken possession of Elmina'.[5] It can certainly be regarded

---

[1] See above, pp. 106–7.

[2] Aided by Pope Hennessy's ill-judged though well-meant action in lifting the em-bargo on the export of munitions to Ashanti (Ellis, op. cit., pp. 276–7). It is not difficult to read a sinister significance into the question put to Plange at the end of his audience in July 1872: 'they asked if there are some guns fixed for the King and where are they?' (Plange to (Le Jeune?), 6 March 1874, *ut supra*). One is tempted, too, to think that not only the king's eagerness for the *kostgeld* but also the growth of his interest in the cash value of the missionaries were stimulated by the need for arms.

[3] This presumably must refer to a message brought down by Ansah on his return from his second visit to Kumasi (Jan.–March 1872), and is in line with the king's remarks to Plange in July (see above, p. 122).

[4] Ramseyer and Kühne, op. cit., pp. 203–5.

[5] Ellis, op. cit., p. 288.

as a continuation of the war of 1863, but, as Claridge (who in turn follows Ellis) says, the transfer 'brought matters to an immediate head and it must be regarded as the actual cause of the resumption of hostilities'.[1]

Up to the beginning of December 1872 the Ashantis played out the comedy of dissimulation for the benefit not only of Plange, but of any who, like the missionaries or the Fantes resident in Kumasi, might be expected to send reports to the Coast. When their preparations were complete, however, 'the mask was thrown off', as the missionaries put it. Not only their intentions but also their motives were made clear. 'War, war against the Coast' was the cry,[2] and the newly-arrived British messenger Dawson was not deceived by the king's declaration that he wanted war with neither white men nor Fantes, but only with Denkyiras, Asins and Akims, 'who are his own slaves and who have turned to rob him so greedily he will not allow'. Dawson was convinced that this was a 'disguise' after hearing the king enumerate his grievances at a private interview on 17 December. The burden of Karikari's complaint was that Elmina Castle, 'in which', he said with great stress, 'I eat' (referring, according to Dawson, to the payment of stipend), had been 'taken' and given to Kwaku Fram, King of Denkyira. He did not hesitate now to speak of 'my Elmina Fort', reviving the claim that it had been taken from the Denkyiras. He paid little attention to Dawson's denial that the castle had been or would be delivered to Kwaku Fram, and when the messenger pointed out that Britain had undertaken to continue, and, indeed, to double the stipend, he answered 'And what became of what was due before?'[3]

In a letter of 20 March 1873 to Colonel Harley, now Governor-in-Chief, Karikari dispelled any remaining doubt as to his position. 'He being the grandson of Osei Tutu,' he declared, 'he owns the Elminas to be his relatives'; and, consequently, the fort at Elmina and its dependencies were 'his'. 'The only thing or way to appease him' was for the British to restore the Denkyiras, Akims and Asins 'back to

[1] Claridge, op. cit., ii, pp. 3-4.
[2] Ramseyer and Kühne, op. cit., pp. 204-5.
[3] Dawson to Harley, 19 Dec. 1872, Kumasi, Parliamentary Papers, *Further Correspondence respecting the Ashantee Invasion* . . . [=P.P. 1873, xlix [C. 819]], pp. 4-7.

their former position as his subjects' *and* to restore 'the Elmina fort and people back in the same manner as they were before. . . '.[1] This was clear enough, even if it was bound up, as the king's complaints to Dawson had also been, with a farrago of accusations against Plange, the alleged bearer of the 'news' that Elmina Castle had been 'given' to the Denkyiras.[2] Some of these accusations *may* have been true,[3] but it is difficult to see Plange as 'the causer of the existing irritation', as Karikari represented him. The missionaries were convinced 'that Mr. Plange was but the pretended cause of the war', while Dawson assured Harley 'that this invasion has purely arisen from the cession of the Elmina Fort and its dependencies. . . '.[4] Even if Plange were guilty of the grossest mis-statement, this had little bearing on the central fact of the situation, namely the king's reassertion of the claim that Elmina was his 'by right', and his consequent and explicit refusal to accept the cession.

There was no doubt amongst the Elminas themselves that the object of the Ashanti invasion was to undo the events of 1872. As early as February 1873 the Dutch consul Le Jeune reported that many of the Elminas sympathized with the Ashantis, believing that an Ashanti victory would mean the return of the Dutch flag to Elmina. Some, indeed, thought that the return of the Dutch was imminent and were on the look-out for a Dutch warship.[5] In the

---

[1] Ibid., p. 3, Karikari to Harley, 20 March 1873, Kumasi.

[2] Ibid., pp. 4–7, Dawson to Harley, 19 Dec. 1872, Kumasi; Plange to (Le Jeune?), 6 March 1874, *ut supra*.

[3] There is a good deal to be said for the opinion of a one-time Administrator of the Gold Coast that 'the English speaking natives that were available as messengers were so untrustworthy or open to be influenced that to engage almost any of them in however humble a capacity was, I may say, not without danger; you rarely got your message honestly conveyed or the answer faithfully returned' (Salmon to C.O., 17 Dec. 1873, Geneva, Parliamentary Papers, *Further Correspondence respecting the Ashantee Invasion (No. 4)* [=P.P. 1874, xlvi [C. 893]], pp. 25–9). On the other hand, the discrediting of messengers for reasons of policy was by now a well-worn Ashanti technique. Ansah had been accused of misrepresentation; later in 1871 Salmon had lapped up a story (apparently from Ashanti sources) that the Dutch recruiting agent de Heer had 'grossly misinterpreted' a letter from Ussher 'and thereby caused most of the subsequent troubles between the Fantees, Elminas and Ashantee' (Salmon to Le Jeune (copy), 7 Nov. 1871, Cape Coast, Afst. V). Now it was Plange's turn to serve first as a pretext for war and then as a scapegoat when retribution seemed near.

[4] Dawson to Harley, 21 March 1873, Kumasi, P.P. 1873, xlix [C. 819], pp. 3–4; Ramseyer and Kühne, op. cit., p. 201.

[5] Le Jeune to M. B. Z. (secret), 26 Feb. 1873, Elmina, Afst. V. According to Harley it was difficult to convince the Elminas that the Dutch had gone for good. For this reason he was anxious to get rid of Le Jeune and his deputy Hamel. It was,

event the invasion brought to a head the division between those former 'Dutch' natives who were willing to throw in their lot with the British and the King of Elmina's 'resistance party'. At a 'palaver' in the castle on 12 March the king, who, as he had informed Karikari, had been 'only waiting on him as he had promised before making any movements',[1] at last laid aside all pretence. Asked to take an oath of allegiance he struck the table with his fist and declared

I am not afraid of your power. You may hang me if you like. I will not sign any paper. Myself and some of the people of Elmina have taken fetish oath to oppose the English Government coming to Elmina, and we have not broken that oath yet.[2]

The invasion was in fact the signal for the 'king's party' to come into the open, and the war that followed saw Elminas actively engaged on both sides.

Among the Fantes, too, it seems to have been accepted that it was the cession that had precipitated the war. The King of Abrah (near Cape Coast) stated that

the causes and purposes of these inroads of the Ashantis are the cession of the Elmina fort, and the Elminas having become the British subjects; because (from what we have repeatedly heard) the king of Ashanti says, that from the time immemorial his ancestors ate and drank at Elmina— *i.e.* he gets all his wants from there[3]—and that the fort is theirs; therefore he will come and take it by force of arms.[4]

3

That the cession was the occasion of the Ashanti War is a proposition for which the weight of evidence is indeed overwhelming. The

---

he said, 'desirable to remove all traces of the former occupation . . . and to let the people understand that the Dutch have been for all purposes and in every sense replaced by Her Majesty's Officers' (Harley to Kimberley (confidential), 16 May 1873, Cape Coast, C.O. 96/99).

[1] Dawson to Harley, 14 April 1873, Cape Coast, Parliamentary Papers, *Further Papers relating to the Ashantee Invasion (No. 1)* [=P.P. 1874, xliv [C. 890]], p. 84.

[2] 'King's statement', enclosed in Harley to Kimberley, 15 March 1873, Cape Coast, Parliamentary Papers, *Despatches from Mr Pope Hennessy . . . Part II* (266–I), p. 325.

[3] It is not clear whether this explanation of Karikari's words is that of the speaker or a subsequent interpolation. Dawson's elucidation of 'eating' as referring to the *kostgeld* (see above, p. 125) seems preferable, for it was only in this sense that the Ashantis got 'their wants' from Elmina in the nineteenth century.

[4] Cited in H. Brackenbury and G. Huyshe, *Fanti and Ashanti* (Edinburgh and London, 1873), p. 73.

first-hand testimony of the missionaries has a unique value, and effectively disposes of the view of ex-Administrator Salmon that

little importance should be attached to the statement of the Ashantee King, that Elmina was his property; it is a figurative way the chiefs have, when speaking of their old allies.[1]

For the *ultimate* cause of the war it may be necessary to look else-where—with the missionaries, to the unfinished business of 1863–4, or, with Nagtglas, to 'the King's desire to avenge the defeat of Dodowa and to get back the authority over Assin and Denkera'. But the historian cannot afford to become obsessed with speculative ultimate causes to the exclusion of concrete proximate ones. This was the trap into which Nagtglas fell in asserting that 'the real cause of the Ashanti invasion is not the claim on Elmina, as many mis-informed people imagine'—if, indeed, this is not to be written off as the special pleading of a man who had staked his reputation on the 'absurdity' of that claim.[2] It was the trap into which, as we shall see, Knatchbull-Hugessen eagerly followed Nagtglas.

In what possible sense, we may well ask, was the fate of Elmina not a 'real' *casus belli*? From the Ashanti point of view, considera-tions of pride, power and prestige all seemed to demand a challenge to the cession. Let us briefly unravel these strands in the Ashanti attitude. The injury done to Ashanti pride by the contemptuous dis-missal of the claim to Elmina called out for redress, even though policy might dictate its temporary 'withdrawal'. From the point of view of power the cession was a blow: with the removal of the benevolently 'neutral' Dutch the assistance of Elmina against the Fantes and the rest could not be relied upon. Prestige was a pecu-liarly important consideration, not merely to overawe neighbours but also hold the federation itself together at a time when grave internal stresses were making themselves felt. Karikari's enstoolment on his accession in 1867 had been delayed by disturbances in Kumasi

---

[1] A decidedly odd assertion from someone who two years earlier thought that Karikari was trying to get his 'authority and jurisdiction over Elmina' acknowledged (see above, p. 107); but Salmon, who had brushed aside warnings of an Ashanti invasion, was on the defensive, attempting to shield himself (and Pope Hennessy) from the charge of lack of foresight: Salmon to C.O., 17 Dec. 1873, Geneva, P.P. 1874, xlvi [C. 893], pp. 25–9.

[2] See his letter in the *Standard*, 18 Feb. 1874.

which nearly led to civil war, and though peace had been restored, the grievances and rivalries which had endangered it had not diminished.[1] It was probably their consciousness of this weakness within as much as anything else which made the chiefs refuse to 'allow the kingdom to be broken up bit by bit'.

To these considerations—enough by themselves, one might think, to provoke so warlike a people—may we perhaps add one more, that of pocket? If there *were* economic reasons for an Ashanti challenge to the cession they were certainly not those suggested by Claridge. Claridge argued that the cession 'struck at the very root of their power and independence' since at any time the roads to Elmina might be closed. For the past half-century, he went on, they

had been dependent (for trade) upon free intercourse with Elmina, and its possible closure to them was, therefore, a matter of vital importance.[2]

Now it is simply not true that the Ashantis had been commercially dependent on Elmina.[3] As Nagtglas said in 1874, the king's objection to the cession could scarcely have been that it put him

in want of a seaport, for the Ashantee traders went always to Cape Coast and Azamboe[4] for this purpose.[5]

He might have added that in any case the transfer made little practical difference, since the Fantes had already demonstrated their ability to shut off Dutch Elmina from Ashanti or any other inland trade.

There is, however, a grain of truth concealed in Claridge's argument. The whole known history of the Ashantis up to this time shows them pressing towards the Coast in an attempt to establish direct trade relations with the Europeans and thus cut out the Fante

---

[1] Claridge, op. cit., i, pp. 555–6.
[2] Ibid., ii, p. 4.
[3] See above, p. 2. The 'trade' in recruits, the ending of which by the cession was thought by some contemporary English commentators to have been an Ashanti grievance, was by this time so unimportant that there had been no Dutch recruiting agent in Kumasi since 1869 (Herman, op. cit., ii, p. 99). From 1867 to 1872 only three shipments of recruits, totalling 219 men in all, were dispatched from Elmina (S. P. L'Honoré Naber, *De Nederlanders in Guineë* . . . p. 40).
[4] Presumably Anamaboe (present-day Anomabu) is meant.
[5] *Standard*, 18 Feb. 1874.

middlemen.[1] At Elmina they had succeeded in their aim, only to find in the nineteenth century that the terms of trade, middlemen or no middlemen, customs duties or no customs duties, were irresistibly better at Cape Coast. There was, it may be added, a good deal of sympathy in Britain for this dislike of middlemen, and some vague idea at the Colonial Office that the cession would facilitate trade with Ashanti, as Kimberley put it, 'through the friendly connexion between the Elminas and the Ashantees'—that is, by cutting out the middlemen of Cape Coast.[2] But the Ashantis can scarcely have seen matters in this light. They may have valued the *possibility* of direct trade through Elmina, even if they failed to avail themselves of it, and probably feared that the British flag went together with the middlemen and would thus put paid to any prospect of a worthwhile direct trade.

All this, while speculative, is at least plausible, which is more than can be said for Claridge's notions; and in this somewhat restricted sense the sixth Ashanti War can perhaps be seen as an instalment of the Ashanti fight against the middlemen. Compared, however, with the compelling political motives for war with which the cession provided Ashanti, these essentially long-term economic considerations seem rather small beer, especially since the precise role of the middlemen at this time is far from clear.[3] This is not to suggest, of course, that the British conduct of the war, and the subsequent change of policy towards the Coast, were entirely unconnected with important economic trends. It is possible to see them as a stage in the European penetration of the interior in search of materials and markets which characterizes this

period of transition from a predominantly slave-trading economy to one based on trade in the raw materials of the West African forest,[4]

---

[1] Cf. Nagtglas to Ussher, 20 Dec. 1870, Elmina, P.P. 1872, lxx [C. 670], pp. 13–14.

[2] Kimberley to Wolseley, 10 Sept. 1873, Parliamentary Papers, *Further Correspondence respecting the Ashantee Invasion (No. 2)* [=P.P. 1874, xlvi [C. 891]], pp. 141–3.

[3] There is much work to be done on the mechanics of trade between the coast and the interior in the nineteenth century. The Fantes could no longer prevent direct contact between the Ashantis (who themselves monopolized the transit trade with the interior) and the coastal merchants—except, of course, in time of war—but they seem to have maintained a sort of intermediacy by acting as hosts and go-betweens for the Ashanti traders, for which services they demanded *from the merchants* a small percentage on their trade.

[4] Dike, op. cit., p. 5.

though such an interpretation would have greatly surprised the men responsible for them. But we cannot say that it was primarily for economic reasons that the cession of Elmina provoked the Ashanti invasion of 1873, and so we cannot write off the war (as did the contemporary Salmon and the near-contemporary Casely Hayford) as a mere trade dispute.[1]

4

The news of the Ashanti invasion was published in London on 6 March 1873. It does not seem to have aroused much interest, except among the apostles of 'non-extension', eager to represent it as yet another example of the evil consequences of the violation of their principle. At first these parliamentary critics got little change out of Kimberley and Knatchbull-Hugessen, who declared their uncertainty of the causes of the invasion and emphasized the care that had been taken to placate Ashanti.[2] On 9 May, however, Knatchbull-Hugessen was able to dispel the mystery. 'The cause of the invasion', he stated,

was placed beyond doubt by a letter from the King of Ashantee to the Administrator,[3] which stated that the invasion was the result of the cession of Elmina by the Dutch to the English Government, and that he was determined to retake it.[4]

The first reaction to Knatchbull-Hugessen's statement came five days later in the debate on a colonial grand-in-aid, when Adderley used it to demonstrate the unwisdom of the annexation. Although rather hazy about the details of this transaction, he was quite clear that

it would have been fortunate for the English, if the agreement had ultimately been, that she should transfer her forts to the Dutch.

This attack seems to have left the Colonial Under-Secretary

---

[1] Salmon to C.O., 17 Dec. 1873, Geneva, P.P. 1874, xlvi (C. 893), pp. 25–9; Casely Hayford, *Gold Coast Native Institutions* (London, 1903), p. 242.
[2] *Hansard*, 3rd ser., ccxv, cols. 151–8, 1560–1.
[3] See above, pp. 125–6.
[4] *Hansard*, 3rd ser., ccxv, col. 1719.

K

unperturbed. He made no attempt to qualify his previous statement of the cause of the invasion, but relied upon the 'Certificate of Apologie' to absolve the government from a charge of heedless provocation. On the larger issue raised by Adderley he came out more plainly against 'ultimate withdrawal' than perhaps any responsible minister had done since 1865. The British West African settlements, he declared, had brought much good to the African, and neither public nor parliamentary opinion was really in favour of withdrawal—witness the popular outcry in 1870 when the cession of the Gambia to France seemed imminent. It was true that the 1865 Committee had recommended it, 'but the publication of that recommendation had not been altogether fortunate'.[1]

Soon, however, it would be not only Adderley and his friends who would need answering. The Ashanti attack on Elmina in June, and Commander Commerell's disaster on the Pra in August, awakened British opinion to the seriousness of the situation on the Coast,[2] and encouraged a close and critical scrutiny of the policy which, by Knatchbull-Hugessen's own admission, had led up to it. In the Cabinet itself a division was revealed between those who defended this policy and those who had doubts.[3] Foremost among its defenders were Kimberley and Cardwell, now at the War Office. These were the ministers who were instrumental in obtaining the appointment as Governor and Commander-in-Chief of Sir Garnet Wolseley, in whose instructions Kimberley declared it beyond a doubt that 'one of the main objects of the invasion was the assertion of Ashantee supremacy over Elmina'.[4] Gladstone himself does not seem to have reflected upon the causes of the war in which his government found itself embroiled until mid-September, when he was prompted to do so by a proposal from Wolseley, forwarded by Cardwell, for building a 'tramway' to facilitate the transport of supplies inland from the Coast. The Prime Minister was 'aghast at the Expenditure', and once more, as when the question of the transfer had first been put up to him three years earlier, he asked for further information. 'Do you not think,' he asked Cardwell,

---

[1] Ibid., cols. 1807–13.
[2] Claridge, op. cit., ii, pp. 44–5.
[3] Viscount Wolseley, *Story of a Soldier's Life,* ii (London, 1903), pp. 261–8.
[4] Kimberley to Wolseley, 10 Sept. 1873, P.P. 1874, xlvi [C. 891], pp. 141–3.

it wd be well if a mem. were prepared in Kimberley's office, yours
or both, to put the C(abine)t. in possession of inform^n wh. at present
is I think almost confined to you two as to the circ^s. of the quarrel and the
local features of the country with the chances they afford? You see the
quivering state of the public mind. Some of our colleagues are I think
uneasy even about what we have done, chiefly perhaps because it was
done upon narrow inform^n.

John Bright[1] in particular was saying that the Ashantis were the only
people 'worth a rap' on the Coast, and that all they wanted was free
access to the sea. Gladstone himself had no views: 'I own myself
very ignorant' was the faintly apologetic note on which he concluded
this letter.[2] Cardwell regretted that he was 'not capable' of explaining 'the circumstances of the quarrel',[3] but the Prime Minister's
qualms, if any, on this subject seem to have been set at rest by a
Colonial Office memorandum emphasizing the 'Certificate of Apologie' and the acquiescence of the Elminas in the cession.[4]

If the 'quivering state of the public mind' filled Gladstone with
apprehension, it opened up for his great rival Disraeli the prospect
of political advantage. The Conservative leader, who in June 1872,
in what his biographer calls 'the famous declaration from which the
modern conception of the British Empire largely takes its rise', had
accused the Liberals of effecting the disintegration of the Empire,[5]
now showed no reluctance to castigate the annexation of the Dutch
Gold Coast. In a letter of 11 September he told Sir Stafford North
cote[6] that he could not take too decided a line on the Ashanti question. 'What is the cause of the quarrel?' he continued:

If the Ash. want commercial access to the coast, wh. they always used
to have, their claim does not seem unreasonable : a matter certainly that

---

[1] The radical statesman had been out of office owing to ill-health since December
1870, and did not formally become a 'colleague' again until he accepted the
Chancellorship of the Duchy of Lancaster on 30 September 1873.

[2] War Office to C.O., 13 Sept. 1873, P.P. 1874, xlvi [C. 891], p. 146; Gladstone
to Cardwell (abstract), 17 Sept. 1873, Add. MSS. 44542; Drus, op. cit., pp. 41–2.

[3] Cardwell to Gladstone (private), 19 Sept. 1873, Add. MSS. 44120.

[4] 'Memorandum as to Affairs of the Gold Coast' (by E. E. Blake), Oct. 1873 (Conf.
Print African No. 37C, in P.R.O. 30/6/86).

[5] G. E. Buckle, *Life of Disraeli*, v (London, 1920), p. 194.

[6] Conservative politician (later first Earl of Iddesleigh) who became Chancellor of
the Exchequer when Disraeli formed his ministry in 1874.

ought to admit of arrangement. . . .There cannot be a more unprofitable, and more inglorious quarrel. . . .[1]

In January 1874, with a general election in the offing, Disraeli gave public expression to these sentiments. He represented the transfer as the 'equivalent' for the Sumatra treaty (as *The Times* and other newspapers, much to Harris's chagrin, had already done),[2] and condemned this bargain which had involved us in a 'most distressing war' and also in the abandonment of the Sultan of Acheh. 'The honour of the country,' he declared,

now requires that we should prosecute that war with the vigour necessary to ensure success; but when that honour is vindicated it will be the duty of Parliament to inquire by what means we were led into a costly and destructive contest, which neither Parliament nor the country have ever sanctioned, and of the necessity of which, in its origin, they have not been made aware.[3]

A public inquest into the causes of the war had thus become more or less inevitable. In the event it was conducted in a less penetrating manner than had at one time seemed probable. By the time that 'honour' had been satisfied by the Treaty of Fomana, signed on behalf of the King of Ashanti in March, the Conservatives were in power, and the ministers, restrained by the responsibilities of office and themselves grappling with the problem of future policy on the Coast,[4] were inclined to leave the task of harrying the late ministry to their back-benchers. The latter seized the opportunity provided when, on 27 April, Mr. Hanbury[5] called attention to the 1865

---

[1] Disraeli to Stafford Northcote (confidential), 11 Sept. 1873, Hughenden Manor, Buckle, op cit., v, pp. 258–9. Similarly, Derby (Conservative leader in the Lords) was reported as having said at this time 'I doubt whether it was wise to take over Dutch Forts . . .' (*Hansard*, 3rd ser., ccxviii, cols. 1592–1663), a remark fully in line with his consistent opposition to colonial annexation.

[2] 'As you are aware this is entirely a mistake. Each Treaty stood on its own merits' : Harris to Granville, 2 Jan. 1874, Hague, P.R.O. 30/29/103.

[3] Address to electors of co. of Buckingham, 24 Jan. 1874, Hughenden Manor, *Standard*, 26 Jan. 1874; ibid., 2 Feb. 1874, Address at Aylesbury, 31 Jan. 1874.

[4] Carnarvon, the new Colonial Secretary, who doubted whether 'on the showing generally of the Parliamentary papers . . . we should make a complete and conclusive case' against the late government, dissuaded Disraeli from initiating a debate on the causes of the war (Carnarvon to Disraeli (private—copy), 6 March 1874, P.R.O. 30/6/11.)

[5] R. W. Hanbury (1845–1903). Conservative member for Tamworth in 1872 at the age of 27.

report and moved that it would not now be desirable to withdraw from the administration of the Gold Coast. A Mr. Holms commented that, on the contrary, Britain should clear out as soon as she could because she was demonstrably doing no good by staying. Brushing aside the 'Certificate of Apologie',[1] he declared that the government had 'entirely ignored the claims of the King of Ashantee and the King of Elmina', and that the House

must look forward with great interest to the statement of the late Government as to what was the real cause of the war.[2]

This discussion was resumed on 4 May, when Hanbury's resolution was put forward as a substantive motion. Member after member rose to suggest that the war had been fundamentally due to the failure of the late government to pay proper heed to the claims and protests of the Ashantis and Elminas, to make, in fact (as one member put it), 'any enquiry as to the nature of the responsibility which we were about to assume'. When Knatchbull-Hugessen rose to defend the late administration, it was easy enough for him to show that the annexation was not at variance with the 1865 Committee's resolutions, and that it had in any case been made necessary by the results of the exchange treaty concluded by a Conservative Government in 1867—though he went altogether too far in claiming that his government had made the execution of the 1871 treaty dependent upon the renunciation of the Ashanti claim.[3] The least convincing part of his speech was that which dealt directly with the causes of the war. A year earlier he had made the perfectly correct but politically tactless statement that the war had resulted from the cession. This was a fact that he was now at great pains to deny, an act of flagrant self-contradiction which seems to have escaped notice. Relying on a letter from Nagtglas which the Standard had published in February, he dilated upon such supposed 'ultimate' causes of the war as the old Ashanti grudges against Britain and their determination

---

[1] See above, pp. 102–3.

[2] Hansard, 3rd ser., ccxviii, cols. 1204–25. This debate gives a good illustration of the apparently ineradicable nature of the notion that the Dutch Gold Coast was 'purchased'. In putting forward his motion Hanbury pointed out that what had taken place was a cession of jurisdiction, not a sale; yet Holms, who followed him, talked blithely of the sum paid for stores as the Dutch 'price'.

[3] See above, pp. 99–102.

to regain Denkyira and Asin.[1] The most that he would allow was that 'the retirement of the Dutch might have precipitated the war', which was *in any case* inevitable and, he added (presumably to ward off the suggestion that in that case the late government should have been better prepared to fight it), unforeseeable. This attempt to shift off responsibility on to inscrutable historical processes did nothing to appease the critics, who remained convinced that, as Mr. Jenkins[2] put it, the 1871 treaty, together with the manner of its execution, was the true cause of the war.[3]

The debate on Hanbury's motion was inconclusive, in that no vote was ever taken on it. From the point of view of party politics such a vote may well have seemed undesirable, for the debate had shown that in 1874, as in 1865, divisions on West African policy were by no means on party lines: there were Conservative 'Little Englanders' and there were 'imperialistic' Liberals. But one conclusion that could be drawn from the debate without very much difficulty was that there was little strong feeling in the Commons in favour of a policy of immediate withdrawal. Indeed, one of the bitterest criticisms of the late government made by the advocates of 'ultimate withdrawal' was that the Ashanti War, by involving Britain more deeply in the affairs of the Coast, had made the achievement of this end more difficult. The new Colonial Secretary, Carnarvon, had already hinted in the Lords that Britain was going to stay on the Coast,[4] and the debate of 4 May must have given him some moderate encouragement.

On 12 May Carnarvon divulged to the Lords the decisions of the government with regard to the future of the Gold Coast. He claimed that moral obligations to the Fantes precluded any possibility of abandonment, and outlined a series of reforms designed to make administration more effective and more beneficial. There was nothing very startling about these detailed proposals, the most important

---

[1] See above, p. 128.

[2] John Edward Jenkins (1838–1910). Radical member for Dundee and a strong imperialist.

[3] *Hansard*, 3rd ser., ccxviii, cols. 1592–1663. Knatchbull-Hugessen's evasions were elaborated by the Colonial Office List for 1875, which achieved the feat of discussing the possible motives for the Ashanti invasion without even mentioning the cession! (pp. 55–8).

[4] *Hansard*, 3rd ser., ccxviii, cols. 394–8.

of which was that the Gold Coast settlements should be removed
from the control of Sierra Leone and combined with Lagos to form
a Crown Colony; but the Colonial Secretary's more general remarks
denoted a significant change of policy. We did not, he said, intend
'to extend our territorial jurisdiction and not materially to extend
our obligations', but throughout his speech there ran the assumption
that the protectorate no less than the settlements involved Britain
in formal rights and formal obligations. That this in fact was Carnarvon's meaning was speedily shown by the steps which he took in
the months that followed to define and regularize the extent and
nature of the protectorate. He was determined, as he told the Lords,
that

as long as we stay there, whether it be long or whether it be short, we
should exercise an effective control—a control beneficial to the natives
themselves and worthy of the history and position of this country.

Hedged round with reservations and qualifications designed to
placate the doubters in the Conservative ranks, Carnarvon's central
concept of 'effective control' of the protectorate, of a sort of *de facto*
sovereignty in fact, was none the less a new departure in British
Gold Coast policy; though, as Grey pointed out in welcoming the
statement, the principle 'of giving control as well as protection' had
been followed long ago on an unofficial level by Maclean. Kimberley
put his finger on the essence of Carnarvon's declaration when he
adjured their Lordships not to imagine

that under the name of protectorate we do not assume all the responsibility
of managing the affairs of the colony. . . .

He also very pertinently pointed out that, although Carnarvon had
assured his hearers that 'it will be open to us at any future time to
reconsider our position upon this Coast', the whole 'tenour of his
statement' in fact 'seemed . . . to point to a permanent administration'.[1] The events of 1867–74 had indeed been a fatal blow for 'ultimate withdrawal', and also for the consistent refusal of the Colonial
Office to undertake the responsibility of governing and defending the
protectorate.[2]

1 Ibid., ccxix, cols. 152–173.
2 See the revealing C.O. minutes printed in W. E. F. Ward, *History of the Gold
Coast* (London, 1948) p. 257.

5

In this chapter we have examined the events which led from the cession of 1872 to the revision of Britain's policy on the Gold Coast in 1874. In so doing we have noted the sweeping indictment made inside and outside Parliament of the treaty of 1871 and of its execution. Was this condemnation in fact justified? Did the unfortunate results of the cession demonstrate that it, like the exchange of 1868, was a gross blunder which might have been avoided if proper attention had been paid to the rights and traditions of the natives?

There is in fact no real analogy between the exchange and the cession. The former was an arrangement made and carried out by the home governments with virtually no consultation of African opinion, which was largely hostile to it. From the point of view of the governments it was undoubtedly desirable, but scarcely necessary. The cession, on the other hand, was highly agreeable to the mass of Africans on the Coast, it was carried out with the explicit consent of those who were directly concerned, and it had in some degree been necessitated by events since 1868. Can it, none the less, be condemned by reason of what followed it? It was certainly the immediate cause of the Ashanti War, whether or not that event was in the long run bound to occur. For this reason we have already criticized Knatchbull-Hugessen's attempt to conceal this connexion by pleading 'inevitability'. On the other hand, there is a good deal to be said for his contention that 'no human being could have foreseen it'. The monotonous wisdom after the event of the critics did scant justice to the care taken by both British and Dutch to see to it that 1872 did not repeat the pattern of 1868. We cannot, it is true, accept Knatchbull-Hugessen's assertion that the British Government made the execution of the treaty dependent upon the formal withdrawal of the Ashanti claim to Elmina; but, this apart, every precaution was taken to ensure that the change of flags would be accepted, if not necessarily welcomed, by those whom it affected. The cession might have taken place without the 'Certificate of Apologie', but scarcely without the acquiescence of the Elminas. Neither British nor Dutch can be greatly blamed for failing to realize that for some of the Elminas this 'acquiescence' was merely simulated, a comedy performed at the prompting of Ashanti until the latter was ready to descend on the Coast.

Had King Kobbena Edjan and his followers steadfastly maintained their refusal to accept the change of flag instead of playing out this comedy, the course of events might have been very different, though perhaps in the long run no more beneficial for Elmina. Lengthy speculation on this point would be of little profit: suffice it to say that, since neither government was willing to use force, and since opinion in Holland would scarcely have tolerated simple abandonment, continued opposition to the cession by the party of resistance would almost certainly have forced the Dutch to remain in Africa. Thus, by pretending to give way the king's party were in a sense the authors of Elmina's subsequent misfortunes; but it is hardly surprising that, with the lesson of 1868 fresh in their minds, they declined to pin their faith to assurances that they would not be 'transferred' against their will.

6

In a sense the breaking of the historic link between the Netherlands and the Gold Coast was little more than a formality, so little positive benefit did it now possess for either Hollander or African. It nevertheless heralded a new phase in the development of the Gold Coast and a new chapter in British colonial history. 'The events of 1867–74,' says a recent writer, 'had so deeply involved Britain in Gold Coast affairs that it no longer seemed possible for her to evacuate'; instead she had to adopt the only other logical solution of her problems there, namely the legal assumption of responsibility for government and defence 'which was already hers in fact'.[1] She had, in fact, abandoned her 'half-and-half' policy on the Coast in favour of a more positive approach; and the events which had forced her to do this had been the outcome of the agreements made in 1867 and 1871 to overcome the difficulties arising from 'mixed possession'. The first of these had been an unqualified disaster, amply fulfilling the most pessimistic prophecies. The second, too, brought conflict

[1] J. D. Fage, *Introduction to the History of West Africa* (Cambridge, 1955), pp. 139–140.

and bloodshed in its train, but at least provided the foundation on which a new and more stable order of things might be built up.

Doubtless the importance of 1874 as a milestone in the relations of Great Britain and the Gold Coast can be exaggerated. Probably some such development was bound to come in due course, and in fact the treaty of 1867, let alone that of 1871, had been scarcely consonant with the still-born policy of 'ultimate withdrawal'. Proposals very much like those adopted by Carnarvon had already been under consideration at the Colonial Office when news came of the Ashanti invasion.[1] Again, the strengthening of British control in 1874 was by no means the signal for an immediate 'forward policy', either on the Coast or in West Africa generally.[2] Britain's position was still somewhat anomalous, her relationship with the rulers of the protectorate was none too clear, while that with Ashanti was satisfactory to neither side. But all these reservations cannot conceal the salient fact that, for the first time in her history, Britain had undertaken to exercise 'effective control' (as Carnarvon put it) of the peoples of what is now southern Ghana. The future was to show that 'effective control', at a time when the 'sublime instinct' of empire-building had become respectable, was to mean the rejection not only of 'ultimate withdrawal' but of 'non-extension' as well. The men who made the treaty of 1867, or even that of 1871, all of them interested in pacification rather than penetration, economy rather than extension, little guessed what would be the outcome of their efforts. 1874, in truth, marks the birth of the British Gold Coast, as opposed to a handful of forts held more or less on sufferance.[3] One need scarcely labour the point that, however insignificant the cession may have seemed to contemporaries, and however fleeting the concern for the Coast awakened by the resulting Ashanti War may have been, the subsequent economic and political growth of the infant of 1874 (of which these events were, so to speak, the midwives) has made and is making its formative years of profound interest to Englishmen of the twentieth century.

[1] Mins. by Knatchbull-Hugessen of 18 Feb. 1873 and of Kimberley of 22 Feb. 1873 on Commons' order paper of 17 Feb. 1873, C.O. 96/104.
[2] This point is well made by A. McPhee, *The Economic Revolution in British West Africa* (London, 1926), p. 22.
[3] It goes without saying that the pioneering work of Maclean was an essential preliminary to this.

It was the failure of the Dutch to come to terms with the changing West African scene which had made possible this development of effective British rule on the Gold Coast. The Dutch settlements never adjusted themselves to the transition from an economy based on slave-trading to one based on 'legitimate' trade. This, as Dr. Dike says, was the 'revolution which swept away the old order of the nineteenth century'.[1] Of this revolution the Dutch were victims, for, while British administrators and merchants made some attempts, however imperfect, to adapt themselves to the new order, the Dutch clung to the old, and especially to the now economically unremunerative and politically disastrous Ashanti 'alliance'. It was typical of the backward-looking mentality of the Dutch on the Coast that they tried, with little success or profit, to prolong the old slave-trading relationship with Ashanti under the guise of 'recruitment'. As a result the Dutch settlements had ceased to be viable, and it was only a mixture of inertia and pride which prevented their earlier abandonment.

It is natural enough that some Dutchmen, noting the subsequent spectacular growth in value of the Gold Coast, have looked back with regret to this abandonment, regarding it as one of the 'lost chances' of Dutch history. It must remain a matter for speculation whether Holland, as Miss Mollema suggests,[2] *could* have played her part in West African colonization if only she had exerted herself. I would venture, however, to criticize her implied censure of the policy of cession as the outcome of a cheese-paring and faint-hearted lack of enterprise. Certainly this policy was determined in large measure by a desire to avoid useless trouble and expense, but mixed up with this there was a genuine concern for the welfare of the African, which the Dutch, rightly or wrongly, had come to feel themselves incapable of promoting. There was no question of 'selling' or 'bargaining away' the Elminas, nor were they *forced* to accept the British flag. On balance the Dutch part in the treaty of 1871 is one of which no civilized nation need feel ashamed.

To admit this is not of course to assert that my story as a whole has cast a particularly edifying light upon Europe's relations with

[1] Dike, op. cit., p. 5
[2] Mollema, op. cit., pp. 240–1.

the Gold Coast in the mid-Victorian era. Muddle, neglect, selfishness, above all apathy, we have seen in plenty. Yet I have come with some surprise to the conclusion that the outcome of this story represents a modest victory for reason and humanity. The sincerity of the quite remarkable preamble to the treaty of cession, in which concern for the welfare of 'the native population' is adduced as the main reason for its conclusion, does not seem to me to be in doubt. This small achievement would not of course have been possible without a favourable conjunction of political and economic forces and attitudes in Britain and the Netherlands; but there are many worse guides to policy than a self-interest which is genuinely enlightened.

BIBLIOGRAPHY

Note: All the documents, published and unpublished, utilized in this work are listed below. The list of secondary publications is more selective, being confined to those to which more than a passing reference is made. Documents and books marked with an asterisk thus * were studied in transcript or abstract through the courtesy of Miss A. M. P. Mollema. Some parts of the *Handelingen der Staten-Generaal* were seen in this way, others in the original.

I. *Unpublished Documents*

(a) Public Record Office:

(i) Colonial Office Papers:

C.O. 96 (Gold Coast, Original Correspondence) /11, 15–19, 34, 37–44, 46, 49–50, 55–57, 72, 76–88, 90–92, 95, 97, 99, 104.

C.O. 267 (Sierra Leone, Original Correspondence, Secretary of State) /56, 65, 73.

C.O. 268 (Sierra Leone, Entry Books etc.) /20.

C.O. 273 (Straits Settlements, Original Correspondence, Secretary of State) /17, 21–22.

C.O. 402 (Gold Coast, Entry Books of Correspondence, etc.) /5, 9, 12–13

(ii) Foreign Office Papers:

F.O. 37 (General Correspondence, Holland and Netherlands) /290–2, 373, 377, 442, 450, 466, 468–9, 478–80, 487, 489–92, 500, 534.

F.O. 97 (Supplement to General Correspondence) /250.

F.O. 238 (Embassy and Consular Archives: Holland and Netherlands, Correspondence) /149, 157–8, 161, 169.

F.O. 361 (Private Collections, Clarendon Papers) /1.

(iii) Private Collections:

P.R.O. 30/6 (Carnarvon Papers) /11.

P.R.O. 30/29 (Granville Papers) /55, 103.

(b) Bodleian Library :

MS. Clar. Dep. (Clarendon MSS. deposited in the Bodleian Library) C. 47–8, C. 68, C. 476, C. 484, C. 500.

(c) British Museum :

Add. MS. (Additional Manuscripts) 44120, 44224, 44539, 44542.

(d) Papers of the Earl of Kimberley :

PC/A/15, 52.

(e) Archives of the Methodist Missionary Society :

G.C. (Gold Coast) 1859–67 and 1868–76.

(f) Algemeen Rijksarchief :

B.Z. (Archieven van het Ministerie van Buitenlandse Zaken, 1813–70) 2999–3002.

*Kol. (Archieven van het Ministerie van Koloniën/Geheime Kabinetstukken betreffende de Nederlandse bezittingen ter Kuste van Guinea) 1868, 1869, 1870, 1871, 1872.

Kabinet des Konings (Archief van de Algemene Staatssecretarie en het Kabinet des Konings) 1871.

G. (Archieven van de Nederlandse Bezittingen ter Kuste van Guinea) 398, 716, 718, 722–30, 792–3.

N.C. Elmina (Nederlandse Consulaten/Elmina) 1, 4–6.

N.L. (Nederlandse Legatiëen/Groot-Brittanië) 198.

Verzameling van Zuylen van Nijevelt, Aanwinst 1946 (Collectie 105) 101.

(g) Dutch Foreign Ministry :

Afst. (Ministerie van Buitenlandse Zaken/B. 79 : Kust van Guinea-Afstand) IV and V.

(h) Ghana National Archives :

ADM. 1 (Original Correspondence) /8–9, 18, 27, 29, 679, 687–8, 834.

ADM. 5 (Sessional Papers) /1.

ACC. (Accessions) 368/51.

2. *Published Documents*

Confidential Prints :

African No. 49, Gold Coast: British Obligations to Native Tribes; memorandum by Mr. Fairfield (1874) (in C.O. 806/11).

African No. 50, Gold Coast: Enquiry of 1865; memorandum by Mr. Hemming (1874) (in C.O. 806/12).

African No. 52, Gold Coast: Exchange of Settlements with the Dutch in 1867; memorandum by Mr. Hemming (1874) (in C.O. 806/14).

Memorandum as to Affairs of the Gold Coast, by E. E. Blake (1873) (in P.R.O. 30/6/86).

Drus, E. (Ed.), *Journal of Events during the Gladstone Ministry 1868–1874, by John, First Earl of Kimberley* (London, 1958: Camden Miscellany, Vol. xxi).

Handelingen der Staten-Generaal (Eerste en Tweede Kamer, met bijlagen), 1864–1874 (=*Hand. S. G.*).

Hansard, 3rd series, Vols. clxxv–vii, ccix, ccxii, ccxv, ccxviii–xix.

'Instructies en Bestuursreglementen nopens het beleid der Regeering ter Kuste van Guinee', *Bijdragen tot de Taal-, Land-, en Volkenkunde van Nederlandsch Indie*, dl. 86 ('s-Gravenhage, 1930).

Netherlands Colonial Ministry, *Verslag van het beheer en den staat der West-Indische bezittingen en van die ter Kuste van Guinea over 1857.* . . .

Ibid., *over 1858.* . . .

Parliamentary Papers [=P.P.] :

1816, iv (470)—Resolution respecting the Annual Vote (Report from the Select Committee on Papers relating to the African Forts).

1842, xii (551)—Report from the Select Committee on the West Coast of Africa. . . .

1865, v (412)—Report from the Select Committee appointed to consider the state of the British Settlements on the Western Coast of Africa. . . .

1865, xxxvii (170)—Report of Colonel Ord, the commissioner appointed to inquire into the condition of the British Settlements on the West Coast of Africa.

1867, xlix (198)—Correspondence relative to the arrest and deportation . . . of King Aggery of Cape Coast . .

1872, lxx [C. 670]—Correspondence relative to the cession by the Netherlands Government of the Dutch Settlements in the West Coast of Africa.

1873, xlix (266)—Despatches from Mr. Pope Hennessy respecting the transfer of the Dutch possessions on the Gold Coast to the British Crown. . . . (Return to an address . . . dated 5 May 1873).

1873, xlix [C. 802]—Despatches on the subject of the Ashantee Invasion, and attack on Elmina.

1873, xlix [C. 819]—Further correspondence respecting the Ashantee Invasion.

1873, xlix (266–I)—Despatches from Mr. Pope Hennessy. . . . Part II.

1874, xlvi [C. 890]—Further correspondence respecting the Ashantee Invasion (No. 1).

1874, xlvi [C. 891]—Further correspondence respecting the Ashantee Invasion (No. 2).

1874, xlvi [C. 893]—Further correspondence respecting the Ashantee invasion (No. 4).

1874, xlvi [C. 941]—Return of revenue and expenditure and imports and exports of the British possessions in West Africa for twenty years. . . .

1874, lxx [C. 1037]—Statistical abstract for the several colonial and other possessions of the United Kingdom, 1858–72.

Ramm, A. (Ed.), *Political Correspondence of Mr. Gladstone and Lord Granville, 1868–76* (London, 1952: Camden Society, 3rd ser., Vols. 81–82).

Ratelband, K. A. (Ed.), *Vijf Dagregisters van het Kasteel Sao Jorge da Mina* ('s-Gravenhage, 1953).

Tweede Rapport der Staatscommissie, benoemd . . . tot het Voorstellen van Maatregelen ten Aanzien van de Slaven in de Nederlandsche Kolonien . . . (s'-Gravenhage, 1856).

Wolteringen, J. (Ed.), *Rijks Geschiedkundige Publicatien: Bescheiden betreffende de Buitenlandse Politiek van Nederland,* 2de Periode, 1ste dl. (in proof).

3. Contemporary Publications

Aa, Robidé van der, *Afrikaansche Studieën: Koloniaal Bezit en particuliere Handel op Afrika's Westkust* ('s-Gravenhage, 1871).

Adderley, Sir C. B., *Review of 'The Colonial Policy of Lord J. Russell's Administration', by Earl Grey, 1853: and of subsequent colonial history* (London, 1869).

African Times (23/5/1867; 24/10/1870).

*Arnhemsche Courant (21/1/1871; 11/2/1871).

Bowdich, T. E., *Mission from Cape Coast to Ashantee* (London, 1873: new edn.).

Brackenbury, H., *The Ashanti War* . . . (Edinburgh and London, 1874).

Cruikshank, B., *Eighteen Years on the Gold Coast of Africa* (London, 1853: 2 Vols.).

Dupuis, J., *Journal of a Residence in Ashantee* (London, 1824).

Gramberg, J. S. G., *De Goudkust* (reprint from *De Gids,* 1868).

                  Schetsen van Afrika's Westkust (Amsterdam, 1861).

Horton, J. A. B., *Letters on the Political Condition of the Gold Coast* . . . (London, 1870).

                  West African Countries and Peoples (London, 1868).

Jeekel, C. A., *Onze Bezittingen op de Kust van Guinea* (Amsterdam, 1868: reprint from *Onze Tijd*).

Jonge, J. K. J. de, *De Oorsprong van Neerland's Bezittingen op de Kust van Guinea* ('s-Gravenhage, 1871).

Marree, J. A. de, *Reizen op en Beschrijving van de Goudkust van Guinea* ('s-Gravenhage and Amsterdam, 1817–18: 2 Vols.).

(Nagtglas, C. J. M.), *What Must the Netherlands do with her Settlements on the Coast of Guinea?* (translation: London (1864)) (in F.O. 37/466).

Nederlandsche Spectator (4/2/1871; 8/7/1871).

*Nieuwe Amsterdamsche Courant (14/7/1870).

*Nieuwe Rotterdamsche Courant (14/2/1871).

*Het Noorden (15/2/1871).

Pall Mall Gazette (22/12/1868).

Ramseyer, F. A., and Kühne, J., *Four Years in Ashantee* (London, 1878: translation, 2nd ed.).

Standard (15 and 26/1/1874; 2 and 18/2/1874).

The Times (28/3/1871; 1/9/1871; 27/1/1872; 6/2/1872).

*Het Vaderland (20/1/1871).

Vreede, *Hoofdartikelen van wijlen Professor Vreede, overgedrukt uit het Utrechtsche Dagblad, 1869–1880* (Leiden, 1906).

Waal, E. de, *Onze Indische Financien (Nieuwe Reeks Aantekeningen)*, dl. 1 ('s-Gravenhage, 1876).

West African Herald (6/4/1872).

4. *Later Publications*

Afrika Instituut (Rotterdam), *Ghana, 6 Maart, 1957* (Rotterdam, 1957).

Benians, E. A., Butler, J. R. M., and Carrington, C. E. (Edd.), *Cambridge History of the British Empire*, iii (Cambridge, 1959).

Buckle, G. E., *Life of Disraeli*, v (London, 1920).

Claridge, W. W., *History of the Gold Coast and Ashanti* (London, 1915: 2 Vols.).

Colenbrander, H. T., *Koloniale Geschiedenis* ('s-Gravenhage, 1925–6).

Dike, K. O., *Trade and Politics in the Niger Delta, 1830–1885* (Oxford, 1956).

Ellis, A. B., *History of the Gold Coast of West Africa* (London, 1893).

Fabius, G., 'De Gebeurtenissen in Guinea gedurende de Laatste drie Jaren, waarin dit Gebied in nederlandsch Bezit was; 1869–1872', *Bijdragen voor Vaderlandsche Geschiedenis en Oudheidkunde*, 8e reeks, dl. IV (1942).

Fage, J. D., 'The Administration of George Maclean on the Gold

L

Coast, 1830–44', *Transactions of the Gold Coast and Togoland Historical Society*, i, 4 (Achimota, 1955).

Hargreaves, J. D., Review article on *Trade and Politics in the Niger Delta* in *Sierra Leone Studies*, n.s. No. 6 (1956).

Herman, H., *Onze Bezittingen op de Kust van Guinea en de Krijgsverrichtingen aldaar*, dl. ii (typescript, 1926) (in Algemeen Rijksarchief).

James, P. G., Summary of M.A. thesis on 'British policy in relation to the Gold Coast from 1815 to 1858', *Bulletin of the Institute of Historical Research*, xiv (1936).

Klerck, E. S. de, *De Atjeh-Oorlog* ('s-Gravenhage, 1912).
            History of the Netherlands East Indies, ii (Rotterdam, 1938).

Koppius, W. J., 'Herman Willem Daendels, Gouv.-Gen. ter Kuste van Guinea', *De Indische Gids*, Oct. and Nov. 1930.

Martin, E. C., *The British West African Settlements, 1750–1821* (London, 1927).

Metcalfe, G. E., 'After Maclean: Some Aspects of British Gold Coast Policy in the mid-Nineteenth Century', *Transactions of the Gold Coast and Togoland Historical Society*, i, 5 (Achimota, 1955).

Mollema, A. M. P., 'De Afstand der Nederlandse Bezittingen ter Kuste van Guinea aan Engeland in 1872', in *Varia Historica* (Assen, 1954).

Naber, S. P. L'Honoré, *De Nederlanders in Guineë en Brazilië* ('s-Gravenhage, 1931).

Vandenbosch, A., *Dutch Foreign Policy since 1815* (The Hague, 1959).

Ward, W. E. F., *History of the Gold Coast* (London, 1948).

Wartemberg, J. S., *Sao Jorge d'El Mina, Premier West Africa Settlement* (Ilfracombe, n.d.).

Welderen, W. J. van, Baron Ringers, *Schets Eener Parlementaire Geschiedenis van Nederland, 1849 tot 1891* ('s-Gravenhage, 1918).

[Unhappily, two articles by Dr. W. D. McIntyre arrived too late to be made use of in this work : 'British Policy in West Africa: The Ashanti Expedition of 1873–4,' *Historical Journal*, v. I (1962). 'Disraeli's Election Blunder : the Straits of Malacca Issue in the 1874 Election,' *Renaissance & Modern Studies*, v. (1961).]

APPENDIX I

(*Parliamentary Papers* 1867, lxxiv (3900))
CONVENTION BETWEEN HER MAJESTY AND THE KING OF THE NETHERLANDS, FOR AN INTERCHANGE OF TERRITORY ON THE GOLD COAST OF AFRICA

Signed at London, 5 March 1867

(Ratifications exchanged at London, 5 July 1867)

Her Majesty the Queen of the United Kingdom of Great Britain and Ireland, and His Majesty the King of the Netherlands, being of opinion that an interchange of territory on the West Coast of Africa would conduce to their mutual advantage, and would promote the interests of the inhabitants, have resolved to conclude a Convention for that purpose. . . .

[Recital of names of Plenipotentiaries follows.]

Article I

Her Britannic Majesty cedes to His Majesty the King of the Netherlands all British forts, possessions, and rights of sovereignty or jurisdiction which she possesses on the Gold Coast to the westward of the mouth of the Sweet River, where their respective territories are conterminous; and His Majesty the King of the Netherlands cedes to Her Britannic Majesty all Netherlands forts, possessions, and rights of sovereignty or jurisdiction which he possesses on the Gold Coast to the eastward of the mouth of the Sweet River, where their respective territories are conterminous. The boundary between the possessions of Her Britannic Majesty and those of His Majesty the King of the Netherlands will be a line drawn true north from the centre of the mouth of the Sweet River as far as the boundary of the present Ashantee kingdom, but with such deviations within three English miles of the coast, as shall be necessary to retain within British territory any villages which have been in habitual dependence on the British Government at Cape Coast, and within Netherland territory any villages which have been in habitual dependence on the Netherlands Government at St. George d'Elmina.

Article II

The two High Contracting Parties agree that the following Tariff of duties of Customs shall be enforced in their respective Possessions upon the Gold Coast :—

	In the British Possessions		In the Netherlands Possessions	
Ale, beer, wine, and all spirits or spirituous liquors	Per old wine gallon	Sixpence	Per litre	Eight cents
Cigars, snuff, or tobacco in any shape	Per pound	One penny	Per kilogramme	Ten cents
Gunpowder	Do.	Do.	Do.	Do.
Fire-arms of every description	Each	One shilling	Each	Sixty cents
On all other goods of every kind	An *ad valorem* duty of three per cent. on the invoice price.			

Article III

In order to prevent frauds in the importation of goods, the High Contracting Parties engage to empower the officers of their respective Customs on the Gold Coast to require the masters of vessels to make declaration of the nature, quantity, and value of any goods which they may be allowed to land.

If the officers of Customs shall be of opinion that the value so to be declared is insufficient, they shall be at liberty to take the goods on public account, on paying to the importer the amount of his valuation, with the addition of ten per cent. thereon, and returning any duty which may have been already paid.

Article IV

The Tariff of Customs duties specified in Article II shall be put into operation from and after a day to be agreed upon between the two Governments*, and shall remain in force for a period of ten years; and further, until the expiration of twelve months after either of the two Contracting Parties shall have given notice to the other of its desire for a revision or termination thereof.

Article V

The Tariff of Customs duties may be enforced or relaxed by the local authorities, at their own discretion, or according to the orders of their respective Governments, in respect of articles imported for the use of those authorities, or the personal use and consumption of officers in the actual service of the Government.

Article VI

The mutual transfer of forts, possessions, and rights of sovereignty or jurisdiction, stipulated in Article I of the present Convention, is dependent upon and subject to the establishment of the proposed Tariff, and shall not take effect until the Government of each country shall have procured the enactment of any Laws or Regulations necessary in order to establish that Tariff for the term and under the conditions hereinbefore described, and shall have actually put the same into operation.

Article VII

After the transfer alluded to in the foregoing Article shall have been made, a map shall be drawn of the new boundary division according to the terms of Article I. Two copies of the said map, duly attested by the Government on either side, shall then be appended to this Convention, for the purpose of showing the boundary, which shall undergo no alteration, even should any of the villages mentioned at the end of Article I be subsequently abandoned, or the Tariff be modified or withdrawn.

Article VIII

The present Convention, after receiving, so far as may be necessary, the approval of the legislative authority, shall be ratified, and the ratifications shall be exchanged at London within a period of four months, or sooner if possible.

In witness whereof the respective Plenipotentiaries have signed the same, and have affixed thereto the seals of their arms.

Done at London, the fifth day of March, in the year of our Lord one thousand eight hundred and sixty-seven.

(L.S.) Carnarvon
(L.S.) Stanley
(L.S.) Bentinck
(L.S.) C. J. M. Nagtglas

* The 1st of January, 1868, has been agreed upon for this purpose.

APPENDIX II

(*Parliamentary Papers* 1872, lxx [C. 670], pp. 43–5)

CONVENTION BETWEEN HER MAJESTY AND THE KING OF THE NETHERLANDS, FOR THE TRANSFER TO GREAT BRITAIN OF THE DUTCH POSSESSIONS ON THE COAST OF GUINEA

Signed at The Hague, 25 February 1871

(Ratifications exchanged at The Hague, 17 February 1872)

HER Majesty the Queen of the United Kingdom of Great Britain and Ireland, and His Majesty the King of the Netherlands, being desirous to proceed with the regulation of the respective interests in their Colonies in the friendly spirit which has constantly marked the relations between both Kingdoms, and taking into consideration that the mixed dominion exercised on the Coast of Guinea by Great Britain and the Netherlands has occasioned the native population much harm, which did not cease after the interchange of territory stipulated by the treaty of March 5, 1867, and the remedy for which is not to be expected until the two Powers shall carry out, with regard to their respective possessions, the principle of abstaining from or giving up mixed dominion or mixed possession, have, with a view of concluding arrangements for that purpose, named as their Plenipotentiaries, that is to say :—

Her Majesty the Queen of the United Kingdom of Great Britain and Ireland, the Honourable Edward Alfred John Harris, Vice-Admiral, Companion of the Most Honourable Order of the Bath, Her Britannic Majesty's Envoy Extraordinary and Minister Plenipotentiary to His Majesty the King of the Netherlands;

And His Majesty the King of the Netherlands, Mr. Joseph Lodewijk Hendrik Alfred Baron Gericke van Herwynen, Commander of the Order of the Netherlands Lion, Knight Grand Cross of the Order of the Oaken Crown of Luxemburg, &c. &c., His Minister of Foreign Affairs;

And Mr. Pieter Philip van Bosse, Commander of the Order of the Netherlands Lion, Knight Grand Cross of the Order of the Oaken Crown of Luxemburg, &c. &c., His Minister for the Colonies;

Who, having communicated to each other their respective full powers, found in good and due form, have agreed upon the following Articles : —

Article I

His Majesty the King of the Netherlands transfers to Her Majesty the Queen of the United Kingdom of Great Britain and Ireland all the rights of sovereignty, jurisdiction, and property which he possesses on the Coast of Guinea.

Article II

Her Majesty the Queen of the United Kingdom of Great Britain and Ireland accepts those rights, and the obligations resulting from them towards the populations hitherto placed under the authority of the King of the Netherlands.

The British Authorities will take care, as far as possible, that no person belonging to these populations, who may during the dominion of the Netherlands, have participated in quarrels or hostilities with independent tribes or tribes dependent on Great Britain, shall be annoyed or troubled on that account.

Any persons who, within a period of six years after the actual transfer of the aforesaid possessions, may wish to remove to other Netherland possessions or to foreign places, shall be considered at liberty to do so by the British authorities.

Article III

In the transfer are comprised all the forts, buildings, and premises, with the grounds appertaining thereto, owned by the Netherland Government, as also all the stores of ordnance, weapons, ammunition, and the like, besides furniture and all other moveable objects, with the exception of those articles which the Netherland authorities at the Coast may deem unfit for transfer.

For the stores and movable articles to be thus transferred, there shall be paid to His Majesty the King of the Netherlands a fair price, not exceeding twenty-four thousand pounds.

The precise amount shall be fixed by persons to be named by both parties immediately after the exchange of the ratifications of the present Convention.

The time and mode of the payment shall be the subject of future arrangement, provided that the sum so fixed shall bear interest at the rate of five per cent. per annum from the day of the transfer to the day of payment.

Article IV

The Africans freed from military service in the Netherland Transatlantic possessions, and who have not made use of the liberty mentioned in Article II to remove from the coast, shall, provided they conform themselves to the laws and regulations introduced or established by the British authorities, be allowed to continue to dwell by themselves, in the manner adopted by a large number of them, in any part of the present Netherland Guinea.

Article V[1]

Netherland subjects, provided they conform themselves to the laws and regulations of the British Government, shall be treated on the Coast of Guinea on the same footing as British subjects, in regard to their right to proceed thereto or to travel therein, or to establish themselves within the same; or to hold temporarily therein any houses, manufactories, warehouses, shops and premises, which may be necessary for the purpose of their residence or trade, by wholesale or retail, carried on either in person or by agents whom they may think fit to employ.

Netherland subjects, Netherland vessels and goods imported or exported in Netherland vessels, shall be treated on the Coast of Guinea on the same footing as British subjects, vessels, and goods, in all that regards commerce, navigation, duties of import or export, local dues, trade duties, prohibitions, impositions, warehousing, bounties and drawbacks, without any distinction as to the respective flags under which articles of lawful commerce may be imported or exported, or as to place of origin, departure or destination.

Article VI

The present Convention, after receiving, so far as may be necessary, the approval of the States-General, shall be ratified, and the ratifications shall be exchanged at the Hague as soon as possible.

In witness whereof the respective Plenipotentiaries have signed the same, and have affixed thereto the seal of their arms.

Done at The Hague, the twenty-fifth day of February, in the year of our Lord one thousand eight hundred and seventy-one.

(L.S.) E. A. J. HARRIS
(L.S.) L. GERICKE
(L.S.) VAN BOSSE

PROTOCOL[2]

The Undersigned, Her Britannic Majesty's Envoy Extraordinary and

---

[1] This article is still in force, according to *Ghana, 6 Maart 1957*, p. 41. See also W. K. Hancock, *Survey of British Commonwealth Affairs*, ii, pt. 2 (London, 1942), p. 308 n.

[2] In 1873 Gericke tried to persuade Harris to get his government to allow the recruitment provided for by this protocol. He argued that thus to remove 'the tribes at Elmina discontented with (British) rule' would be of benefit to Britain, as well as

Minister Plenipotentiary to His Majesty the King of the Netherlands, and His Netherland Majesty's Ministers of Foreign Affairs and of the Colonies, having recognized the utility of an additional stipulation to the Convention concluded on the 25th February 1871 between the respective Plenipotentiaries, for the transfer to Her Majesty the Queen of the United Kingdom of Great Britain and Ireland, of the rights which His Majesty the King of the Netherlands possesses on the Coast of Guinea, have, as duly empowered thereto, agreed on the following :—

If at any time the British Government should allow the recruitment of free labourers in the British possessions on the Coast of Guinea, and their exportation to British Colonies, such recruitment and exportation from those British possessions shall also, on the same conditions, be secured to the Netherlands in behalf of the Netherland Colonies.

This stipulation shall be considered as having the same force and value as the aforesaid Convention of the 25th February 1871.

In witness whereof the Undersigned have confirmed the present Protocol by their signatures and the seals of their arms.

Done at the Hague, the second day of November, in the year of our Lord, one thousand eight hundred and seventy-one.

(L.S.) E. A. J. HARRIS
(L.S.) L. GERICKE
(L.S.) VAN BOSSE

---

helping the Dutch Government to disarm opposition at a time when a violent attack from the opponents of the cession was expected (Harris to Granville (copy), 30 July 1873, Hague, ACC. 368/51). This was followed by an equally fruitless approach in 1876, and for some time after this Dutch consular agents on the Coast continued to investigate the possibilities of recruitment; the relevant correspondence is collected in N. C. Elmina 5–6.

INDEX

PRINTED IN GREAT BRITAIN BY
BILLING AND SONS LIMITED,
GUILDFORD AND LONDON

DATE DUE